SCORN

MATTHEW PARRIS worked for the Foreign Office before serving as an MP. He now writes as a columnist for *The Times* and the *Spectator*, and has won Best Political Journalist at the British Press Awards 2015. He is the author of several books, including the longstanding travel-book success, *Inca Kola*, his autobiography *Chance Witness* and the bestselling *The Spanish Ambassador's Suitcase*.

SCORN

The WITTIEST and WICKEDEST INSULTS in HUMAN HISTORY

MATTHEW PARRIS

PROFILE BOOKS

This paperback edition published in 2017

First published in Great Britain in 2016 by
PROFILE BOOKS LTD
3 Holford Yard
Bevin Way
London
WC1X 9HD
www.profilebooks.com

10 9 8 7 6 5 4 3 2

Typeset in Quadraat by MacGuru Ltd

Printed and bound in Great Britain by CPI Group (UK) Ltd, Croydon CR0 4YY

A CIP catalogue record for this book is available from the British Library.

ISBN 978 1 78125 730 2
eISBN 978 1 78283 297 3

List of Contents

Introduction

This is a new anthology. The original *Scorn*, first published in 1994, prospered, was expanded, occasionally updated, and over the years appeared in a series of editions under different imprints, the last published eight years ago.

It was time for a clearout and re-stock. My assistant Robbie Smith and I decided to remove all the entries which seemed to us to have lost freshness or currency, and replace them with new material: some of it classic, some modern, some (given a British referendum and an election year in America) very recent indeed. This time we had the social media to plunder too; and two more prime ministers and half a dozen more party leaders as richly scorned as those that went before. And we wanted to beef up the entries on sport, a cornucopia of verbal abuse which I had hitherto neglected.

But the concept and basic format of the book remain the same. This is a whimsical and quirky collection, not a comprehensive dictionary. Nor is it a roll-call of literary merit. Silvio Berlusconi's view of Angela Merkel – 'an unfuckable lard-arse' – is more lump-hammer than it is stiletto, and David

Cameron's alleged dalliance with a dead pig's head drew a rich harvest of unprintables for us to print. But Noel Gallagher has given us more blade than bludgeon in his estimation of his brother Liam ('a man with a fork in a world of soup') and of Russell Brand ('I couldn't see him overthrowing a table of drinks').

As before, we have not strung out the entries. Nor have we attempted to divide them into neat sections – 'attacks on honour', 'attacks on appearance', 'attacks on ability', etc. – or where would you put the remark that a man's an incompetent, warty scoundrel? Instead we have tried to order these quotations in a way that allows them to speak, one to another.

Scanning our chosen remarks, many struck us as voices answering, echoing or rebuking each other down the ages. Often there seemed to be a dialogue going on, sometimes between people who had never heard of each other, sometimes between people who had. So we have tried to arrange our quotations as a sort of conversation, a 'rally'. Often – not always – this works well. Sometimes the thread linking the dialogue is tenuous. Occasionally it may break. Rallies are not continuous. More than once a new voice will take the ball and run with it to a different court. But the feelings and ideas which link human expressions of scorn have enough in common to bounce these quotations off each other in a verbal sport which, at least sometimes, finds meaning and momentum.

The direction of the conversation has been signposted, by topic, very broadly in the heading at the beginning of each chapter. But we hope that this dialogue of voices has enough shape to invite its being read as a play, rather than consulted as a directory.

A play or directory of what? There are many excellent anthologies of insult, which we have consulted freely, some of which are credited in the Acknowledgements. But they leave so much out. 'Insult' is restrictive. 'Scorn' became our chosen title, for language can be used to express anger, hatred or disapprobation in a range of ways, of which simple insult is only a part. When Job curses the day he was conceived, he scorns life itself, but this is not really an insult. When Hobbes describes human society as 'nasty, brutish, and short', that is scorn, not insult. Neither is 'witty'. Neither are 'put-downs'. Wit and put-down – taking a verbal dig at others – are part of scorn, but not the whole of it. What we have tried to explore has been the dark side of language: humorous or serious, the use of the spoken and written word to hurt, wound or ridicule – to decry not just other persons but things too: and art, and life, and God himself.

The language of scorn, though vast, finds itself pursuing one or more of only four purposes. The first purpose is part factual, part polemical: the indictment – the conveying of hurtful facts or a hurtful argument. The literature is enormous and a little outside our theme; it finds a handful of examples in this book, such as Burke's indictment of Warren Hastings and Geoffrey Howe's of Margaret Thatcher.

The second is not to persuade or inform but to discomfort by a reference to existing, agreed knowledge: mockery – words which allude to something already known or suspected but whose mention, precisely because it is known, is hurtful. It could be, for example, a reference to someone's big nose or humble parentage, or a physical or moral defect, a failing.

A third purpose of scorn comprises the very simplest form of abuse: the nose-thumb or snarl. This is the use of language in circumstances where the alternative might be to spit, an expression of pure hatred: 'I loathe you' or 'ya-boo-sucks'. Such abuse conveys neither reason nor justification for the scorn; it conveys the scorn alone.

And finally the most curious of the four: the curse – a verbal formula used to invoke some malign external power to hurt one's victim. This uses words as we might use a pin to stick in a voodoo doll.

It is fascinating to observe the decline in the potency and frequency of real cursing between ancient times and our own. God and the prophets do a great deal of it in the Old (and to some extent the New) Testament. Judaism and Islam use the curse. So did the ancient Egyptians – we include here a desecrator's curse. In early times, in primitive cultures now, and very strongly in Eastern European cultures today, the use of language to curse is rich and lively, while the use of wit, indictment and other verbal abuse is often disappointingly crude.

As faith in the supernatural declines, so does the living curse. It degenerates into a notional curse ('damn you', 'a plague on both your houses') which neither alludes to any actual failing nor conveys real information. It takes the form of a curse but is not a true curse: it is just a snarl. Modern cursing, though common, is uninteresting and routine because its soul is dead. We have lost our link with the supernatural. Correspondingly, other forms of scorn have been getting cleverer and wittier since the ancients. Words, stripped of the innate magical powers invoked by the simple act of pronouncing them, are obliged to carry interest and meaning in their own right.

As we gathered material for this book it became clear that the curse is really a subject on its own, and needs an anthology of its own; it cannot be properly integrated into other forms of verbal abuse. But it is too interesting to ignore. We have therefore included, along with ancient, primitive and folk abuse, a short section in which a sampler of curses, from ancient to modern times is assembled more as a list than as a dialogue.

Scorn has not been difficult to collect. The British Library, the Cambridge University Library, and appeals for suggestions to some 500 people in public or academic life have brought in a wealth of material. The problem, as ever, has been what to leave out. For a short book one must leave out most. This collection is therefore utterly and unapologetically idiosyncratic.

We have had a problem with Shakespeare. His work alone yields a treasury of insult, and such a collection has already been published. But, though he provides both wit and argument in his scorning, Shakespeare is really outstanding for his simple, schoolboyish, but verbally dazzling mockery. A glance at his vocabulary of insult gives the impression of relentless verbal heavy-shelling of a gloriously crude kind: 'Thou drone, thou snail, thou slug, thou sot', 'breath of garlic-eaters!', 'these mad mustachio purple-hued maltworms!', 'leathern-jerkin, crystal-button, not-pated, agate-ring, puke-stocking, caddis-garter, smooth-tongue, Spanish pouch!', 'Whoreson, obscene, greasy tallow-catch', 'oh polished peturbation!', 'you Banbury cheese!', 'show your sheep-biting face', 'stale old mouse-eaten dry cheese', 'I will smite his noddles!', 'you whoreson upright rabbit!', 'you fustilarian! I'll tickle your catastrophe!' You could fill a book with this; we have decided to let others do so. Fascinating – to us – has been what, in Shakespeare's case, the insults reveal about the insulter. Scorn tells us much – unwittingly – about the tastes and prejudices of the scorner. Shakespeare's real horror was of grossness. Flick from the Shakespearean insults above to our insults from Britain's 2016 EU referendum. Look on pp. 413–14 at the volley of tweets responding to Michael Gove. 'Pork mannequin', 'incompetent ventriloquist-dummy-faced spunktrumpet' ... literally meaningless yet glorying in the sheer sound and image, this was a fusillade of which the Bard would have been proud.

Scorn also reveals much about the offensive-defensive divide. Its literature is crammed full – starting spectacularly with the Romans – of anti-homosexual invective, the key image being that of the effeminate, passive gay man who is buggered by others. Later, we begin to find confident answering scorn from the gay camp. There is much anti-Semitic insult, less insult returned. Anti-black invective is prodigious and rich; anti-white invective is edgy, defensive and scarce.

Eschewing political correctness, we've included much. Finally, attribution has often been a problem. A handful of individuals in political and literary history – Dr Johnson,

Disraeli, Churchill, Dorothy Parker, for instance – have become so famous for their wit and scorn that the world has begun to attribute to them sayings which more careful research revealed were not theirs. The internet has only intensified this phenomenon, as Albert Einstein's endlessly expanding list of witticisms and bon mots continues to demonstrate. Further, famous scorners begin to attract their Boswells, and find their conversation recorded and remembered, where ours would be forgotten, or unattributed. It seems that if you acquire a sufficiently powerful reputation for insult, the reputation will begin to grow by its own momentum, as everything you say is noted, and extra sayings of unknown authorship are attributed, speculatively, to you.

Gathering this collection has been fun. But many months of staring at unremitting lists of unpleasant remarks does, eventually, lower the spirits. We are looking forward to raising our eyes at last from the bucketful of misery and spite which follows.

Matthew Parris & Robbie Smith
Limehouse

Humanity

As I looked out into the night sky, across all those infinite stars, it made me realise how unimportant they are.
Peter Cook

Life starts out with everyone clapping when you take a poo and goes downhill from there.
Sloane Crosley

Life is a moderately good play with a badly written third act.
Truman Capote

Life itself is a universally fatal sexually transmitted disease.
Petr Skrabanek

You're far from a perfect creature. But as far as natural selection is concerned, you'll do, and that's why you're here.
Alice Roberts

Life doesn't imitate art. It imitates bad television.
Woody Allen

Expecting the world to treat you fairly because you are a good person is like expecting the bull not to attack you because you are a vegetarian.
Dennis Wholey

So hard to teach but so easy to deceive.
Greek Stoic philosopher on mankind

It is not enough to succeed. Friends must fail.
Gore Vidal

I have always felt that life was simply a series of personal humiliations relieved, occasionally, by the humiliations of others.
Lorrie Moore

Happiness is an agreeable sensation arising from contemplating the misery of another.
Ambrose Bierce

Insensitivity.
Tennessee Williams's definition of happiness

We become moral when we are unhappy.
Marcel Proust

It is foolish to tear one's hair in grief, as though sorrow would be made less by baldness.
Cicero

It is pretty hard to tell what does bring happiness: poverty and wealth have both failed.
Frank McKinney Hubbard

Have I not reason to hate and to despise myself? Indeed I do; and chiefly for not having hated and despised the world enough.
William Hazlitt, On the Pleasure of Hating

There is no fate that cannot be surmounted by scorn.
Albert Camus

Trying is the first step towards failure.
Homer Simpson

I have no patience whatever with these Gorilla damnifications of humanity.
Thomas Carlyle on Charles Darwin

Only two things are infinite, the universe and human stupidity, and I'm not sure about the former.
Albert Einstein

Think of how stupid the average person is, and realise half of them are stupider than that.
George Carlin

Those who can, do. Those who can't, teach. Those who can't teach, teach gym.
Woody Allen

There is no expedient to which a man will not resort to avoid the real labour of thinking.
Sir Joshua Reynolds

The human mind treats a new idea the same way the body treats a strange protein: it rejects it.
Anatomist P.B. Medawar

The majority of minds are no more to be controlled by strong reason than plumb-pudding is to be grasped by sharp pincers.
George Eliot

Those who know their minds do not necessarily know their hearts.
François de la Rochefoucauld

Many people would sooner die than think. In fact, they do.
Bertrand Russell

Life is tough, but it's tougher when you're stupid.
John Wayne

Real stupidity beats artificial intelligence every time.
Terry Pratchett

To err is human but to really foul up, you need computers.
Anonymous

Computers are useless. They only give you answers.
Picasso

If we had a keen vision and feeling of all ordinary human life,
it would be like hearing the grass grow and the squirrel's heart
beat, and we should die of that roar that stretches on the other
side of silence. As it is, the quickest of us walk about well-
wadded with stupidity.
George Eliot, Middlemarch

Drinking when we are not thirsty and making love all year
round, madam; that is all there is to distinguish us from other
animals.
Pierre-Augustin Caron de Beaumarchais, Le Mariage de Figaro

The human race, to which so many of my readers belong.
G.K. Chesterton

He grew up from manhood into boyhood.
Ronald Knox on G.K. Chesterton

It must be a sign of our times that I was asked to observe two
minutes' silence at my local library.
Doug Meredith on Remembrance Day

Society is now one polish'd horde,
Form'd of two mighty tribes, the Bores and Bored.
Lord Byron, Don Juan, XIII

All charming people have something to conceal, usually their
total dependence on the appreciation of others.
Cyril Connolly

Style, like sheer silk, too often hides eczema.
Albert Camus, The Fall

I sometimes think that God, in creating man, somewhat
overestimated his ability.
Oscar Wilde

A certain type of man is only stirred to the heights of passion
by administrative inconvenience.
Anthony Powell

No one ever lacks a good reason for suicide.
Cesare Pavese, who committed suicide in 1950

Millions long for immortality who do not know what to do
with themselves on a rainy Sunday afternoon.
Susan Ertz

No arts; no letters; no society; and which is worst of all, continual fear and danger of violent death; and the life of man, solitary, poor, nasty, brutish, and short.

Thomas Hobbes, Leviathan

Extreme hopes are born of extreme misery.

Bertrand Russell

No lesson seems to be so deeply inculcated by the experience of life as that you never should trust experts. If you believe the doctors, nothing is wholesome: if you believe the theologians, nothing is innocent: if you believe the soldiers, nothing is safe. They all require to have their strong wine diluted by a very large admixture of insipid common sense.

Lord Salisbury

If it stinks it's chemistry. If it wiggles, it's biology. If it doesn't work, it's physics.

Anon

The world is formed by unreasonable men. A reasonable man looks at the world and sees how he can fit in with it. An unreasonable man looks at the world and sees how he can change it to fit in with him.

George Bernard Shaw

All of man's unhappiness stems from his inability to stay in a room alone.

Pascal

Hell is other people.
Jean-Paul Sartre

Hull is other people.
Jonathan Cecil, British actor

There is not a more mean, stupid, dastardly, pitiful, selfish, envious, ungrateful animal than the public. It is the greatest of cowards, for it is afraid of itself.
William Hazlitt, On Living to One's-Self

People like Coldplay and voted for the Nazis. You can't trust people.
From Peep Show

The only people we think of as normal are those we don't know very well.
Sigmund Freud

People who say others are difficult are usually difficult themselves.
Van Morrison

For what do we live but to make sport of our neighbours, and laugh at them in our turn?
Jane Austen, Pride and Prejudice

The belief in the supernatural source of evil is not necessary; men alone are quite capable of every wickedness.
Joseph Conrad, Under Western Eyes

A desperate man never forgives a favour.
Dominic Lawson

If you pick up a starving dog and make him prosperous, he will not bite you. That is the principle difference between a dog and a man.
Mark Twain

He has all the characteristics of a dog except loyalty.
Sam Houston, American politician, on fellow-politician Thomas Jefferson Green.

Man is the only animal that blushes. Or needs to.
Mark Twain

If a dog whines it does it because it's in pain or is hungry. But if a human being whines, nine times out of ten it's doing it because it enjoys it.
Julie Burchill

Depend upon it that if a man talks of his misfortunes there is something in them that is not disagreeable to him.
Dr Johnson

Horse sense is the thing a horse has which keeps it from
betting on people.
W.C. Fields

The man who tells you truth does not exist is asking you not to
believe him. So don't.
Roger Scruton

I like animals. It's people who like animals I don't like.
Jean Genet

I love mankind: it's people I can't stand.
Peanuts character Linus van Pelt

Mirrors and copulation are abominable, for they multiply the
number of men.
Jorge Luis Borges

Maybe this world is another planet's hell.
Aldous Huxley

Tis not contrary to reason to prefer the destruction of the
whole world to the scratching of my finger.
David Hume

Tragedy is when I cut my finger. Comedy is when you fall into
an open sewer and die.
Mel Brooks

The surest sign that intelligent life exists elsewhere in the universe is that it has never tried to contact us.
Bill Watterson

Progress means bad things happen faster.
Terry Pratchett

Shyness is just egotism out of its depth.
Penelope Keith

The problem with people who have no vices is that generally you can be pretty sure they're going to have some pretty annoying virtues.
Elizabeth Taylor

You take somebody that cries their goddam eyes out over phoney stuff in the cinema and nine times out of ten they're mean bastards at heart.
J. D Salinger, The Catcher in the Rye

A friend in need is an acquaintance.
Mariella Frostrup

If friendship were cars, then women would constantly be out there tinkering with them, polishing them, servicing them – whereas men would just let them rust away in the front garden.
Christopher Middleton

The difference between perseverance and obstinacy is that one comes from a strong will, and the other from a strong won't.
Henry Ward Beecher

Trying to be popular in high school is like trying to be mayor of a city that won't exist in four years.
Jenny Holzer

Man is the only animal that can remain on friendly terms with the victims he intends to eat until he eats them.
Samuel Butler

In most of mankind gratitude is merely a secret hope for greater favours.
Duc de la Rochefoucauld

History is the sum total of the things that could have been avoided.
Konrad Adenauer

History is gossip.
Robert Frost

History is irony on the move.
Emil Cioran

It is difficult at times to repress the thought that history is about as instructive as an abattoir.
Seamus Heaney

History is about arrogance, vanity and vapidity. Who better than me to present it?
David Starkey

What is history?
Manuscript scrawl by W.E. Gladstone in a book margin against its author's mention of 'history'

God cannot alter the past; only historians do that.
Simon Jenkins

Historians are like deaf people who go on answering questions that no one has asked them.
Leo Tolstoy

If it were not for quotations, conversation between gentlemen would consist of an endless succession of 'what-hos!'
P.G. Wodehouse

The ability to quote is a serviceable substitute for wit.
W. Somerset Maugham

It is better to be quotable than to be honest.
Tom Stoppard

I hate quotations. Tell me what you know.
Ralph Waldo Emerson

All quotation is out of context.

Enoch Powell, *responding to a complaint that he had quoted someone 'out of context'*

There is nothing so ill-bred as audible laughter, with its disagreeable noise and shocking distortion of the face.

Lord Chesterfield

The world itself is but a large prison, out of which some are daily led to execution.

Sir Walter Raleigh, *after his trial for treason. Attrib.*

I am told I am a true cosmopolitan. I am unhappy everywhere.

Stephen Vizinczey, *in the* Guardian

I am a Renaissance man, but only in the sense that I wear mauve pantaloons and have tertiary syphilis.

Simon Blackwell

Be yourself. Well, maybe someone a little nicer.

Barbara Bush

If you look like your passport photo, you're too ill to travel.

Joe Pasquale

Should not the Society of Indexers be known as Indexers, Society of, The?

Keith Waterhouse

A spa hotel? It's like a normal hotel, only in reception there's a picture of a pebble.
Rhod Gilbert

Camping is nature's way of promoting the motel business.
Dave Barry

Often it seems a pity Noah and his party didn't miss the boat.
Mark Twain

A week in which a bunch of loser jihadists slaughtered 132 innocents in Paris to prove the future belongs to them, rather than a civilisation like France.

I can't say I fancy their chances. France, the country of Descartes, Boulez, Monet, Sartre, Rousseau, Camus, Renoir, Berlioz, Cézanne, Gauguin, Hugo, Voltaire, Matisse, Debussy, Ravel, Saint-Saëns, Bizet, Satie, Pasteur, Molière, Zola, Balzac, Poulenc, cutting-edge science, world-class medicine, fearsome security forces, nuclear power, Coco Chanel, Château Lafite, coq au vin, Daft Punk, Zizou Zidane, Juliet Binoche, liberté, égalité, fraternité and crème brûlée.

Versus what? Beheadings, crucifixions, amputations, slavery, mass murder, medieval squalor and a death cult barbarity that would shame the Middle Ages.

Well, IS or Daesh or ISIS or ISIL or whatever name you are going by, I'm sticking with IS – as in Islamist Scumbags. I think the outcome is pretty clear to everyone but you. You will lose. In a thousand years' time, Paris, that glorious city of lights, will still be shining bright as will every other city like it.

And you will be as dust, along with the ragbag of fascist Nazis and Stalinists that previously dared to challenge democracy and failed.

Andrew Neil, following the ISIS terrorist attack on Paris

I have never killed a man, but I have read many obituaries with great pleasure.

Clarence Darrow

Maybe all one can do is hope to end up with the right regrets.

Arthur Miller

God and Religion

If triangles invented a god, they would make him three-sided.
Baron de Montesquieu, Lettres persanes

God can stand being told by Professor Ayer and Marghanita
Laski that He doesn't exist.
J.B. Priestley, in the Listener

If it turns out that there is a God, I don't think that he's evil.
But the worst that you can say about him is that basically he's
an underachiever.
Woody Allen

It is clearly absurd that it should be possible for a woman to
qualify as a saint with direct access to the Almighty while she
may not qualify as a curate.
Mary Stocks

Man is quite insane. He wouldn't know how to create a
maggot and he creates Gods by the dozen.
Michel de Montaigne, Essais

God is the immemorial refuge of the incompetent, the
helpless, the miserable. They find not only sanctuary in
His arms, but also a kind of superiority, soothing to their
macerated egos; He will set them above their betters.
H.L. Mencken

An inordinate fondness for beetles.
*J.B.S. Haldane, when asked what inferences could be drawn about the nature
of God from a study of his works*

God in his wisdom made the fly. And then forgot to tell us why.
Ogden Nash

Forgive, O Lord, my little jokes on Thee
And I'll forgive Thy great big one on me.
Robert Frost

[God] invented the giraffe, the elephant, and the cat. He has
no real style, He just goes on trying other things.
Pablo Picasso

Operationally, God is beginning to resemble not a ruler but
the last fading smile of a Cheshire Cat.
*Julian Huxley, biologist and first director-general of UNESCO, Religion
without Revelation*

Many people believe that they are attracted by God, or by Nature, when they are only repelled by man.
William Ralph Inge, More Lay thoughts of a Dean

The whole religious complexion of the modern world is due to the absence from Jerusalem of a lunatic asylum.
Havelock Ellis

Religion is a temper, not a pursuit.
Harriet Martineau

Religion is the source of all imaginable follies and disturbances; it is the parent of fanaticism and civil discord; it is the enemy of mankind.
Voltaire

The godless arch scoundrel Voltaire is dead – dead like a dog, like a beast.
Wolfgang Amadeus Mozart

It is the opium of the people.
Karl Marx on religion

All religions are the same; religion is basically guilt, with different holidays.
Cathy Ladman

When, and how, and at what stage of our development did spirituality and our strange notions of religion arise? The

need for worship which is nothing more than our frightened
refuge into propitiation of a Creator we do not understand?
A detective story, the supreme Who-done-it, written in
indecipherable hieroglyphics, no Rosetta stone supplied,
by the consummate mystifier to tease us poor fumbling
unravellers of his plot.
Vita Sackville-West

All religions are equally sublime to the ignorant, useful to the
politician and ridiculous to the philosopher.
Lucretius

All wise men have the same religion. As to what it is, wise men
never say.
Benjamin Disraeli

I am not attacking any particular version of God or gods. I am
attacking God, all gods, anything and everything supernatural,
wherever and whenever they have been or will be invented.
Richard Dawkins

Imagine someone holding forth on biology whose only
knowledge of the subject is the *Book of British Birds*, and you
have a rough idea of what it feels like to read Richard Dawkins
on theology.
Terry Eagleton

Saying atheism is a belief system is like saying not going skiing is a hobby.

Ricky Gervais

If we take in our hand any volume; of divinity or school metaphysics, for instance; let us ask, Does it contain any experimental reasoning, concerning matter of fact and existence? No. Commit it then to the flames; for it can contain nothing but sophistry and illusion.

David Hume, An Enquiry Concerning Human Understanding, 1748

Oysters are more beautiful than any religion ... There's nothing in Christianity or Buddhism that quite matches the sympathetic unselfishness of an oyster.

Andrei Dimitrievich Sakharov

My prayer to God is a very short one: 'Oh Lord, make my enemies ridiculous.' God has granted it.

Voltaire

To ask that the laws of the universe be annulled on behalf of a single petitioner confessedly unworthy.

Ambrose Bierce's definition of 'pray'

Anything too stupid to be said should be sung.

Voltaire

When I'm sitting on the woolsack in the House of Lords I amuse myself by saying 'bollocks', *sotto voce*, to the bishops.
Lord Hailsham, Lord Chancellor

I asserted – and I repeat – that a man has no reason to be ashamed of having an ape for his grandfather. If there were an ancestor whom I should feel shame in recalling it would rather be a man – a man of restless and versatile intellect – who, not content with an equivocal success in his own sphere of activity, plunges into scientific questions with which he has no real acquaintance, only to obscure them by an aimless rhetoric, and distract the attention of his hearers from the real point at issue by eloquent digressions and skilled appeal to religious prejudice.
T.H. Huxley, biologist, replying to Bishop Wilberforce in an Oxford debate on Darwin's theory of evolution

Illness is a consequence of sin.
Archbishop Paul Cordes, head of the Vatican Agency for Humanitarian Relief, presenting the Papal Message for Lent, 2002

For a priest to turn a man when he lies a-dying, is just like one that has a long time solicited a woman, and cannot obtain his end; at length makes her drunk, and so lies with her.
John Selden

Utter nonsense.
Eleanor Roosevelt, spoken to the nurse who told her she would die when the reason God put her on earth was fulfilled

Every day people are straying away from the church and going back to God. Really.

Lenny Bruce

While I cannot be regarded as a pillar, I must be regarded as a buttress of the church, because I support it from the outside.

Lord Melbourne. Attrib.

Fuckin Abbot.

Written by a monk on a 1528 manuscript of De Officiis

We must preserve the Church of England. It's our only defence against real religion.

Anon British politician

It is hard to tell where the MCC ends and the Church of England begins.

J.B. Priestley, of the Marylebone Cricket Club, in the New Statesman

You can't exactly lapse when you're C of E. You don't lose your faith; you just can't remember where you left it.

Jeremy Hardy

Like many C of E folks I am merely tinged with faith, like those white paint-shades with 'a hint of peach'.

Janice Turner

The Church is like a swimming-pool: most of the noise comes from the shallow end.
Theologian W.H. Vanstone

It is no accident that the symbol of a bishop is a crook and the sign of an archbishop is a double-cross.
Dom Gregory Dix

When the last trumpet shall sound, a commission will be set up on the significance of the trumpet, the financial implication of the trumpet, and for a report to come back in three years' time.
John Sentamu, Archbishop of York, on The Church of England

The numerous vermin of mendicant friars, Franciscans, Dominicans, Augustins, Carmelites, who swarmed in this century [the 13th], with habits and institutions variously ridiculous, disgraced religion, learning, and common sense. They seized on scholastic philosophy as a science particularly suited to their minds; and, excepting only Friar Bacon, they all preferred words to things. The subtle, the profound, the irrefragable, the angelic, and the seraphic Doctor acquired those pompous titles by filling ponderous volumes with a small number of technical terms, and a much smaller number of ideas. Universities arose in every part of Europe, and thousands of students employed their lives upon these grave follies.
Edward Gibbon on medieval Christendom

I call Christianity the one great curse, the one great innermost corruption, the one great instinct of revenge, for which no means is poisonous, stealthy, subterranean, small enough – I call it the one immortal blemish of mankind.
Friedrich Nietzsche, The Antichrist

In passing, also, I would like to say that the first time Adam had a chance he laid the blame on a woman.
Nancy Astor

Abstinence makes the Church grow fondlers.
Placard at a London anti-Pope rally

I have to believe in the Apostolic Succession. There is no other way of explaining the descent of the Bishop of Exeter from Judas Iscariot.
Sydney Smith

Frankly I'm amazed it survived the invention of the tambourine.
Jack Dee on Christianity

The Christian religion not only was at first attended with miracles, but even at this day cannot be believed by any reasonable person without one.
David Hume, Essays, 'Of Miracles'

Hearing nuns' confessions is like being pecked to death by ducks.
Catholic chaplain quoted by Chris Patten

Bad weather is God's way of telling us to burn more Catholics.
Rowan Atkinson, Blackadder

We know these new English Catholics. They are the last word in Protest. They are Protestants protesting against Protestantism.
D.H. Lawrence, letter to Lady Cynthia Asquith

I am a devout ex-Catholic. Every Sunday, come rain or shine, I remember not to go to church.
Big Issue founder John Bird

A single friar who goes counter to all Christianity for a thousand years must be wrong.
Charles V, Holy Roman Emperor, on Martin Luther, at the Diet of Worms

A Lutheran's foot has six toes.
Polish insult

Puritanism – the haunting fear that someone, somewhere, may be happy.
H.L. Mencken

Mencken, with his filthy verbal haemorrhages, is so low down in the moral scale, so damnable dirty, so vile and degenerate,

that when his time comes to die it will take a special
dispensation from Heaven to get him into the bottommost pit
of Hell.
Letter to H.L. Mencken, in the Jackson News

Faith may be defined briefly as an illogical belief in the
occurrence of the improbable.
H.L. Mencken

Mr Mencken did not degenerate from an ape, but an ass. And
in the process of 'evolution' the tail was eliminated, the ears
became shorter, and the hind parts smaller; but the ability
to bray was increased, intensified, amplified, and otherwise
assified about one million times.
J.D. Tedder on H.L. Mencken

The chief contribution of Protestantism to human thought is
its massive proof that God is a bore.
H.L. Mencken

The Puritan hated bear-baiting, not because it gave pain to the
bear, but because it gave pleasure to the spectators.
Thomas Babington Macaulay, History of England

Martyrdom ... the only way in which a man can become
famous without ability.
George Bernard Shaw

Sir, the pretending of extraordinary revelations and gifts of the Holy Ghost is a horrid thing, a very horrid thing.
Bishop Joseph Butler to John Wesley

Saints should always be judged guilty until proved innocent.
George Orwell

A saint is a person whose life has been under-researched.
Theologian Henry Chadwick

A thieving, fanatical Albanian dwarf.
Christopher Hitchens on Mother Teresa

An ugly little charlatan … if you gave [him] an enema, he could be buried in a matchbox.
Christopher Hitchens on evangelical pastor Jerry Falwell

No visit to Dove Cottage, Grasmere, is complete without examining the outhouse where Hazlitt's father, a Unitarian minister of strong liberal views, attempted to put his hand up Dorothy Wordsworth's skirt.
Alan Coren

Tell my clergy when I've gone to weep no tears –
I'll be no deader than they have been for years.
Bishop Montgomery Campbell, Bishop of London

I've heard of the milk of human kindness but I've never met the cow before.
Henry Montgomery Campbell, after staying the night at a vicarage

I'm taking steps to have the Thames widened.
Bishop Montgomery Campbell, Bishop of London, on the news of Mervin Stockwood's appointment as Bishop of Southwark, over the river

No kingdom has ever had as many civil wars as the kingdom of Christ.
Baron de Montesquieu, Lettres persanes

HECKLER: Christianity has been on the earth for 2,000 years, and look at the state of the world today.
DONALD SOPER: Water has been on the earth longer than that, and look at the colour of your neck.

It was just one of those parties which got out of hand.
Lenny Bruce on the Crucifixion

If Jesus Christ were to come today, people would not even crucify him. They would ask him to dinner, and hear what he had to say, and make fun of it.
Thomas Carlyle

Things have come to a pretty pass when religion is allowed to invade the sphere of private life.
Lord Melbourne. Attrib.

CLERGYMAN: How did you like my sermon, Mr Canning?
GEORGE CANNING: You were brief.
CLERGYMAN: Yes, you know I avoid being tedious.
CANNING: But you were tedious.

Yes, about ten minutes.

Duke of Wellington, asked by a vicar whether there was anything he would like his sermon to be about

Parson, I have, during my life, detested many men; but never anyone so much as you ... Priests have, in all ages, been remarkable for cool and deliberate and unrelenting cruelty; but it seems to be reserved for the Church of England to produce one who has a just claim to the atrocious pre-eminence. No assemblage of words can give an appropriate designation of you; and therefore, as being the single word which best suits the character of such a man, I call you Parson ...

William Cobbett to Thomas Malthus

When the white man came we had the land and they had the Bibles; now they have the land and we have the Bibles.

Dan George, Canadian Indian Chief, who acted in a number of films, including Little Big Man

That revolting odious Jew production, called Bible, has been for ages the idol of all sorts of blockheads, the glory of knaves, and the disgust of wise men. It is a history of lust, sodomies, wholesale slaughtering, and horrible depravity, that the vilest parts of all other histories, collected into one book, could not parallel. Priests tell us that this concentration of abominations was written by a god; all the world believe priests, or they would rather have thought it the outpourings of some devil.

Charles Southwell in the Oracle of Reason, an openly atheistic weekly newspaper, 1841. Southwell was fined £100 and imprisoned for a year.

Jesus was a crackpot.

Bhagwan Shree Rajneesh

A parish demagogue.

Percy Bysshe Shelley on Jesus

It is so stupid of modern civilisation to have given up believing in the devil when he is the only explanation of it.

Ronald Knox, Catholic priest and writer, Let Dons Delight

Even in the valley of the shadow of death, two and two do not make six.

Leo Tolstoy on his deathbed, refusing to reconcile himself with the Russian Orthodox Church

This is no time for making new enemies.

Voltaire, on being asked to renounce the Devil on his deathbed

Show me just what Muhammed brought that was new, and there you will find things only evil and inhuman ...

Pope Benedict XVI, quoting the Byzantine Emperor Manuel II Paleologus

'What's it like being a Muslim?' Well it's hard to find a decent halal pizza place and occasionally there's a hashtag calling for your genocide.

@boycotthumans, on Twitter

I am not a self-hating Jew. I just hate myself.

Woody Allen

A very old political monk shuffling around in Gucci shoes.

Rupert Murdoch on the Dalai Lama

Morality

Prisoner, God has given you good abilities, instead of which you go about the country stealing ducks.
William Arabin, judge

Anger is just and love is just but justice is not just.
D.H. Lawrence

In the history of the world no one has ever washed a rented car.
Harvard President, Lawrence Summers

Conscience is the inner voice that warns us somebody may be looking.
H.L. Mencken

Common sense is the deposits of prejudice laid down in the mind before the age of eighteen.
Albert Einstein

Moral indignation is in most cases two per cent moral, 48 per cent indignation and 50 per cent envy.
Vittorio De Sica

We know of no spectacle so ridiculous as the British public in one of its periodical fits of morality.
Thomas Babington Macaulay

Truth is like sunlight: people used to think it was good for you.
From King of the Hill, US cartoon

Some men love truth so much that they seem to be in continual fear lest she should catch a cold on overexposure.
Samuel Butler

He that shall follow truth too close at the heels – it shall happily kick out his teeth.
Thomas Hobbes

Not to threaten visiting lecturers with pokers.
Karl Popper to Ludwig Wittgenstein, after the latter had waved a poker in Popper's face and demanded an example of a moral rule in a heated discussion at Cambridge

And whoever walks a mile full of false sympathy walks to the funeral of the whole human race and whoever forces himself to love anybody begets a murderer in his own body.
D.H. Lawrence: reply to Jesus

An orgy looks particularly alluring seen through the mists of righteous indignation.
Malcolm Muggeridge

Frivolity is the privilege of the secure, or the refuge of the desperate.
Matthew d'Ancona, British journalist

'SLUT (noun): A woman with the morals of a man'
Anon.

It's always tempting to impute/Unlikely virtues to the cute.
P.J. O'Rourke

Nations

The great nations have always acted like gangsters, and the small nations like prostitutes.
Stanley Kubrick

If people behaved in the way nations do, they would all be put in straightjackets.
Tennessee Williams

National character is only another name for the particular form which the littleness, perversity and baseness of mankind take in every country. Every nation mocks at other nations, and all are right.
Arthur Schopenhauer

'My country, right or wrong' is a thing no patriot would think of saying. It is like saying, 'My mother, drunk or sober.'
G.K. Chesterton

All men should have a drop of treason in their veins, if nations are not to go soft like so many sleepy pears.
Rebecca West

What is patriotism but the love of the good things we ate in our childhood?
Lin Yutang

Patriotism is, fundamentally, a conviction that a particular country is the best in the world because you were born in it.
George Bernard Shaw

A diplomat is a person who can be disarming, even though his country isn't.
Adage

I offer a toast to this gracious lady. Up your bottom.
Andrei Gromyko, Soviet Foreign Minister, to Mrs Dean Rusk at the 1979 Vienna Summit, after he had refused the assistance of a translator

The perfidious, haughty, savage, disdainful, stupid, slothful, inhospitable, inhuman, English.
Julius Caesar Scaliger on England

You must look out in England that you are not cheated by the charioteers.
Marcus Tullius Cicero

The most significant British contribution to the European Community to date is BSE.
The German newspaper Allgemeine Zeitung

Britain is the only country now dominated by an elite of anti-elitists.
George Walden

He has one of those characteristic British faces that, once seen, is never remembered.
Oscar Wilde

Big ideas murdered my grandmother. I like small, British ideas.
Daniel Finkelstein

It is related of an Englishman that he hanged himself to avoid the daily task of dressing and undressing.
Johann Wolfgang von Goethe

The English think soap is civilization.
Heinrich von Treitschke

One of the most precious freedoms of the British is the freedom from culture.
Lord Goodman

A demon took a monkey to wife – the result by the Grace of God was the English.
Indian saying

In England we have come to rely upon a comfortable time-lag of fifty years or a century intervening between the perception that something ought to be done and a serious attempt to do it.
H.G. Wells

England, the heart of a rabbit in the body of a Lion. The jaws of a serpent in an abode of popinjays.
Eustache Deschamps, fourteenth century writer, on England

England is not a bad country – it's just a mean, cold, ugly, divided, tired, clapped-out, post-imperial, post-industrial, slag heap covered in polystyrene hamburger cartons.
Margaret Drabble

... where the Greeks had modesty, we have cant; where they had poetry, we have cant; where they had patriotism, we have cant; where they had anything that exalts, delights, or adorns humanity, we have nothing but cant, cant, cant.
Thomas Love Peacock, Crotchet Castle, on the English

A ready means of being cherished by the English is to adopt the simple expedient of living a long time. I have little doubt that if, say, Oscar Wilde had lived into his nineties, instead of dying in his forties, he would have been considered a

benign, distinguished figure suitable to preside at a school prize-giving or to instruct and exhort scoutmasters at their jamborees. He might even have been knighted.
Malcolm Muggeridge

The English have an extraordinary ability for flying into a great calm.
Alexander Woollcott

The English don't mind people pissing on them, provided it's from a great height.
Anonymous Greek greengrocer

Thirty million, mostly fools.
Thomas Carlyle, when asked what the population of England was. Attrib.

But of all nations in the world the English are perhaps the least a nation of pure philosophers.
Walter Bagehot

Britain is the only country where people will introduce you to a friend by saying: 'This is my mate Barry, he's a bit of a twat.'
Reginald D. Hunter

They're not a cynical people, the Americans. They want you to do quite well, whereas in Britain they just want you to fall flat on your face.
Piers Morgan

The English are the only people who can experience schadenfreude at their own misfortunes.
Tony Judt

Continental people have love lives; the British have hot water bottles.
George Mikes

I love the British summer, it's my favourite day of the year.
Kathy Lette

In all the four corners of the earth one of these three names is given to him who steals from his neighbours; brigand, robber or Englishman.
Les Triades de l'Anglais

The English often kill themselves. It is a malady caused by the humid climate.
Napoléon Bonaparte

That sweet enemy.
Sir Philip Sidney on France

A small acquaintance with history shows that all Governments are selfish and the French Governments more selfish than most.
Lord Eccles

I do not dislike the French from the vulgar antipathy between neighbouring nations, but for their insolent and unfounded airs of superiority.

Horace Walpole

Never doubt the courage of the French. They are the ones who discovered snails are edible.

Doug Larson

France was a long despotism tempered by epigrams.

Thomas Carlyle, History of the French Revolution

Poltroons, cowards, skullers and dastards.

Eustache Deschamps on the English

France is a dog-hole.

William Shakespeare, All's Well That Ends Well

England is a nation of shopkeepers.

Napoléon Bonaparte

Frenchmen are like gunpowder, each by itself smutty and contemptible, but mass them together and they are terrible indeed.

Samuel Taylor Coleridge

It is unthinkable for a Frenchman to arrive at middle age without having syphilis and the Cross of the Legion of Honour.

André Gide

They are short, blue-vested people who carry their own onions when cycling abroad, and have a yard which is 3.37 inches longer than other people's.
Alan Coren on the French

I found there a country with thirty-two religions and only one sauce.
Talleyrand on America

He is a silk stocking filled with dung.
Napoléon Bonaparte on Talleyrand

Nobody can simply bring together a country that has 365 kinds of cheese.
Charles de Gaulle on France

One cannot trust people whose cuisine is so bad ... The only thing they have ever done for European agriculture is mad cow disease ... After Finland, it is the country with the worst food.
Jacques Chirac, French President, on Britain

Cheese-eating surrender monkeys.
Groundsman Willie in The Simpsons, on the French

It was wonderful to find America, but it would have been more wonderful to miss it.
Mark Twain

When an American heiress wants to buy a man, she at once

crosses the Atlantic. The only real materialistic people I have
ever met are the Europeans.
Mary McCarthy

One in three Americans weigh as much as the other two.
David Sedaris

There is a providence that protects idiots, drunkards, children
and the United States of America.
Otto von Bismarck. Attrib.

America is the only nation in history which miraculously
has gone from barbarism to degeneration without the usual
interval of civilization.
Georges Clemenceau

The essential American soul is hard, isolate, stoic, and a killer.
It has never yet melted.
D.H. Lawrence

The American people generally do the right thing ... after first
exhausting every available alternative.
Winston Churchill

Be nice to America – or we'll bring you democracy.
Bumper sticker in the USA

Wherever there is suffering, injustice and oppression, the

Americans will show up, six months late, and bomb the country next to where it is happening.
P.J. O'Rourke

Kick all America in the guts: they need it ... Spit on every neurotic ... All that arty and literacy crew, I know them, they are smoking, steaming shits.
D.H. Lawrence on America

America is one long expectoration.
Oscar Wilde

It is absurd to say that there are neither ruins nor curiosities in America when they have their mothers and their manners.
Oscar Wilde

No one can be as calculatedly rude as the British, which amazes Americans, who do not understand studied insult and can only offer abuse as a substitute.
Paul Gallico

Most of American life is driving somewhere and then driving back wondering why the hell you went.
John Updike

The trouble with America is that there are far too many wide open spaces surrounded by teeth.
Charles Luckman

America is just a big version of [the] Westfield [shopping centre] but with witty people around the edges and a desert in the middle.
Kevin Maher

America is a large, friendly dog in a very small room. Every time it wags its tail it knocks over a chair.
Arnold Toynbee

Americans are people who laugh at African witch doctors and spend 100 million dollars on fake reducing systems.
L.L. Levinson

As always the British shudder at the latest American vulgarity, and then embrace it with enthusiasm two years later.
Alistair Cooke

There is nothing the matter with Americans except their ideals. The real American is all right; it is the ideal American who is all wrong.
G.K. Chesterton

The Americans often appease their enemies, but they always betray their friends.
Anonymous Middle East Ruler

What you do to your enemies today, you will do to your friends tomorrow.
Afghan proverb

The average American is just like a child.
Richard Nixon

Walking is uniquely un-American.
Bill Bryson

What America calls 'globalisation' the rest of the world call 'Americanisation'.
Henry Louis Gates Jnr

Knavery seems to be so much the striking feature of its inhabitants that it may not in the end be an evil that they will become aliens to this country.
George III on America

Not so much an axis of evil, more an arc of insufferability.
US pundit describing America's European allies

Paralytic sycophants, effete betrayers of humanity, carrion-eating servile imitators, arch-cowards and collaborators, gang of women-murderers, degenerate rabble, parasitic traditionalists, playboy soldiers, conceited dandies.
Approved terms of abuse in 1953 for East German Communist speakers when describing Britain

The Earth contains no race of human beings so totally vile and worthless as the Welsh.
Walter Savage Landor, letter to Robert Southey

'The Welsh,' said the Doctor, 'are the only nation in the world that has produced no graphic or plastic art, no architecture, no drama. They just sing,' he said with disgust, 'sing and blow down wind instruments of plated silver.'
Evelyn Waugh, Decline and Fall

Last Sunday I came – a man whom the Lord God made – to the town of Flint, with its great double walls and rounded bastions: may I see it all aflame! An obscure English wedding was there, with but little mead – an English feast! And I meant to earn a shilling solid reward for my harper's art. So I began with ready speed, to sing an ode to the kinsmen; but all I got was mockery, spurning of my song, and grief.
Lewis Glyn Cothi or Tudur Penllyn, tr. from the Welsh by Kenneth Jackson, The English Wedding

But Lord! to see the absurd nature of Englishmen, that cannot forbear laughing and jeering at everything that looks strange.
Samuel Pepys, Diary

A Welshman is a man who prays on his knees on Sunday and preys on his friends the rest of the week.
Insult, probably of English origin

The land of my fathers. My fathers can have it.
Dylan Thomas on Wales

There are still parts of Wales where the only concession to gaiety is a striped shroud.

Gwyn Thomas

The Welsh are so damn Welsh that it looks like affectation.

Sir Walter Alexander Raleigh to D.B. Wyndham Lewis

The relationship between the Welsh and the English is based on trust and understanding. They don't trust us and we don't understand them.

Dudley Wood

Fucking Welsh.

Tony Blair, reported by his press secretary Alastair Campbell

Other people have a nationality. The Irish and the Jews have a psychosis.

Brendan Behan

Put an Irishman on the spit and you can always get another Irishman to turn him.

George Bernard Shaw

I return your seasonal greeting card with contempt. May your hypocritical words choke you and may they choke you early in the New Year, rather than later.

Professor Kennedy Lindsay, a Vanguard member of the Northern Assembly, returning a Christmas card from the Minister for Foreign Affairs, Dr Garret FitzGerald, in the Irish Times

Ireland is the old sow that eats her farrow.
James Joyce, A Portrait of the Artist as a Young Man

An Irish queer is a fellow who prefers women to drink.
Sean O'Faolain

I speak Spanish to God, Italian to women, French to men, and German to my horse.
Charles V, Holy Roman Emperor. Attrib.

An ass in Germany is a professor in Rome.
German Song

Life is never so bad that Germany is better.
Jeremy Clarkson

German humour is no laughing matter.
Mark Twain

I like Germany so much, I think there should be two of them.
François Mauriac on German reunification

Ah, so next time we shall not be able to hear them coming.
Pierre Mendès-France, former French Prime Minister, on news that German soldiers' jackboots were now fitted with rubber soles, 1960

Germany is too big for Europe, too small for the world.
Henry Kissinger

To the small extent that it still exhibits a smiling countenance it is, as Hofmannsthal said, because it no longer has any muscles in its face. There has indeed always been something feminine about Vienna, perhaps because of the strong Slav elements in its population, and the combination of aimlessness and femininity has unfortunate results. It makes it a sad and rather mean town. The people seem to lack charity towards each other. They rather enjoy denouncing each other for minor breaches of the regulations. They give vent to explosions of rage when inconvenienced in small ways. They cling to what they think of as their old traditions, treacly and anaemic though these were for the most part. The dowdy clothes, the grim municipal tenement buildings and the general grubbiness make Vienna at certain times of the year look more like an Iron-Curtain town than one which belongs to the West. Indeed the inhabitants of Prague and of Budapest seem to me to walk with a jauntier step than do the Viennese. There is certainly no more depressing sight than that of the self-conscious crowds of businessmen and their ladies at the famous opera ball, supposedly the glittering climax of a brilliant carnival season. Austria has the highest published suicide-rate of any country in the world and Vienna makes a disproportionate contribution to this record.

Sir Anthony Rumbold, British ambassador to Austria, on Vienna

The devil take these people and their language! They take a dozen monosyllabic words in their jaws, chew them, crunch them and spit them out again, and call that speaking.

Fortunately they are by nature fairly silent, and although they gaze at us open-mouthed, they spare us long conversations.
Heinrich Heine on the English

German is a language which was developed solely to afford the speaker the opportunity to spit at strangers under the guise of polite conversation.
National Lampoon

Unmitigated noodles.
Kaiser Wilhelm II of Germany on the English

One thing I will say for the Germans, they are always perfectly willing to give somebody else's land to somebody else.
Will Rogers

The English are, in my opinion, perfidious and cunning, plotting the destruction of the lives of foreigners, so that even if they humbly bend the knee, they cannot be trusted.
Leo de Rozmital, 1456

I have the feeling this is all going to end very badly.
General Charles de Gaulle, to an aide, on first seeing California

The immense popularity of American movies abroad demonstrates that Europe is the unfinished negative of which America is the proof.
Mary McCarthy, American novelist

We are terribly afraid that some Americans spit on the floor, even when that floor is covered by good carpets. Now all claims to civilisation are suspended till this secretion is otherwise disposed of. No English gentleman has spit upon the floor since the Heptarchy.

Sydney Smith

An Englishman's way of speaking absolutely classifies him. The moment he talks he makes some other Englishman despise him.

Alan Jay Lerner, My Fair Lady

Oh, if the Queen were a man, she would like to go and give those horrid Russians whose word one cannot trust such a beating.

Queen Victoria, letter to Disraeli

The English take their pleasures sadly, after the fashion of their country.

Maximilien de Béthune, Duc de Sully

On the Continent people have good food: in England people have good table manners.

George Mikes

The Japanese have perfected good manners and made them indistinguishable from rudeness.

Paul Theroux

The French have made of ingratitude – as of most things in life – an art.
Charles Krauthammer, Washington Post

The English are the people of consummate cant.
Friedrich Nietzsche, Twilight of the Idols

Pakistan has many of the characteristics of mid-Victorian England – few, unfortunately, of the better ones.
John Bushell, British Ambassador to Pakistan

The departure of the Wise men from the East seems to have been on a more extensive scale than is generally supposed, for no one of that description seems to have been left behind.
Sydney Smith on the East

The only good that comes from the east is the sun.
Portuguese saying

I must confess that hitherto I had never been able to take the Lebanese entirely seriously. Poised uneasily between Europe and the Orient, Christianity and Islam, the country, for all its beauty, seemed not really to belong anywhere. It appeared to be inhabited by a kind of quintessential wog with a rich patina of French chic, ready to trade with anyone in any commodity at his own price, existing in a kind of perpetual Nescafé society, hoping that the problems of the real world would somehow

disappear if not looked at too closely, and concentrating on the sensible occupation of making money.
Sir Paul Wright, British Ambassador to Lebanon

In Italy for thirty years under the Borgias they had warfare, terror, murder, bloodshed – they produced Michelangelo, Leonardo da Vinci and the Renaissance. In Switzerland they had brotherly love, five hundred years of democracy and peace, and what did they produce? The cuckoo clock.
Orson Welles, The Third Man

Since both its national products, snow and chocolate, melt, the cuckoo clock was invented solely in order to give tourists something solid to remember it by.
Alan Coren on Switzerland

Oats. A grain, which in England is generally given to horses, but in Scotland supports the people.
Samuel Johnson, Dictionary of the English Language

It is never difficult to distinguish between a Scotsman with a grievance and a ray of sunshine.
P.G. Wodehouse

Norway, too, has noble wild prospects; and Lapland is remarkable for prodigious noble wild prospects. But, Sir, let me tell you, the noblest prospect which a Scotchman ever sees, is the high road that leads him to England.
Samuel Johnson, A Journey to the Western Islands of Scotland

Of course I want political autonomy but not cultural autonomy. You just have to watch the Scottish Baftas to want to kill yourself.
Muriel Gray

I have been trying all my life to like Scotchmen, and am obligated to desist from the experiment in despair.
Charles Lamb

His sayings are generally like women's letters; all the pith is in the postscript.
William Hazlitt on Charles Lamb

The Scotchman is one who keeps the Sabbath and every other thing he can lay his hands on.
Lyndon Johnson

It raises the average IQ of both countries.
Robert Muldoon, Prime Minister of New Zealand, commenting on an exodus of New Zealanders emigrating to Australia

Acquaintances seemed to steer slap through his consciousness and were gone with the wind.
D.H. Lawrence comparing the Australian mind with the Flying Dutchman

Pass a law to give every single whingeing bloody Pommie his fare home to England. Back to the smoke and the sun shining ten days a year and shit in the streets. Yer can have it.
Thomas Keneally, The Chant of Jimmie Blacksmith

I find it hard to say, because when I was there it seemed to be shut.
Clement Freud on being asked his opinion of New Zealand

You must remember that the Australian voter has a short memory span ... less than fourteen days in most cases.
John Howard, Australian Prime Minister

Frustrate a Frenchman, he will drink himself to death; an Irishman, he will die of angry hypertension; a Dane, he will shoot himself; an American, he will get drunk, shoot you, then establish a million dollar aid programme for your relatives. Then he will die of an ulcer.
Stanley Rudin

American intellectuals became afraid to collect their thoughts lest they be accused of unlawful assembly.
Historian Charles Beard on McCarthyite hysteria in America

The English approach to ideas is not to kill them but to let them die of neglect.
Jeremy Paxman

England is perhaps the only great country whose intellectuals are ashamed of their own nationality.
George Orwell

The English think of an opinion as something which a decent

person, if he has the misfortune to have one, does all he can to hide.

Margaret Halsey, American writer

Canada is useful only to provide me with furs.

Madame de Pompadour after the fall of Quebec

The gloomy region, where the year is divided into one day and one night, lies entirely outside the stream of history.

W.W. Reade on Canada, 1872

Canada is a country built against any common, geographical, historic or cultural sense.

Pierre Trudeau, Canadian Prime Minister

I don't even know what street Canada is on.

Al Capone

A country the size of a piece of snot.

Chen Tan-Sun, Taiwanese Foreign Minister, on Singapore

In China, when you're one in a million, there are 1,300 other people just like you.

Bill Gates

The general level of intelligence of the Thais is rather low, a good deal lower than ours and much lower than that of the Chinese.

Sir Anthony Rumbold, British ambassador to Thailand

Decayed garbage left for months on the side of the roads; stagnant canals that serve both as cesspools and as the dumping ground for dead dogs; buses and lorries that belch uncontrolled clouds of diesel fumes; scarcely a pavement without potholes and open manholes to break the legs of the unwary; bag-snatchers in every block; assault and violence a way of life; prostitution and every form of natural and unnatural vice on a scale astonishing even in Asia; a city of 4 million with only one park, and that littered with refuse and infested with thieves; unplanned hideous ribbon development; no proper drainage, so that in the rainy season large areas of the city remain flooded for weeks on end; and the whole set in a flat mournful plain without even a hillock in sight for a 100 miles in any direction: this is Bangkok, the vaunted Venice of the East.

Sir Arthur de la Mare, British Ambassador to Thailand

God made serpents and rabbits and Armenians.

Turkish insult

Do not trust a Hungarian unless he has a third eye in his forehead.

Czech insult

Half an Italian is one too many in a house.

German and French insult

I saw the new Italian navy. Its boats have glass bottoms so they can see the old Italian navy.

Peter Secchia, President Bush's nominee for US Ambassador to Italy, during Senate confirmation hearings, 1989

In Milan traffic lights are instructions. In Rome they are suggestions. In Naples they are Christmas decorations.

Italian Defence Minister, Antonio Martino

Apart from cheese and tulips, the main product of Holland is advocaat, a drink made from lawyers.

Alan Coren, The Sanity Inspector

The indigested vomit of the sea
Fell to the Dutch by just propriety.

Andrew Marvell, 'The Character of Holland'

There are few virtues which the Poles do not possess and there are few errors they have ever avoided.

Winston Churchill

Did hogs feast or did Lithuanians have a feast here?

Polish saying

Beer is the Danish national drink and the Danish national weakness is another beer.

Clementine Paddleford

Fuck off, Norway.
Paul Gascoigne, when asked by live Norwegian television if he had a message for the Norwegian people before the England-Norway World Cup qualifier

It could plausibly be argued that it is a misfortune for anybody but a Finn to spend three years in Finland, as I have just done. Even the Finns who can afford it are happy to make frequent escapes to sunnier climes. Finland is flat, freezing, and far from the pulsating centres of European life. Nature has done little for her and art not much more. Until yesterday the country was inhabited only by peasants, foresters, fishermen and a small class of alien rulers who spent most of their money elsewhere. The rich cultural past of Europe has left fewer traces in Finland in the shape of public and private buildings of quality and the objects of art which adorn them than anywhere else in the Western world save perhaps Iceland. Finnish cooking deserves a sentence to itself for its crude horror; only the mushrooms and the crayfish merit attention.
Sir Bernard Ledwidge, British Ambassador to Finland

How do you tell the difference between a Finnish introvert and a Finnish extrovert? One looks at his own feet when he's talking to you, the other will look at yours.
Finnish joke

The Greeks – dirty and impoverished descendants of a bunch of la-de-da fruit salads who invented democracy and then forgot how to use it while walking around dressed up like girls.

P.J. O'Rourke, in the National Lampoon

The people of Crete unfortunately make more history than they can consume locally.

Saki

Just compare with the vast monuments of this vital aqueduct network those useless pyramids or the good-for-nothing tourist attractions of the Greeks.

Frontinus, superintendent of Roman aqueducts

In Sao Paulo it is now said to be quicker and safer to rob a bank than to try to cash a cheque in one.

Sir John Russell, British Ambassador to Brazil

Poor Mexico, so far from God and so near to the United States!

Porfirio Díaz

There is, I fear, no question but that the average Nicaraguan is one of the most dishonest, unreliable, violent and alcoholic of the Latin Americans – and after nearly 21 years of Latin American experience I feel I can speak with some authority on the subject.

Roger Pinsent, British Ambassador to Nicaragua

Bolivians are merely metamorphosed llamas who have learned to talk but not think.
Chilean Admiral José Toribio Merino

Realizing that they will never be a world power, the Cypriots have decided to settle for being a world nuisance.
George Mikes

A nation is a society united by a delusion about its ancestry and by a common hatred of its neighbours.
William Ralph Inge, The Perpetual Pessimist

If I had to choose between betraying my country and betraying my friend, I hope I should have the guts to betray my country.
E.M. Forster, Two Cheers for Democracy, 'What I Believe'

Patriotism is the last refuge of the scoundrel.
Samuel Johnson

When Dr Johnson described patriotism as the last refuge of the scoundrel, he ignored the enormous possibilities of the word Reform.
US Senator Roscoe Conkling

Places

I come from Des Moines, Iowa. Somebody had to.

The opening line to Bill Bryson's first book

I'm out of here, I'm better than all of you.

Tracey Emin on her home town of Margate

You gotta live somewhere.

Jimmy Brogan, a suggested motto for Cleveland, USA

Come, friendly bombs, and fall on Slough
It isn't fit for humans now.
... Come, friendly bombs, and fall on Slough
To get it ready for the plough.
The cabbages are coming now;
The earth exhales.

John Betjeman, Continual Dew, 'Slough'

I see you come from Slough. You can go back there. It is a terrible place.

Mr Justice Melford Stevenson, to a prisoner acquitted of rape

Erith isn't twinned with anywhere, but it does have a suicide pact with Dagenham.

Linda Smith

In 1956 the population of Los Angeles was 2,243,901. By 1970 it had risen to 2,811,801, 1,650,917 of whom are currently up for a series.

Fran Lebowitz on Los Angeles

The difference between yoghurt and Los Angeles is that yoghurt has a living culture.

Sean Penn

She's blended right in – not necessarily a compliment around here.

A member of the public after seeing Gwyneth Paltrow in London's Kilburn High Road

Suburbia is where the developer bulldozes out the trees, then names the streets after them.

Bill Vaughan

Can pigs grow wings and fly, unwonton birds?
Can the salt sea grow black with grazing herds?
Can the lean thistle blossom into figs?

Or Oxford aught produce save fools and prigs?
Geoffrey Howard on Oxford

Home of lost causes, and forsaken beliefs, and unpopular
names, and impossible loyalties!
Matthew Arnold on Oxford

So this is Winnipeg. I can tell it's not Paris.
Bob Edwards on Winnipeg

From 20,000 feet in the air, on the way to Paris.
*Australian Prime Minister Paul Keating, asked the best way to see Darwin,
Northern Territory*

One has no great hopes from Birmingham. I always say there
is something direful in the sound.
Jane Austen, Emma

When a man is tired of Birmingham he is entirely right.
Hannah Betts

Getting drunk is the quickest way out of it.
Anonymous High Court Judge on Manchester

Manchester is, in the main, dull and workmanlike, the
majority of its people live between the workshop, the racing
columns of the newspapers, the organized banality of the
music hall and the mean street.
D.L. Kelleher, The Glamour of Manchester, 1920

He chose to live in Manchester, a wholly incomprehensible choice for a free man to make.
Mr Justice Melford Stevenson, of a man in a divorce case

Not such a nice place.
Queen Elizabeth II on Manchester, during a visit to St Petersburg, 1994

The best thing that comes out of Yorkshire is the road to Lancashire.
Dame Thora Hird

Never ask a man if he comes from Yorkshire. If he does, he will tell you without asking. If he does not, why humiliate him?
Sydney Smith

They see themselves whenever possible as victims, and resent their victim status; yet at the same time they wallow in it. Part of this flawed psychological state is that they cannot accept that they might have made any contribution to their misfortunes, but seek rather to blame someone else for it, thereby deepening their sense of shared tribal grievance against the rest of society.
Editorial in the Spectator. The editor, Boris Johnson, took responsibility. It was alleged that the journalist Simon Heffer was involved in drafting the column.

Here we are, in one of the most depressed towns in Southern

England, a place that is arguably too full of drugs, obesity, underachievement and Labour MPs.
Boris Johnson on Portsmouth

An inverted pyramid of piffle.
Boris Johnson on allegations against himself

A small nodule of erupted spleen at the eastern edge of England.
Camilla Long on Thanet

They will steal the very teeth of your mouth as you walk the streets. I know it from experience.
Judge William Arabin on the people of Uxbridge

New York ... That unnatural city where everyone is an exile, none more so than the American.
Charlotte Perkins Gilman

Any time three New Yorkers get into a cab without an argument, a bank has just been robbed.
Phyllis Diller

I am faced with a typically New York problem, which is how to bring my mediocrity before the public.
Kurt Vonnegut

London, that great cesspool into which all the loungers of the Empire are irresistibly drained.

Sir Arthur Conan Doyle, A Study in Scarlet

I don't know what London's coming to – the higher the buildings, the lower the morals.

Noël Coward

Rome's just a city like anywhere else. A vastly overrated city, I'd say. It trades on belief just as Stratford trades on Shakespeare.

Anthony Burgess, Inside Mr Enderby

The young Cambridge group, the group that stood for 'freedom' and flannel trousers and flannel shirts open at the neck, and a well-bred sort of emotional anarchy, and a whispering, murmuring sort of voice, and an ultra-sensitive sort of manner.

D.H. Lawrence, Lady Chatterley's Lover

You will hear more good things on the outside of a stagecoach from London to Oxford than if you were to pass a twelve-month with the undergraduates, or heads of colleges, of that famous university.

William Hazlitt, The Ignorance of the Learned

Oxford is on the whole more attractive than Cambridge to the ordinary visitor; and the traveller is therefore recommended to visit Cambridge first, or to omit it altogether if he cannot visit both.

Baedeker's Great Britain

Too often travel, instead of broadening the mind, merely lengthens the conversation.

Elizabeth Drew

Bugger Bognor.

George V, alleged last words when told by his doctor that he would soon be well enough to visit Bognor Regis; also claimed as the king's response to the proposal to rename the town Bognor Regis in honour of its recuperative effect on His Majesty

Brighton looks like a town which is helping police with their enquiries.

Keith Waterhouse, in the Evening Standard

Very flat, Norfolk.

Noël Coward, Private Lives

Roast beef in human form.

Horace Walpole on the inhabitants of Norfolk

Shake a bridle over a Yorkshireman's grave and he will rise and steal a horse.

Lancashire saying

California is a place in which a boom mentality and a sense of Chekhovian loss meet in uneasy suspension.
Joan Didion

The continental United States slopes gently from east to west, with the result that everything with a screw loose rolls into California.
John Naughton

In Marseilles they make half the toilet soap we consume in America, but the Marseillaise only have a vague theoretical idea of its use, which they have obtained from books of travel.
Mark Twain

If I owned Texas and Hell, I would rent out Texas and live in Hell.
General Philip Sheridan

Race

We are all beautiful (except white people, they are full of and made of shit)...

Imamu Amiri Baraka, Black Magic, 'A school of prayer'

One of the things that makes a Negro unpleasant to white folks is the fact that he suffers from their injustice. He is thus a standing rebuke to them.

H.L. Mencken

I wouldn't know, I'm from Alabama.

An African-American responds to President Nixon, having been asked, at a celebration of Ghana's independence, what it felt like to be free.

I have almost reached the regrettable conclusion that the Negro's great stumbling block in his stride toward freedom is not the White Citizen's Councillor or the Ku Klux Klanner, but the white moderate, who is more devoted to order than to justice.

Martin Luther King

I fucking hate niggers, I wish we could put them all in a concentration camp with the kikes and be done with the lot.

'Tay', a Microsoft bot designed to learn how to communicate authentically on Twitter. It took just fifteen hours for the bot to become racist.

[A person is] a male Person, including an Indian and excluding a person of Mongolian or Chinese race.

Canada Franchise Act 1885

We have every kind of mixture you can have. I have a black, I have a woman, two Jews and a cripple.

James Watt, US Interior Secretary on the balanced composition of an advisory board

Porkie.

Jamaican term of abuse for white people

What negroes want is tight pussy, loose shoes and a warm place to shit.

Earl Butz, US Secretary for Agriculture in the Nixon administration

When black man thief, him steal half a bit; but when white man thief, him steal a whole sugar plantation.

Black American slave. Attrib.

When the white man is about to leave a garden for good, he wrecks it.

Yoruba proverb

Making love to a white man is like making love to a skinned animal.
Anonymous Nigerian woman

The white race is the cancer of all human history. It is the white race and it alone, its ideologies and inventions, which eradicate autonomous civilizations wherever it spreads.
Susan Sontag, Partisan Review

You gotta say this for the white race – its self-confidence knows no bounds. Who else could go to a small island in the South Pacific where there's no poverty, no crime, no unemployment, no war and no worry – and call it a 'primitive society'?
Dick Gregory

I have no purpose to introduce political and social equality between the white and black races. There is a physical difference between the two which, in my judgement, will probably for ever forbid their living together upon the footing of perfect equality; and inasmuch as it becomes a necessity that there must be a difference, I ... am in favour of the race to which I belong having the superior position.
Abraham Lincoln

White people say to me 'Isn't there anything good about us?' and I reply 'Yes. You sure can ski. You're beautiful skiers.'
Paul Mooney

The Sioux Indians are a set of miserable, dirty, lousy, blanketed, seething, lying, sneaking, murdering, graceless, faceless, dog-eating SKUNKS as the Lord ever permitted to infect the earth, and whose immediate and final extermination all MEN, excepting Indian agents and traders, should pray for.
Topeka Weekly Daily, 1869

I'm a coloured, one-eyed Jew.
Sammy Davis, Jr., when asked what his handicap was during a game of golf

There is only one race greater than the Jews – and that is the Derby.
Victor Sassoon

All those who are not racially pure are mere chaff.
Adolf Hitler, Mein Kampf

His 140,000 words were 140,000 offences against the spirit of the German language.
Leon Feuchtwanger on Hitler's Mein Kampf

They are more like animals than human beings. Those of them who live deep in the north – between the end of the even climates and the end of the habitable world – have been so affected by the extreme distance of the sun from the Zenith above their heads, resulting in cold climate and thick atmosphere, that their temperatures have become chilly and their humours rude. Consequently their bodies are huge, their colour pale and their hair long. For the same reason they lack keenness in intelligence

and perspicacity and are characterized by ignorance and
stupidity. Folly and mental blindness prevail among them.
Sai'd, eleventh-century Muslim scientist, on Northern Europeans

If a Jew can have the rope free of charge he will let himself be
hanged.
Russian insult

If the Jew is of gold, his testicles are of copper.
Moorish insult

The gentleman will please remember that when his half-
civilized ancestors were hunting the wild boar in Silesia, mine
were princes of the earth.
*Judah Benjamin, replying to an anti-Semitic remark by a senator of German
origin. Attrib.*

Of all the bigotries that savage the human temper there is
none so stupid as the anti-Semitic.
David Lloyd George

... a tendency – from which I suffer myself – to presume that
anyone of any eminence at all is Jewish, unless he or she can
show definitive proof to the contrary.
Chaim Bermant

No, not really. Except this: We think they're stupid.
*Dominic Lawson, when asked at a Spectator lunch whether Jews held any
prejudice against Gentiles comparable to anti-Semitism*

Class and Courtesy

Actually I vote Labour, but my butler's a Tory.

Earl Mountbatten to a canvasser during the 1945 election

The difference between us is that my family begins with me,
whereas yours ends with you.

Iphicrates, Athenian general and the son of a cobbler, replying to a descendant
of the Athenian hero Harmodius who mocked his lowly origins

Of course they have, or I wouldn't be talking to you.

Barbara Cartland, when asked by BBC reporter Sandra Harris in a radio
interview whether she thought English class barriers had broken down

You can't expect a boy to be vicious till he's been to a good school.

Saki

Aristocrats spend their childhood being beaten by fierce
nannies and their later years murdering wildlife, so it's hardly
surprising their sex lives are a bit cock-eyed.

Jilly Cooper, Men and Super Men

In the British aristocracy the gene pool has always had a shallow end.

Former US ambassador Raymond Seitz

The English aristocracy is a wonderful institution, not for its power, which is nothing, nor for its achievements, which are few, but for the gigantic impression it is able to make upon weak minds. Practically, its power has dwindled to the prerogative of occasionally obstructing a theological measure for a limited period ... [but it is] one of the stock nightmares of morbid brains. It takes its place with Antichrist and irremissible sin among the dismal spectres that haunt a disturbed imagination.

Lord Salisbury

He was educated at Eton and at Oxford, so Watson, bring the gun.

Sherlock Holmes

These bloody people. I can't bear that man. I mean, he's so awful, he really is.

Prince Charles on Royal Correspondent, Nicholas Witchell

Good breeding consists in concealing how much we think of ourselves and how little we think of the other person.

Mark Twain

Good manners is the art of making people uncomfortable.

Craig Brown

How do you keep the natives off the booze long enough to get them past the test?

The Duke of Edinburgh to a driving instructor in Scotland

An aristocracy in a republic is like a chicken whose head has been cut off; it may run about in a lively way, but in fact it is dead.

Nancy Mitford, Noblesse Oblige

How beastly the bourgeois is
especially the male of the species – ...
Nicely groomed, like a mushroom
standing there so sleek and erect and eyeable –
And a fungus, living on the remains of bygone life
sucking his life out of the dead leaves of greater life than his
        own.
And even so, he's stale, he's been there too long.
Touch him, and you'll find he's all gone inside
just like an old mushroom, all wormy inside, and hollow
under a smooth skin and an upright appearance.
Full of seething, wormy, hollow feelings
rather nasty –
How beastly the bourgeois is! ...

D.H. Lawrence, Pansies, How beastly the bourgeois is

The bourgeois prefers comfort to pleasure, convenience to liberty, and a pleasant temperature to the deathly inner consuming fire.

Hermann Hesse

Poor Matt. He's gone to heaven, no doubt, but he won't like God.
Robert Louis Stevenson on Matthew Arnold

Let them eat cake.
Marie-Antoinette repeating an old saying when told the people had no bread to eat

Voting and buying drugs: the two activities that will drag a professional person into a place where people live on land owned by the council.
Giles Coren in The Times

If you've seen one city slum you've seen them all.
Spiro T. Agnew

MY LORD, – Now I am recovering from an illness of several months' duration, aggravated no little by your lordship's rude reception of me at the Cascine, in presence of my family and innumerable Florentines. I must remind you in the gentlest terms of the occurrence. We are both of us old men, my lord, and are verging on decrepitude and imbecility. Else my note might be more energetic. I am not unobservant of distinctions. You, by the favour of a minister, are Marquis of Normanby, I by the grace of God am.
WALTER SAVAGE LANDOR
W.S. Landor, letter to Lord Normanby, who had cut him

I've been offered titles, but I think they get one into disreputable company.

George Bernard Shaw

When you are down and out, something always turns up – and it is usually the noses of your friends.

Orson Welles

Not really. Experience has taught us that those who matter don't mind and those who mind don't matter.

Ambassador to a dinner guest who had forced her fellow guests to swap seats after discovering precedence ought to accord her a place closer to the Ambassador. She had said to him: 'I expect you find these questions of precedence very troublesome, Your Excellency.'

We invite people like that to tea, but we don't marry them.

Lady Chetwode on her future son-in-law, John Betjeman

I would rather cry in the back of a BMW than laugh on your bicycle.

Chinese reality TV contestant

What you need is a couple of aspirates.

F.E. Smith to Jimmy Thomas, who never pronounced his h's. He had complained of an 'eadache

No writer before the middle of the 19th century wrote about the working classes other than a grotesque or as pastoral decoration. Then when they were given the vote certain writers started to suck up to them.

Evelyn Waugh

Like most liberals, I will do anything for the working classes, anything – apart from mix with them.

Kevin Day

I never knew the working classes had such white skins.

Lord Curzon, seeing some troops bathing during the First World War

Kings, Queens and Commoners

Becket parts company from Henry II and Louis VII, after a stormy meeting.

From The Becket Leaves

A hereditary monarch is as absurd a proposition as a hereditary doctor or mathematician.

Thomas Paine

... a pig, an ass, a dunghill, the spawn of an adder, a basilisk, a lying buffoon, a mad fool with a frothy mouth ... a lubberly ass ... a frantic madman ...
Martin Luther on Henry VIII

Because half-a-dozen grasshoppers under a fern make the field ring with their importunate chink, whilst thousands of great cattle, reposed beneath the shadow of the British oak, chew the cud and are silent, pray do not imagine that those who make the noise are the only inhabitants of the field; that of course they are many in number; or that, after all, they are other than the little shrivelled, meagre, hopping, though loud and troublesome insects of the hour.
Edmund Burke

It is the folly of too many, to mistake the echo of a London coffee-house for the voice of the kingdom.
Jonathan Swift

One has often wondered whether upon the whole earth there is anything so unintelligent, so unapt to perceive how the world is really going, as an ordinary young Englishman of our upper classes.
Matthew Arnold, Culture and Anarchy

The aristocratic disdain for work is the one legacy they've left that's really worth something.
John Cooper Clarke

The king blew his nose twice, and wiped the royal perspiration repeatedly from a face which is probably the largest uncivilized spot in England.

Oliver Wendell Holmes on William IV

Good-morning, gentlemen both.

Elizabeth I, addressing a group of eighteen tailors

To promote a Woman to beare rule, superioritie, dominion, or empire above any Realme, nation, or Citie, is repugnant to nature; contumelie to God, a thing most contrarious to his reveled will and approved ordinance; and finallie, it is the subversion of good Order, of all equitie and justice ... For who can denie but it is repugneth to nature, that the blind shall be appointed to leade and conduct such as do see? That the weake, the sicke, and impotent persons shall norishe and kepe the hole and the strong? And finallie, that the foolishe, madde, and phrenetike shall governe the discrete, and give counsel to such as be of sober mind? Of such be all women, compared unto man in bearing of authoritie. For their sight in civile regiment is but blindness; their strength, weakness; their counsel, foolishness; and judgement, phrensie, if it be rightlie considered ...

John Knox, First Blast of the Trumpet against the Monstrous Regiment of Women

The most notorious whore in all the world.

Peter Wentworth on Mary Queen of Scots

Most gracious Queen we thee implore
To Go Away and sin no more
But if that effort be too great
To go away, at any rate.
Anonymous epigram on Queen Caroline, wife of George IV

The bloom of her ugliness is going off.
Colonel Disbrowe on the ageing looks of Queen Charlotte

Beauty is only skin deep, but ugliness goes clean to the bone.
Dorothy Parker

Anne ... when in good humour, was meekly stupid, and when in bad humour, was sulkily stupid.
Thomas Babington Macaulay on Queen Anne

One of the smallest people ever set in a great place.
Walter Bagehot on Queen Anne

The wisest fool in Christendom.
Henri IV of France on James I of England. Attrib.

One of the moral monsters of history.
Samuel Taylor Coleridge on Charles II

Henry VIII perhaps approached as nearly to the ideal standard of perfect wickedness as the infirmities of human nature will allow.
Sir James Mackintosh

A blot of blood and grease upon the History of England.
Charles Dickens on Henry VIII

Here lies our mutton-loving King
Whose word no man relies on
Who never said a foolish thing
And never did a wise one.
John Wilmot on Charles II

This is very true: for my words are my own, and my actions are
my ministers.
Charles II

Throughout the greater part of his life, George III was a kind
of consecrated obstruction.
Walter Bagehot

The Radical MP John Wilkes at a formal dinner in the presence
of the Prince of Wales proposed a toast to the King's health, a
thing which no one had ever known him do before. The Prince
asked Wilkes how long he had shown such concern for his
father's well-being. Wilkes replied: 'Since I had the pleasure of
your Royal Highness's acquaintance.'
John Wilkes on the Prince of Wales, later on George IV

The two most powerful men in Russia are Tsar Nicholas II and
the last person who spoke to him.
Anonymous

Never was a person less mourned by his fellow men than the late King ... if ever George IV had a friend, a true friend, in any social class, so we may claim that his or her name never reached our ears.

The Times, *commentary*

Who's your fat friend?

George 'Beau' Brummell to Beau Nash, who had introduced the Prince Regent

Queen Victoria was like a great paperweight that for half a century sat upon men's minds, and when she was removed their ideas began to blow all over the place haphazardly.

H.G. Wells

Strip your Louis Quatorze of his king gear and there is left nothing but a poor forked radish with a head fantastically carved.

Thomas Carlyle on Louis XIV

Nowadays, a parlour maid as ignorant as Queen Victoria was when she came to the throne, would be classed as mentally defective.

George Bernard Shaw on Queen Victoria

Very sorry can't come. Lie follows by post.

Telegram from Charles Beresford to the Prince of Wales, later Edward VIII, following a dinner invitation at short notice

No thank you; I only smoke on special occasions.

Anonymous commoner, confused and overawed, on being asked by George VI at a banquet whether he cared for a cigar

Thank God for the Civil Service.

George VI on Labour's 1945 election victory

Born into the ranks of the working class, the new King's most likely fate would have been that of a street-corner loafer.

James Keir Hardie, Labour leader, on George V

For seventeen years he did nothing at all but kill animals and stick in stamps.

Harold Nicolson, biographer of George V, on his subject

My father was frightened of his mother, I was frightened of my father, and I am damned well going to see to it that my children are frightened of me.

King George V

He will go from resort to resort getting more tanned and more tired.

Westbrook Pegler on the abdication of Edward VIII, quoted by Alistair Cooke, Six Men

God grant him peace and happiness but never understanding of what he has lost.

Stanley Baldwin on the abdication of Edward VIII

[A] wife capable of behaving in this way: tantrums and suicide charades – anyone trying to do it with paracetamol isn't trying – is a witless little girl unfit for marriage to anyone. And the wife capable of exploiting her position to get revenge through mass publicity is a destructive little chancer emotionally located in the foothills of adolescence. The footling story of Diana Spencer makes a bitter republican point, the liability of fairy tales to have been written by the Brothers Grimm! ...

Charles has claims to be a victim of the Asiatic fixing of his family. No wife brought from Karachi to Southall by imperious parents-in-law could better respect an arranged marriage than the English rose heavily urged for the Crown Prince. She was English (after much public scorn of the former Teutonic norm), a virgin and thus free from all tattle, and she looked good. The facts: that she is virtuoso of on-camera tears, that her delight in life is the nightclub and that she seems to have no mind at all, were disregarded. An intelligent man has been fettered in 'a suitable marriage' to a frothball and has sought to live his life apart from her. What sharper intimation of the shabbiness of monarchy could there be?

There are many reasons for dispensing with monarchy, but two will suffice. The job could be done better; and monarchy, just by existing, induces pathetic impulses in other people. There has to be something wrong with an institution which assembles, in various degrees of competitive abjectness, Lord St John of Fawsley, in whom I have real difficulty believing, Sir Alastair Burnet and Lord Rees-Mogg.

These Firbankian grotesques, prime fruit of the trees of

deference, can be relied upon to squelch noisily under royal foot. Happy calling someone twenty years younger 'Sir' or 'Maa-am' they proclaim a social pyramid in which their own status is secured by guileful proximity to the apex. They fawn and teach us to fawn. Unlike the late Richard Dimbleby, grand under-butler to the nation, they do not tell us that the Queen looks radiant, but they are lit by all the royal refection into which they can creep.

Such courtiers only echo the sick adoration of part of the nation. Royalty has done a roaring trade since the war in glossy iconic tosh, books about royal lives, houses, tours, weddings, ancestry and interior décor, books, God help us, about royal dogs. The appetite of silly people for living vicarious, reverential lives through this assembly of low-octane duds in jodhpurs is tragic.

Edward Pearce, the Guardian, *'The Aspirin of the People'*

Prince Charles is an insensitive, hypocritical oaf and Princess Diana is a selfish, empty-headed bimbo. They should never have got married in the first place. I blame the parents.

Richard Littlejohn, in the Sun

Harlot and trollop

Alleged remarks by Prince Philip in letter to Diana. Officially denied.

So thick and yet so thin.

Comedian Linda Smith on Princess Diana

A sort of social hand grenade, ready to explode, leaving unsuspecting playboys legless and broken.
Trevor Philips on the Princess of Wales, shortly before her death

Shea was a master of evasion, more slippery than a Jacuzzi full of KY jelly. You might say he was the first Sensitol-lubricated PR man – particularly appropriate when you consider where he has spent most of his life.
Richard Littlejohn on Michael Shea, the Queen's former press secretary, in the Sun

I'm prepared to take advice on leisure from Prince Philip. He's a world expert on leisure. He's been practising for most of his adult life.
Neil Kinnock on Prince Philip, in the Western Mail

Why don't you naff off!
Princess Anne to reporters, in the Daily Mirror

He is a man of many ideas, most of them bad.
Oliver Kamm on Prince Charles

It's no wonder you're deaf.
Prince Philip, to children from the British Deaf Association as they stood next to a Caribbean steel band

My, you must have fun chasing the soap around the bath.
Diana, Princess of Wales, shaking hands with a one-armed man in Australia, 1983

People, Politicians and Government

In all ages, whatever the form and name of government, be it monarchy, republic, or democracy, an oligarchy lurks behind the façade.
Ronald Syme

I'm starting to think that the Facebook status update I liked has had absolutely no influence on Government policy at all.
@RogerQuimbly

We have screwed up. Not a little but a lot. No country in Europe has screwed up as much as we have. It can be explained. We have obviously lied throughout the past 18 to 24 months. It was perfectly clear that what we were saying was not true ... I almost perished because I had to pretend for 18 months that we were governing. Instead we lied morning, noon and night.
Ferenc Gyurcsány, Hungarian Prime Minister, recorded in a private meeting to his party in 2006. The broadcast caused riots.

It is a peculiarity of our times that we want politicians to be
more human, and then, when they screw up, we demand they
be more professional.
Ann Treneman

I have found some of the best reasons I ever had for remaining
at the bottom simply by looking at the men at the top.
Frank More Colby

He was a man of splendid abilities but utterly corrupt. Like
rotten mackerel by moonlight, he shines and stinks.
John Randolph on fellow-US-politician Edward Livingstone

The urge to power is a personality disorder in its own right,
like the urge to sexual congress with children or the taste for
rubber underwear.
Auberon Waugh

One baby is a patient baby, and waits indefinitely until its
mother is ready to feed it. The other baby is an impatient baby
and cries lustily, screams and kicks and makes everybody
unpleasant until it is fed. Well, we know perfectly well which
baby is attended to first. That is the whole history of politics.
Emmeline Pankhurst

Generosity is part of my character, and I therefore hasten to
assure this Government that I will never make an allegation of

dishonesty against it wherever a simple explanation of stupidity will suffice.
Leslie Lever

Being in politics is like being a football coach. You have to be smart enough to understand the game and dumb enough to think it is important.
Eugene J. McCarthy

If I had known Henry was going to be President I would have sent him to school.
A 19th-century President of Bolivia's mother

There exists no politician in India daring enough to attempt to explain to the masses that cows can be eaten.
Indira Gandhi

No party in Ireland is prepared to accept anything except the impossible.
W.E. Gladstone

Sire, I have other sons.
Lord Stanley, at the Battle of Bosworth, having been told by Richard III that his son would be executed if Stanley did not support him

They are nothing else but a load of kippers – two-faced, with no guts.
Eric Heffer on the Conservative Government

A liberal is just a conservative who hasn't been mugged.
Hilton Hamman, South African self-defence expert

A liberal is a man too broad-minded to take his own side in a quarrel.
Robert Frost

A liberal is someone whose interests are not threatened at the moment.
Ann Leslie

A liberal is a conservative who's been arrested.
Tom Wolfe

Have I said something foolish?
Phocion, to his friend, Diogenes Laertius, after the crowd applauded a point in his speech, 150 BC

First rate men will not canvas mobs: and mobs will not elect first rate men.
Lord Salisbury

The people would be just as noisy if they were going to see me hanged.
Oliver Cromwell, referring to a noisy crowd of admirers

True terror is to wake up one morning and realise that your high school class is running the country.
Kurt Vonnegut

The penalty of success is to be bored by people who used to snub you.
Nancy Astor

Far better to keep your mouth shut and let everyone think you're stupid than to open it and leave no doubt.
Norman Tebbit to Dennis Skinner

We had lost the art of communication – but not, alas, the gift of speech.
Gordon Brown, then Shadow Chancellor, on the Labour Party's 1983 election campaign, 1997

The reason academic politics are so bitter is that so little is at stake.
Sayre's law, as summarised by Henry Kissinger

He is undoubtedly living proof that a pig's bladder on a stick can be elected as a member of parliament.
Tony Banks on fellow MP Terry Dicks

Since a politician never believes what he says, he is surprised when others believe him.
Charles de Gaulle. Attrib.

A horrible voice, bad breath and a vulgar manner – the characteristics of a popular politician.
Aristophanes

Politics is the gentle art of getting votes from the poor and campaign contributions from the rich by promising to protect each from the other.
Edward Bennet Williams, US political campaign organiser

An election is coming. Universal peace is declared, and the foxes have a sincere interest in prolonging the lives of the poultry.
George Eliot, Felix Holt

He brings to the fierce struggle of politics the tepid enthusiasm of a lazy summer afternoon at a cricket match.
Aneurin Bevan on Clement Attlee

Reform? Reform? Aren't things bad enough already?
The Duke of Wellington

Too bad all the people who know how to run the country are busy driving cabs and cutting hair.
George Burns

It is easier to cancel a nuclear submarine than a civil servant's parking space.
Simon Jenkins

One fifth of the people are against everything all the time.
Robert Kennedy

It's a sure sign of political backwardness when any movement is led by students.
A.J.P. Taylor

Every great cause begins as a movement, becomes a business, and eventually deteriorates into a racket.
Eric Hoffer

Kill your enemies with cream.
Peter Mandelson's favourite saying

The reason there are so few female politicians is that it is too much trouble to put make-up on two faces.
Maureen Murphy

It is now known ... that men enter local politics solely as a result of being unhappily married.
Cyril Northcote Parkinson, Parkinson's Law

Politics, as a practice, whatever its professions, had always been the systematic organization of hatred.
Henry Adams, The Education of Henry Adams

Politicians can forgive almost anything in the way of abuse; they can forgive subversion, revolution, being contradicted, exposed as liars, even ridiculed, but they can never forgive being ignored.
Auberon Waugh, in the Observer

For a nation to try to tax itself into prosperity is like a man standing in a bucket and trying to lift himself up by the handle.
Winston Churchill

Under every stone lurks a politician.
Aristophanes

The soft bigotry of low expectations.
George W. Bush on the welfare state

Our human stock is threatened ... These mothers ... single parents from classes 4 and 5, are now producing a third of all births. If we do nothing the nation moves towards degeneration.
Sir Keith Joseph, Conservative politician. The speech ended his hope of leadership.

For every difficult intractable problem there's a solution that's neat, plausible and wrong.
H.L. Mencken

Only constant repetition will finally succeed in imprinting an idea on the memory of the crowd.
Adolf Hitler, Mein Kampf

Would that the Roman people had one neck!
Gaius Caesar, commonly known as Caligula

I was elected by a bunch of fat, stupid, ugly old ladies that watch soap operas, play bingo, read tabloids and don't know the metric system.

Tom Alcieri on his election as a Republican member of the New Hampshire state legislature

Democracy has been served – the people have spoken, (*sotto voce*) the bastards.

Wendell Willkie on hearing of his defeat by President Roosevelt

There is nothing more tyrannical than a strong popular feeling among a democratic people.

Anthony Trollope

Democracy is the process by which people choose who to blame.

Bertrand Russell

Democracy, which means despair of finding any Heroes to govern you.

Thomas Carlyle

Athenian democracy is destroying itself because it taught its citizens to regard disrespect as a right, lawlessness as a liberty, impertinence as equality and anarchy as enjoyment.

Socrates

Drop dead, you little cretin.

Nicolas Sarkozy after a man rejected his handshake in a crowd and shouted 'Don't touch me, you will make me dirty'.

A committee is a group of people who individually can do nothing but as a group decide nothing can be done.
Fred Allen

The broad mass of a nation ... will more easily fall victim to a big lie than to a small one.
Adolf Hitler, Mein Kampf

That garrulous monk.
Benito Mussolini on Adolf Hitler

A group is always more easily deceived than an individual.
Pío Baroja

When a politician changes his position it's sometimes hard to tell whether he has seen the light or felt the heat.
Robert Fuoss

Oratory: the art of making deep noises from the chest sound like important messages from the brain.
H.I. Phillips

Politicians are people who, when they see light at the end of the tunnel, order more tunnel.
John Quinton, a banker

Few things are as immutable as the addiction of political groups to the ideas by which they have once won office.
John Kenneth Galbraith, The Affluent Society

In a dying civilisation, political prestige is the reward not of the shrewdest diagnostician but of the man with the best bedside manner.
Eric Ambler

A common definition of gaffe is when a politician tells the truth.
Alexander Chancellor

Well, you might try getting crucified and rising again on the third day.
Talleyrand on what might impress the French peasantry

Out of the crooked timber of humanity no straight thing can ever be made.
Immanuel Kant, Idee zu einer allgemeinen Geschichte in weltbürgerlicher Absicht

The people long eagerly for just two things – bread and circuses.
Juvenal, Satires

Without exaggerating, the miners' leaders were the stupidest men in England, had we not had frequent occasion to meet the mine owners.
Lord Birkenhead

Two kinds of government chair correspond with the two kinds

of minister: one sort folds up instantly and the other sort goes round and round.

Sir Humphrey Appleby, the fictional senior civil servant, in Yes, Prime Minister

The urge to pass new laws must be seen as an illness, not much different from the urge to bite old women.

Auberon Waugh

There ain't nothing in the middle of the road but yellow lines and dead armadillos.

Texan politician on 'middle of the road' politics

Consensus: the process of abandoning all beliefs, principles, values and policies in search of something in which no one believes.

Margaret Thatcher

The hottest places in hell are reserved for those who, in times of great moral crisis, maintain their neutrality.

Dante

I prefer the cacophony of the playground to the tortured prose of Whitehall but both answer to a need: that of a child to say something and a bureaucrat to say nothing.

Simon Jenkins

The business of the Civil Service is the orderly management of decline.
William Armstrong, Head of the Civil Service 1968–74

Guidelines for bureaucrats: (1) When in charge, ponder;
(2) When in trouble, delegate; (3) When in doubt, mumble.
James H. Boren

A government bureau is the nearest thing to eternal life we will ever see on this Earth.
Ronald Reagan

A tree's a tree. How many do you need to look at?
Ronald Reagan on plans to expand California's Redwood National Park 1967

Saying sorry is becoming fashionable ... because it's something government can do without raising taxes.
Joe Rogaly

A diplomat ... is a person who can tell you to go to hell in such a way that you actually look forward to the trip.
Caskie Stinnett

Diplomacy is the art of saying 'Nice Doggie' until you can find a rock.
Will Rogers

The great Unwashed.
Lord Henry Brougham. Attrib.

The whole aim of practical politics is to keep the populace alarmed (and hence clamorous to be led to safety) by menacing it with an endless series of hobgoblins, all of them imaginary.

H.L. Mencken

Freedom's just another word for nothing left to lose.

Kris Kristofferson, American actor and singer

I have more than once pointed out that no organisation with 'liberation' in its title has ever, or ever will, liberate anyone or anything.

Bernard Levin

Watching the eurozone countries trying to resolve their debt crisis has been like watching 17 people in oven gloves manipulating a Rubik's cube.

John Lichfield

The only person alive actually famed for his obscurity.

Hugo Rifkind on Herman Van Rompuy, first President of the European Council

All the charisma of a damp rag and the appearance of a low-grade bank clerk.

Nigel Farage on Herman Van Rompuy

I believe there is something out there watching over us. Unfortunately it's the government.

Woody Allen

Left and Right

Welcome to Britain's New Political Order. No passion ... No Right. No Left. Just multi-hued blancmange.
Austin Mitchell

The facile leather-tongued oracle of the ordinary bourgeois intelligence.
Karl Marx on Jeremy Bentham

The world would not be in such a snarl, had Marx been Groucho instead of Karl.
Irving Berlin on Karl Marx

The left always has an orgasm when it sees a crowd.
Simon Jenkins

The voice of the discontented wealthy.
Nick Cohen on Russell Brand

You can read Russell Brand's autobiography and dismiss it as

rubbish, if you like. Or you can dismiss it as rubbish without reading it, to save time.
Stewart Lee

I couldn't see him overthrowing a table of drinks.
Noel Gallagher on Russell Brand

As with the Christian religion, the worst advertisement for Socialism is its adherents.
George Orwell

An idea isn't responsible for the people who believe in it.
Don Marquis

We should have had socialism in this country long ago, if it were not for the bloody people who became socialists.
George Bernard Shaw

Conservative ideal of freedom and progress: everyone to have an unfettered opportunity of remaining exactly where they are.
Geoffrey Madan

That dreary tribe of high-minded women and sandal-wearers and bearded fruit-juice drinkers who come flocking towards the smell of 'progress' like bluebottles to a dead cat.
George Orwell on left-wing intellectuals

I would rather consult my valet than the Conservative conference.
Arthur Balfour

My son is 22 years old. If he had not become a communist at 22, I would have disowned him. If he is still a communist at 30, I will do it then.
Georges Clemenceau

There are lots of ways to get socialism, but I think trying to fracture the Labour party by incessant contest cannot be one of them.
Neil Kinnock

We know that the organised workers of the country are our friends. As for the rest, they don't matter a tinker's cuss.
Emanuel Shinwell, Labour politician

My epitaph must be: 'Died of writing inane letters to empty-headed Conservative Associations'. It is a miserable death to look forward to.
Lord Salisbury

They are political Calibans on Prospero's island, chanting their subversive songs only to each other.
Jenny McCartney on the Left

After God had finished the rattlesnake, the toad, and the vampire, he had some awful substance left with which he made a scab. A scab is a two-legged animal with a corkscrew soul, a water brain, a combination backbone of jelly and glue. Where others have hearts, he carries a tumor of rotten principles.

Jack London on strikebreakers

The trouble with socialism is that it takes up too many evenings.

Oscar Wilde

A conservative is a man with two perfectly good legs who has never learned how to walk forward.

Franklin D. Roosevelt

Why do Republicans hate gay marriage so much? They certainly don't hate gay prostitutes.

Margaret Cho

Its relationship to democratic institutions is that of the death-watch-beetle – it is not a Party, it is a conspiracy.

Aneurin Bevan on the Communist Party

Russian communism is the illegitimate child of Karl Marx and Catherine the Great.

Clement Attlee

I shall be an autocrat: that's my trade. And the good Lord will forgive me: that's his.

Catherine the Great. Attrib.

The most radical revolutionary will become a conservative on the day after the revolution.
Hannah Arendt

Russia is a collapse, not a revolution.
D.H. Lawrence

Every revolution evaporates and leaves behind it only the slime of a new bureaucracy.
Franz Kafka

It would have been better if the experiment had been conducted in some small country, to make it clear it was a Utopian idea.
Boris Yeltsin on Communism

The Party line is that there is no Party line.
Milovan Djilas on reforms to the Yugoslavian Communist Party

It is a Party shackled by tradition; all the cautious people, all the timid, all the unimaginative, belong to it. It stumbles slowly and painfully from precedent to precedent with its eyes fixed on the ground.
Lord Salisbury on the Conservative Party

We will bury you.
Nikita Khrushchev at a Kremlin reception

A pig-eyed bag of wind.

Frank L. Howley on Nikita Khrushchev

When you are skinning your customers, you should leave some on to grow so that you can skin them again.

Nikita Khrushchev to British businessmen

No amount of cajolery, and no attempts at ethical and social seduction, can eradicate from my heart a deep burning hatred for the Tory Party ... So far as I am concerned they are lower than vermin.

Aneurin Bevan

I Told You So You Fucking Fools.

Kingsley Amis's suggested name change for a republication of Robert Conquest's The Great Terror. Conquest had been attacked by the left as a Cold War propagandist at the time of the original publication.

The Pope! How many divisions has he got?

Joseph Stalin, when urged by Pierre Laval to tolerate Catholicism in the USSR to appease the Pope

The most eminent mediocrity in the party.

Leon Trotsky on Joseph Stalin

Pathological exhibits ... human scum ... paranoiacs, degenerates, morons, bludgers ... pack of dingoes ... industrial outlaws and political lepers ... ratbags. If these people went to Russia, Stalin wouldn't even use them for manure.

Arthur Calwell, Australian Minister of Immigration, on Australian Communists

When I give food to the poor, they call me a saint. When I ask why the poor have no food, they call me a communist.

Brazilian archbishop Hélder Câmara

That all men are equal is a proposition to which at ordinary times, no sane individual has ever given his assent.

Aldous Huxley, Proper Studies

To be absolutely honest, what I feel really bad about is that I don't feel worse. That's the ineffectual liberal's problem in a nutshell.

Michael Frayn

Wonderful theory, wrong species.

Biologist E.O. Wilson on Marxism

Stupid asses.

Karl Marx and Friedrich Engels on the proletariat, private correspondence

If the workers had an inkling of the sacrifices that were necessary for this work, which was written only for them and for their sakes to be completed they would perhaps show a little more interest.

Jenny Marx, frustrated by the lack of attention given to the publication of her husband's magnum opus, Das Kapital.

The trouble with socialism is that eventually you run out of other people's money.
Margaret Thatcher

'To borrow and to borrow and to borrow' is not Macbeth with a heavy cold: it is Labour Party policy.
Margaret Thatcher

Communism is the longest path from capitalism to capitalism.
Russian joke

It is too early to say.
Zhou Enlai, 20th-century Chinese Party Chairman, asked for his assessment of the 1789 French Revolution. But he may have thought the question was about revolutionary French students.

An ideological movement is a collection of people, many of whom could hardly bake a cake, fix a car, sustain a friendship or a marriage, or even do a quadratic equation, yet they believe they know how to rule the world.
Professor Kenneth Minogue

I've been married to one Marxist and one fascist, and neither one would take the garbage out.
Actor Lee Grant

British Politics

What shall we do with this bauble? There, take it away.

Oliver Cromwell, dismissing Parliament, 1653

SIR,
I have received your letter with indignation and with scorn
return you this answer ... I scorn your proffer; I disdain your
favour; I abhor your treason; and am so far from delivering up
this island to your advantage, that I shall keep it to the utmost
of my power, and, I hope, to your destruction. Take this for
your final answer, and forbear any further solicitations; for if
you trouble me with any more messages of this nature, I will
burn your paper, and hang up your messenger.
DERBY

*The Earl of Derby, a Royalist holding the Isle of Man, to General Henry Ireton,
Cromwell's son in law*

... consider into the commission of what crimes, impieties,
wickednesses, and unheard of villanies, we have been led,
cheated, cozened, and betrayed, by that grand impostor, that

loathsome hypocrite, that detestable traitor, that prodigy of nature, that opprobrium of mankind, that landscape of iniquity, that sink of sin, and that compendium of baseness, who now calls himself our Protector. What have we done, nay, what have we not done, which either hellish policy was able to contrive, or brutish power to execute? We have trampled underfoot all authorities; we have laid violent hands upon our own Sovereign; we have ravished our Parliaments; we have deflowered the virgin liberty of our nation; we have put a yoke, an heavy yoke of iron, upon the necks of our own countrymen; we have thrown down the walls and bulwarks of the people's safety; we have broken often repeated oaths, vows, engagements, covenants, protestations; we have betrayed our trusts; we have violated our faiths; we have lifted up our hands to heaven deceitfully; and that these our sins might want no aggravation to make them exceedingly sinful, we have added hypocrisy to them all; and ... like the audacious strumpet, wiped our mouths, and boasted that we have done no evil ...
Anabaptist address to Charles II, attacking Cromwell shortly before his death

Sir, the atrocious crime of being a young man, which the honourable gentleman has, with such spirit and decency, charged upon me, I shall neither attempt to palliate nor deny; but content myself with wishing that I may be one of those whose follies may cease with their youth, and not of those who continue ignorant in spite of age and experience ... Much more, Sir, is he to be abhorred, who, as he has advanced in age, has receded from virtue, and become more wicked with less temptation: who prostitutes himself for money which he cannot enjoy, and spends the remains of his life in the ruin of his country.

William Pitt, speech, after entering Parliament, to Horace Walpole, who had mocked his youth

Gentlemen, I received yours and am surprised by your insolence in troubling me about the Excise. You know, what I very well know, that I bought you. And I know, what perhaps you think I don't know, you are now selling yourselves to somebody Else; and I know, what you do not know, that I am buying another borough. May God's curse light upon you all: may your houses be as open and common to all Excise Officers as your wives and daughters were to me, when I stood for your scoundrel corporation. Yours, etc., Anthony Henley

Letter from Anthony Henley, MP for Southampton (1727–34), to his constituents, following their protests over the Excise Bill

Mr Speaker, I said the honourable member was a liar it is true and I am sorry for it. The honourable member may place the punctuation where he pleases.

Richard Brinsley Sheridan on being asked to apologise for calling a fellow MP a liar. Attrib.

Therefore I charge Mr Hastings with having destroyed, for private purposes, the whole system of government by the six provincial Councils, which he had no right to destroy.

I charge him with taking bribes of Gunga Govind Sing.

I charge him with not having done that bribe-service which

fidelity, even in iniquity, requires at the hands of the worst of men.

I charge him with having robbed those persons of whom he took the bribes.

I charge him with having fraudulently alienated the fortunes of widows.

I charge him with having, without right, title or purchase, taken the lands of orphans and given them to wicked persons under him.

I charge him with having removed the natural guardians of a minor Raja, and given his zamindary to that wicked person, Deby Singh.

I charge him – his wickedness being known to himself and all the world – with having committed to Deby Singh the management of three great provinces; and with having thereby wasted the country, destroyed the landed interest, cruelly harassed the peasants, burnt their houses, seized their crops, tortured and degraded their persons, and destroyed the honour of the whole female race of that country.

Edmund Burke, peroration on Warren Hastings, 1788

As he rose like a rocket, he fell like a stick.

Thomas Paine on Edmund Burke

When I get into Parliament, I will pledge myself to no party, but write upon my forehead in legible characters 'To Be Let'.

Tom Sheridan to his father, Richard Brinsley Sheridan

And under it, Tom, write 'Unfurnished'.
Richard Sheridan's reply

With death doomed to grapple
Beneath this cold slab, he
Who lied in the Chapel
Now lies in the Abbey.
Lord Byron on William Pitt

... two vultures sick for battle,
Two scorpions under one wet stone,
Two bloodless wolves whose dry throats rattle,
Two crows perched on the murrained cattle,
Two vipers tangled into one.
Percy Bysshe Shelley, similes for two political characters of 1819 – the Home
Secretary Sidmouth, and Foreign Secretary and Leader of the Commons, Castlereagh

Why is a pump like Viscount Castlereagh? –
Because it is a slender thing of wood,
That up and down its awkward arm doth sway,
And coolly spout and spout and spout away,
In one weak, washy, everlasting flood.
Thomas Moore on Viscount Castlereagh

I met Murder on the way – He had a mask like Castlereagh ...
Percy Bysshe Shelley, The Mask of Anarchy

Posterity will ne'er survey
A nobler grave than this;

Here lie the bones of Castlereagh:
Stop here traveller, and piss.
Lord Byron on Viscount Castereagh, who killed himself

Honest in the most odious sense of the word.
Benjamin Disraeli on W.E. Gladstone

I don't object to the Old Man always having the ace of trumps
up his sleeve, but merely to his belief that God Almighty put it
there.
Henry Labouchere on W.E. Gladstone

An old man in a hurry.
Lord Randolph Churchill on W.E. Gladstone

Gladstone ... founded the great tradition ... in public to speak
the language of the highest and strictest principle, and in
private to pursue and possess every sort of woman.
Peter Wright on W.E. Gladstone

Mr Peter Wright,
Your Garbage about Mr Gladstone in 'Portraits and Criticisms'
has come to our knowledge. You are a liar. Because you
slander a dead man, you are a coward. Because you think the
public will accept invention from such as you, you are a fool.
GLADSTONE

I associate myself with this letter.

H.N. GLADSTONE

W.E. Gladstone's son

The Right Honourable Gentleman's smile is like the silver fittings on a coffin.

Benjamin Disraeli on Sir Robert Peel

... the powers of a first-rate man and the creed of a second-rate man.

Walter Bagehot on Sir Robert Peel

Mrs Thatcher is a woman of common views but uncommon abilities.

Julian Critchley on Margaret Thatcher

If a traveller were informed that such a man was the Leader of the House of Commons, he might begin to comprehend how the Egyptians worshipped an insect.

Benjamin Disraeli on Lord John Russell

He has committed every crime that does not require courage.

Benjamin Disraeli on the Irish agitator Daniel O'Connell

He is a liar. (Cheers) He is a liar in action and in words. His life is a living lie. He is a disgrace to his species ... He is the most degraded of his species and kind; and England is degraded in tolerating or having upon the face of her society a miscreant of his abominable, foul and atrocious nature. (Cheers)

Daniel O'Connell on Benjamin Disraeli, at a meeting of trades unions in Dublin

London, May 6 [1835]
Mr O'Connell:
Although you have long placed yourself out of the pale of
civilization, still I am one who will not be insulted, even by a
Yahoo, without chastising it ... Listen, then, to me. If it had
been possible for you to act like a gentleman, you would have
hesitated before you made your foul and insolent comments
... With regard to your taunts as to my want of success in my
election contests, permit me to remind you that I had nothing
to appeal to but the good sense of the people ... I am not
one of those public beggars that we see swarming with their
obtrusive boxes in the chapels of your creed ...

We shall meet at Philippi; and ... I will seize the first
opportunity of inflicting upon you a castigation which will
make you at the same time remember and repent the insults
you have lavished upon
BENJAMIN DISRAELI
Benjamin Disraeli to Daniel O'Connell

As I sat opposite the Treasury Bench, the Ministers reminded
me of one of those marine landscapes not very unusual on
the coast of South America. You behold a range of exhausted
volcanoes, not a flame flickers on a single pallid crest, but the
situation is still dangerous. There are occasional earthquakes,
and ever and anon the dark rumbling of the sea.
Benjamin Disraeli on the Liberal Government

There is not a criminal in an European gaol, there is not
a cannibal in the South Sea Islands, whose indignation

would not rise and boil at the recital of that which has been done, which has too late been examined, but which remains unavenged; which has left behind all the foul and all the fierce passions that produced it, and which may again spring up, in another murderous harvest, from the soil soaked and reeking in blood, and in the air tainted with every imaginable deed of crime and shame. That such things should be done once, is a damning disgrace to the portion of our race which did them; that a door should be left open for their ever-so-barely possible repetition would spread that shame over the whole ...

W.E. Gladstone on the Turks, Bulgarian Horrors and the Question of the East

He made his conscience not his guide but his accomplice.

Benjamin Disraeli on W.E. Gladstone

... What should we do with others to confront this threat to our citizens, our nation, other nations and the people who suffer under the yoke, the cruel yoke, of Daesh?

... We know that in June four gay men were thrown off the fifth storey of a building in the Syrian city of Deir ez-Zor. We know that in August the 82-year-old guardian of the antiquities of Palmyra, Professor Khaled al-Assad, was beheaded, and his headless body was hung from a traffic light. And we know that in recent weeks there has been the discovery of mass graves in Sinjar, one said to contain the bodies of older Yazidi women murdered by Daesh because they were judged too old to be sold for sex ... Given that we know what they are doing, can we really stand aside ... ?

Hilary Benn MP, Shadow Foreign Secretary, defending air-strikes on Syria in a Commons Speech on 2 Dec 2015

He has not a single redeeming defect.

Benjamin Disraeli on W.E. Gladstone

If Gladstone fell into the Thames, that would be a misfortune, and if anybody pulled him out that, I suppose, would be a calamity.

Benjamin Disraeli on W.E. Gladstone asked to distinguish misfortune and calamity

He was without any rival whatever, the first comic genius who ever installed himself in Downing Street.

Michael Foot on Benjamin Disraeli

A sophistical rhetorician, inebriated with the exuberance of his own verbosity, and gifted with an egotistical imagination, that can at all times command an interminable and inconsistent series of arguments, malign an opponent and glorify himself.

Benjamin Disraeli on W.E. Gladstone, parodying his style

Gladstone ... spent his declining years trying to guess the answer to the Irish Question; unfortunately whenever he was getting warm, the Irish secretly changed the question.

W.C. Sellar and R.J. Yeatman in 1066 and All That

Mr Gladstone speaks to me as if I were a public meeting.
Queen Victoria on W.E. Gladstone

If you weren't such a great man you'd be a terrible bore.
Mrs W.E. Gladstone to her husband

Mr Gladstone read Homer for fun, which I thought served him right.
Winston Churchill on W.E. Gladstone

He spent his whole life in plastering together the true and the false and therefrom extracting the plausible.
Stanley Baldwin on David Lloyd George

Not even a public figure. A man of no experience. And of the utmost insignificance.
Lord Curzon on Stanley Baldwin

A lot of hard-faced men who look as if they had done very well out of the war.
Stanley Baldwin, referring to the post-First-World-War Commons

English policy is to float lazily downstream, occasionally putting out a diplomatic boathook to avoid collisions.
Lord Salisbury

He occasionally stumbled over the truth, but hastily picked himself up and hurried on as if nothing had happened.
Winston Churchill on Stanley Baldwin

Like a cushion, he always bore the impress of the last man who sat on him.

David Lloyd George on Lord Derby; also attrib. to Lord Haig

This goat-footed bard, this half-human visitor to our age from the hag-ridden magic and uncharted woods of Celtic antiquity.

John Maynard Keynes on David Lloyd George

He aroused every feeling except trust.

A.J.P. Taylor on David Lloyd George

The tenth possessor of a foolish face.

David Lloyd George on any aristocrat

When they circumcised Herbert Samuel they threw away the wrong bit.

David Lloyd George. Attrib.

He could not see a belt without hitting below it.

Margot Asquith on David Lloyd George

The Right Honourable gentleman has sat so long on the fence that the iron has entered his soul.

David Lloyd George on Sir John Simon. Attrib.

It is fitting that we should have buried the Unknown Prime Minister by the side of the Unknown Soldier.

Herbert Asquith at Andrew Bonar Law's funeral. Attrib.

For twenty years he has held a season-ticket on the line of least resistance.
Leo Amery on H.H. Asquith

If I am a great man, then a good many of the great men of history are frauds.
Andrew Bonar Law. Attrib.

I must follow them; I am their leader.
Andrew Bonar Law

I met Curzon in Downing Street, from whom I got the sort of greeting a corpse would give to an undertaker.
Stanley Baldwin. Attrib.

One could not even dignify him with the name of a stuffed shirt. He was simply a hole in the air.
George Orwell on Stanley Baldwin

I would rather be an opportunist and float, than go to the bottom with my principles round my neck.
Stanley Baldwin

Decided only to be undecided, resolved to be irresolute, adamant for drift, solid for fluidity, all-powerful to be impotent.
Winston Churchill on Stanley Baldwin

He has the lucidity which is the by-product of a fundamentally

sterile mind ... Listening to a speech by Chamberlain is like paying a visit to Woolworth's; everything in its place and nothing above sixpence.
Aneurin Bevan on Neville Chamberlain

The people of Birmingham have a specially heavy burden for they have given the world the curse of the present British Prime Minister.
Sir Stafford Cripps on Neville Chamberlain

There but for the grace of God goes God.
Winston Churchill on Sir Stafford Cripps

Well, he seemed such a nice old gentleman, I thought I would give him my autograph as a souvenir.
Adolf Hitler on Neville Chamberlain

He saw foreign policy through the wrong end of a municipal drainpipe.
Winston Churchill on Neville Chamberlain; also attrib. to David Lloyd George

He was a meticulous housemaid, great at tidying up.
A.J.P. Taylor on Neville Chamberlain

WANTED! Dead or alive! Winston Churchill. 25 years old. 5 feet 8 inches tall. Indifferent build. Walks with a bend forward. Pale complexion. Red-brownish hair. Small

toothbrush moustache. Talks through his nose and cannot
pronounce the letter 'S' properly.
Jan Smuts on Winston Churchill

I thought he was a young man of promise; but it appears he
was a young man of promises.
*Arthur James Balfour, writing in his diary of Winston Churchill's entry into
politics*

His style ... is not very literary, and he lacks force.
The Daily News on Winston Churchill's Maiden Speech

His impact on history would be no more than the whiff of
scent on a lady's purse.
David Lloyd George on Arthur Balfour

Wherever Sir Stafford Cripps has tried to increase wealth and
happiness, grass never grows again.
Colm Brogan, in 'Our New Masters'

I remember, when I was a child, being taken to the celebrated
Barnum's Circus, which contained an exhibition of freaks and
monstrosities; but the exhibit on the programme which I most
desired to see was the one described 'The Boneless Wonder'.
My parents judged that the spectacle would be too revolting
and demoralizing for my youthful eyes, and I have waited
fifty years to see The Boneless Wonder sitting on the Treasury
Bench.
Winston Churchill on Ramsay MacDonald

Sit down, man. You're a bloody tragedy.

James Maxton, Scottish Labour leader, heckling Ramsay MacDonald during the latter's last Commons speech. Attrib.

Winston had devoted the best years of his life to preparing his impromptu speeches.

F.E. Smith on Winston Churchill

Tell the Lord Privy Seal I am sealed to my privy, and can only deal with one shit at a time.

Winston Churchill when interrupted on the toilet in his wartime bunker and told the Lord Privy Seal wished to see him. Attrib.

A glass of port in his hand and a fat cigar in his mouth, with a huge and bloody red steak which he puts in his mouth in big chunks, and chews and chatters and smokes until the blood trickles down his chin – and to think this monster comes of a good family.

Joseph Goebbels on Winston Churchill

A sheep in sheep's clothing.

Winston Churchill on Clement Attlee

A tardy little marionette.

Randolph Churchill on Clement Attlee

Dear Randolph, utterly unspoilt by failure.

Noël Coward on Randolph Churchill

A triumph of modern science – to find the only part of Randolph that wasn't malignant and remove it.

Evelyn Waugh on Randolph Churchill after an operation

An empty taxi arrived at 10 Downing Street, and when the door was opened Attlee got out.

Winston Churchill (attrib.) on Clement Attlee. But Kenneth Harris (Attlee, 1982) says Churchill denied the quote.

He will be as great a curse to this country in peace as he was a squalid nuisance in time of war.

Winston Churchill on Aneurin Bevan

Christopher, I don't think Mr Mikardo is such a nice man as he looks.

Winston Churchill to his parliamentary private secretary, Christopher Soames, about Ian Mikardo, who was a famously ugly MP

He has a brilliant mind, until he makes it up.

Margot Asquith on Sir Stafford Cripps, Autobiography

I must say that (Profumo) never struck me as a man at all like a cloistered monk; and that Miss Keeler is a professional prostitute. There seems to me to be a basic improbability about the proposition that their relationship was purely platonic. What are whores about? (turning to Macmillan) What is to happen now? We cannot just have business as usual ... I certainly will not quote at him the savage words of Cromwell, but perhaps some word of Browning might be appropriate:

'... let him never come back to us!
There would be doubt, hesitation and pain.
Forced praise on our part – the glimmer of twilight,
Never glad confident morning again.'
Nigel Birch MP on Harold Macmillan: Commons speech

Above any other position of eminence, that of Prime Minister
is filled by fluke.
Enoch Powell

Defeat comes from God, victory comes from the Government.
Aneurin Bevan on Winston Churchill

I have only one purpose, the destruction of Hitler, and my life
is much simplified thereby. If Hitler invaded Hell, I would
make at least a favourable reference to the Devil in the House
of Commons.
Winston Churchill

I have never seen a human being who more perfectly
represented the modern conception of a robot.
Winston Churchill on Molotov

He never spares himself in conversation. He gives himself
so generously that hardly anybody else is permitted to give
anything in his presence.
Aneurin Bevan on Churchill

I stuffed their mouths with gold!
Aneurin Bevan, explaining how he persuaded doctors to accept the National Health Service. Attrib.

MPs love letting fly at each other. The Speaker often struggles to police their language. Since the Official Report commenced in 1861, we can read a bewildering variety of judgements from the chair. What is or is not acceptable as Parliamentary scorn seems to depend on the Speaker's digestion. Take, for instance, rulings on how far a Member may go in calling another Member a liar. The following have been disallowed:

1862 a Member's statement was 'entirely false and without foundation' (Speaker: 'The hon. Member should express himself in proper language.')
1863 'scandalous and unfolded'
1868 'doing dodges'
1870 'false'
1881 'hardly credible'
1883 'resorting to trickiness'
1884 'shuffling'
1886 'dishonest and hypocritical'
1887 'foul calumny' and 'gigantic falsehood'
1888 'flippant mendacity'
1909 'cold and calculated lie'
1914 'mendacious'
     'infamous lie'
     'wilful falsehood'
1932 'perverter of the truth'

1945 'dishonest evasion'
1946 'abdominal lies'
1952 'a wicked misstatement of the truth'
1953 'dishonest'
1961 'untrue'
1963 'duplicity'
1966 'deliberate fabrication'
1967 'twister'
1976 'fiddling the figures'
1978 'arch confidence trickster'
    'spoke with a forked tongue'
1987 'economical with the truth'
1988 'numerological inexactitude'
    'organized mendacity'
1992 'telling porkies' (Speaker: 'I think we will not have that
    word. It escaped my notice last week. I had to look it up
    in the dictionary, but now I know what it means the hon.
    Member should please withdraw it.')
1993 'dishonest'

But these slipped through:

1864 'a calumnious [sic] statement'
1946 'devoid of any truth'
1959 'cooking the figures'
1988 'shameless lack of candour'
1994 'tissue of lies'

And the following lived a half-life, appearing in the first

edition of Hansard then disappearing from a Defence minister's lips, and the bound volume, after the Speaker declared it could not be verified on audio recordings:

2008 'absolute bollocks'
(However, in 2016 Emily Thornberry MP, Shadow Defence Minister, got away with mouthing the word)

It is similarly out of order to accuse another Member of being drunk. All the following having been ruled out of order:

1935 'Have you been drinking?'
1945 'Take him out, he's drunk!'
1951 'alcoholic jeers'
'not sober ...'
1974 'the appearance of being slightly inebriated'
1976 'a semi-drunken Tory brawl'
1983 'in this condition' (Claire Short, MP, of the minister Alan Clark. I was there. He was drunk. But the Deputy Speaker reprimanded Short.)
1987 'in a drunken stupor'

However, in 1974 James Wellbeloved did slip past the Chair this half-retraction: 'I am not suggesting that they are drunk, I am merely suggesting that they are giving a very good imitation of it.'

Comparing another Member with an animal is also unwise. In 1976 the Speaker (Selwyn Lloyd) was clear: 'I always object to the use of animal terminology when applied to Members of this House.' He was banning a description by an MP of the Members opposite as 'laughing hyena'. Withdrawing the words, the MP substituted 'laughing Ken Dodds opposite', which the Chair found satisfactory. How Lloyd would view Michael Foot's description of Norman Tebbit as a 'semi house-trained polecat' we shall never know. Hansard's first recorded animalistic references consisted only of noises. These, and terms in the list which follows, have been ruled out of order:

1872 'amid the general confusion were heard imitations of the crowing of cocks, where at the Speaker declared the scenes unparliamentarily, and gross violations of order'
1884 'bigoted, malevolent young puppy'
1885 'jackal'
1886 'Tory skunks'
1923 'chameleon politician'
1930 'insolent young cub'
1931 'lie down, dog!'
'noble and learned camels' (of the Lords)
1936 'swine'
1946 'silly ass'
1948 'dirty dog'
1949 'stool pigeons'
1952 'you rat'
1953 'cheeky young pup'
1955 'rat'
1977 'snake'
1978 'bitchy' (of Mrs Thatcher)
1985 'baboons'

'his shadow spokesman's monkey'
1986 'political weasel and guttersnipe'
1987 'the morals of tom cats'
1989 'political skunk'

And these were allowed by the Chair:

1989 'the attention span of a gerbil'
     'the wolf of Dagenham'
1992 'the hamster from Bolsover' (of Dennis Skinner)
     'cruel swine' (of Kenneth Baker)

A surprising permission was the Speaker's declining to stop an MP describing Margaret Thatcher as 'behaving with all the sensitivity of a sex-starved boa constrictor'.

I have been helped in the selection of these examples by the research of parliamentary writer Phil Mason, whose book *Nothing Good Will Ever Come of It* quotes more than a century of MPs' recorded predictions, most of them hilariously off-target. Drawing on Mason's files, there follows a selection of various other Speakers' rulings on questionable language:

DISALLOWED
1861 'very insolent and scornful' (of the Chancellor)
1867 'returned by the refuse of a large constituency' (of an MP)
1872 'three peaceful shepherds had already turned their pipes behind him' (Speaker: 'not becoming expression')
1875 'Villains' (Samuel Plimsoll describing shipowners)

1877 Speaker: 'It is not proper to impute what of straight-
forwardness or courage to any Member or to imply
that a Member was not actuated by the feelings of a
gentleman.'

1878 'damnable character'

1880 Speaker: 'It is not in accordance with Parliamentary
usage to say that members of this House are on the side
of Atheism, irreligion and immorality.'

1881 'poltroon'

1884 'seditious blasphemer'
'ruffianism'

1885 'insolence'
'indecent purpose'

1887 'damned lot of cads'
'bad, mean, pettifogging' (of the House of Lords)

1888 'Judas'

1897 'tommy rot'

1900 'language of the pot-house'

1901 'fool'
'orgy of unbridled ruffianism'

1902 'pharisees and hypocrites'

1906 'the offscourings of Bristol' (of constituents)

1908 'vicious and vulgar'
'coward and a cad'

1910 'half pantaloon and half highwayman'

1911 'traitor'

1914 'swindlers' (of government)
'vulgar cad'

1924 'leader of a murder gang' (of a minister)

1926 'the minister of death' (of Minister of Health)
    'a mind on all fours with a London County Council
    sewer'

1928 'Pecksniffian cant'

1931 'blethering'
    'impertinent dog'
    'dirty rot'
    'sponger'

1939 'bunch of robbers'

1944 'unspeakable blackguard'

1946 'source of infection'

1949 'freelance demagogue'

1950 'yahoos opposite'

1951 'rabble', 'stooge'

1955 'nosey parker'

1956 'murderer'
    'traitorous defeatist'

1958 'I'll see you outside'
    'stinker'

1959 'dunderhead'
    'smart Alec'

1960 'oafish'

1961 'lousy'
    'slippery'
    'get back to the gutter'
    'white livered'

1965 'Quisling'
    'sheer, concentrated humbug'

1968 'A British Herr Himmler'

'scoundrel'
1969 'mean bastards'
1972 'the Right honourable cheat'
1975 'bunch of damned hypocrites'
'buffoon'
'grubby and squalid'
1976 'idiots'
'racialists'
'hooligan'
1978 'arch confidence trickster'
'ignorant bigot'
'the biggest basket of them all' (of Prices minister)
1980 'mass murderer'
1983 'two-faced'
1984 'supercilious git'
'mealy-mouthed hypocrisy'
'a load of bullshit'
'pompous sod' (Dennis Skinner of David Owen. Skinner
offered to withdraw 'pompous')
1985 'creeps'
1986 'bollocks'
'cretin'
'twerp'
'boring old twat'
'wimp'
1987 'bugger all'
'giggling idiot'
'go to hell'
'arrogant bastards'

    'fat bounder' (of Nigel Lawson)
    'bumptious balloon' (of Nigel Lawson)
    'Pakistani umpire'
1988 'bugger'
    'political shyster'
    'tweak his goolies'
    'poached bullshit'
    'sneak'
    'berk'
    'wicked'
    'cheat'
    'objectionable lout'
1989 'freak'
    'barmy'
1990 'ignorant twat'
    'poppycock, bunkum and balderdash'
    'scabs'
    'freeloading scroungers'
    'paid hack'
    'arrogant little shit'
    'spiv'
    'parasite'
    'Mr Oil Slick'
    'front bench yobo'
    'jerk'
    'kinnocchio'
1991 'trifler and opportunist'
1992 'little squirt'
    'like a 50p piece: two-faced and seven-sided'

'hack, obedient, lickspittle Tory member'

'clever little sod'

'stool pigeons'

1994 'shifty' (when used to describe a member but allowed for a policy)

'unctuous slob'

'ethically challenged'

'prat'

'stupid cow'

1995 'dimwit'

'nitwit'

1998 'gormless alien'

'the honourable anorak'

'piddling' (the alternative offered, 'two-bit', was also ruled out of order)

1999 'riff raff' (compare with page 152 'waifs and strays', 1996, which was challenged and deemed in order)

'bastard' (when used to describe a policy rather than a person)

2000 (to do) 'sod all'

'Whips' narcs'

2001 'con man'

2002 'coward'

2004 'little sod'

2009 'monster' (when referring to another Member)

2010 'pipsqueak'

2012 'sod'

2013 'conman'

2015 'idiot'

'crap' was allowed in July 1991, but ruled out of order just 5 months later. In 2015, it was allowed again, on the grounds that the Member was reporting the opinion of a constituent: '... the school had become a haven for every crap teacher in the north-east'.

ALLOWED

1931 'nonsensical twaddle' (Speaker: Use of nonsensical 'a matter of taste'. No judgement on twaddle)
'bunk'
'humbug'

1936 'tripe'

1947 'clear your ears out'

1949 'official stooge'
'Quisling'

1953 'unclean'

1957 'near treachery'
'bribery'

1958 'blather'

1959 'a card sharper and confidence trickster'

1966 'tame hacks'

1968 'go back to Moscow'

1970 'carpet bagger'

1971 'shower' (the Government)

1978 'political thug'

1985 'snivelling little git'

1986 'a Government of petty crooks'
'old Etonian twerp'
'Gauleiter'

'pathetic Member'

'wally'

'weak-minded'

1987 'a boot up the backside'

'arrogant little basket'

1988 'wet-necked twits'

'two-faced as hell'

1989 'be quiet, silly old fool'

'absolute bull'

'fathead'

'utter crap'

'street hooligan'

'yankee lickspittle'

'freaks' (as a description of opposing members. In the same year, the singular was ruled out of order as this was deemed to reflect upon an individual member)

Since 1990:

'twit'

'don't be so bloody stupid'

'bloodthirsty louts'

'too bloody mean'

'you mean and silly woman'

'shut up, you old windbag'

'[the minister] does not give a fart'

'witless, blind and stupid ...'

'Polly Pot in No 10' (of Mrs Thatcher)

1990 'pig's bladder on a stick'

1991 'bloodthirsty louts' (again, allowed as it did not refer to a
     particular individual)
1992 'mad fool, loony half-mad cretin'
     'millionaire's mammy boy' (ruled 'not wholly
     unparliamentary')
1995 'twaddle'
1996 'chancer'
     'waifs and strays'
     'school sneaks'
     'pygmy'
1997 'claptrap'
1998 'Sweet FA' (Mr Speaker confessed to be 'not certain
     whether this was unparliamentary, but most
     undesirable')
     [speaking] 'with forked tongue'
1999 'Stepford Wives' (as a description of opposing members)
     'Quislings' (the ruling in 1965 outlawing the same insult
     was on the singular which made all the difference)
     'to blackmail' (allowed as the speaker was accusing
     the Government of doing the deed, not an individual
     Member)
2000 'chopping off their goolies'
     'villain of the piece'
2002 'Oh, shit' (when used in quotation)
     'barmy'
2003 'getting well and truly shafted' (when used as a
     quotation from a constituent)
     'would have been well duffed up in that debate' (no
     admonition from the Chair when the speaker claimed

this to be unparliamentary)

'hypocritical sophistry', 'deceit' and 'lies' (all on the grounds that they were not being used to refer to individual Members but to opponents collectively)

'creating a great deal of wind' (criticising an opponent's line of argument)

2004 'knackered'

'a mafia' (as a description of an opposing party)

2005 'bonkers'

'bunkum'

2006 'total cock-up'

'toe-rags' (used to describe fraudsters, not other members)

'claptrap'

'culturally bananas'

2007 'shit' (when used as a noun)

'nincompoop'

2013 'bigot'

'untrue' (when accusing a Member of giving untrue information. It was permitted as, the chair explained, '[while] it would be wrong to say that the shadow Minister had intentionally misled the House ... to argue that he does not understand the matter and therefore says things that are untrue is not unparliamentary'.)

2014 'puerile and superficial' (when referring to a Member's views rather than to their personality)

2015 'a couple of Muppets' (referring to other Members)

2016 'wazzock' (in a debate on whether US Presidential candidate Donald Trump should be banned from

. coming to Britain, allowed presumably because the
speaker was not referring to a fellow Member)

And finally:
'that amiable dumb bell' (of Sir Geoffrey Howe).

The mild-mannered Sir Geoffrey Howe, Margaret Thatcher's
first Chancellor of the Exchequer and later Foreign Secretary,
finally turned against her in November 1990. His resignation
speech is quoted at some length below, not for the savagery of
its invective – the restrained prose makes for a less than
scorching read – but for its effect, which was the more
explosive in coming from a much-put-upon and
undemonstrative politician. Many would trace Thatcher's
downfall back to this Commons moment, which to witness
was stunning ...

[Sir Geoffrey reflects positively on his time as Margaret
Thatcher's first Chancellor of the Exchequer, but goes on to
say that the Prime Minister is failing to understand Britain's
relationship with European allies] ...
The European enterprise is not and should not be seen like
that – as some kind of zero sum game ... [a] ... nightmare
image sometimes conjured up by my right hon. Friend, who
seems sometimes to look out upon a continent that is
positively teeming with ill-intentioned people, scheming, in
her words, to 'extinguish democracy', to 'dissolve our national
identities' and to lead us 'through the back-door into a federal
Europe'. How on earth are the Chancellor and the Governor of

the Bank of England, commending the hard ecu as they strive to, to be taken as serious participants in the debate against that kind of background noise? ... It is rather like sending your opening batsmen to the crease only for them to find, the moment the first balls are bowled, that their bats have been broken before the game by the team captain ... but the task has become futile: trying to stretch the meaning of words beyond what was credible, and trying to pretend that there was a common policy when every step forward risked being subverted by some casual comment or impulsive answer. The conflict of loyalty ... to my right hon. Friend the Prime Minister ... and ... to what I perceive to be the true interests of the nation, has become all too great. I no longer believe it possible to resolve that conflict from within this Government. That is why I have resigned. In doing so, I have done what I believe to be right for my party and my country. The time has come for others to consider their own response to the tragic conflict of loyalties with which I have myself wrestled for perhaps too long.

Sir Geoffrey Howe, resigning from the government

How can one best summon up the exquisite, earnest tedium of the speech of Sir Geoffrey Howe in yesterday's South African debate? It was rather like watching a much-loved family tortoise creeping over the lawn in search of a distant tomato.

David McKie on Sir Geoffrey Howe

He is not only a bore, but he bores for England.

Malcolm Muggeridge on Sir Anthony Eden

Muggeridge, a garden gnome expelled from Eden, has come to rest as a gargoyle brooding over a derelict cathedral.
Kenneth Tynan on Malcolm Muggeridge

Harold Wilson was one of the men who ruined post-war Britain. He was a small posturing visionless politician, personally pleasant to his friends and even his enemies, amusing, irreverent and apparently kind. But his public work was a long strung-out disaster, overlaid by the impression at the time that it was at least dextrously accomplished.
Hugo Young

I'd like it translated.
Harold Macmillan during an address to the UN General Assembly after Nikita Khrushchev took off his shoe and banged the heel on the table

It was almost impossible to believe he was anything but a down-at-heel actor resting between engagements at the decrepit theatres of minor provincial towns.
Bernard Levin on Harold Macmillan, The Pendulum Years

Greater love hath no man than this, that he lay down his friends for his life.
Jeremy Thorpe after Harold Macmillan's 1962 Cabinet reshuffle

One can never escape the suspicion, with Mr Macmillan, that all his life was a preparation for elder statesmanship.
Frank Johnson on Harold Macmillan, in The Times

SIR ALEC DOUGLAS-HOME: Tell me, Mr Chairman, what do you think would have happened if Mr Khrushchev had been assassinated and not President Kennedy?
CHAIRMAN MAO: I do not believe Mr Onassis would have married Mrs Khrushchev.
Exchange at an official dinner

He is going around the country stirring up apathy.
William Whitelaw on Harold Wilson

If ever he went to school without any boots it was because he was too big for them.
Ivor Bulmer-Thomas on Harold Wilson's claims to an impoverished childhood

From Lord Hailsham we have had a virtuoso performance in the art of kicking a friend in the guts. When self-indulgence has reduced a man to the shape of Lord Hailsham, sexual continence involves no more than a sense of the ridiculous.
Reginald Paget MP on Lord Hailsham, following the Profumo scandal

'What have you done?' cried Christine,
'You've wrecked the whole party machine!
'To lie in the nude may be rude,
'But to lie in the house is obscene!'
Anonymous on John Profumo, about the Profumo scandal

The Conservative Party has two states: complacency and panic.
William Hague

If you were hanging from a ledge by your fingers, he'd stamp on them.
Edward Pearce on James Callaghan

A little boy sucking his misogynist thumb and blubbing and carping in the corner of the front bench below the gangway is a mascot which parliament can do without.
Nicholas Fairbairn MP on Edward Heath

A shiver looking for a spine to run up.
Harold Wilson on Edward Heath

Like being savaged by a dead sheep.
Denis Healey, referring to the attack by Sir Geoffrey Howe on his Budget proposals, in the Listener

A perfectly good second-class chemist, a Beta chemist ... she wasn't an interesting person, except as a Conservative ... I would never, if I had amusing, interesting people staying, have thought of asking Margaret Thatcher.
Dame Janet Vaughan (former tutor at Somerville College, Oxford) on Margaret Thatcher

I am not a doctor.
Edward Heath, declining to speculate on why Mrs Thatcher disliked him

Headstrong, obstinate and dangerously self-opinionated.
ICI personnel report on the 22-year-old Margaret Roberts (later Thatcher)

That fucking stupid, petit bourgeois woman.
Lord Carrington on Margaret Thatcher. Attrib.

The one thing I learnt as Margaret Thatcher's chief whip was that there is no limit to the capacity of human beings to absorb flattery.
Lord Wakeham

I don't mind how much my Ministers talk, as long as they do what I say.
Margaret Thatcher

They'll have the same as me.
Margaret Thatcher (in puppet form in the TV satire Spitting Image) while dining with her ministers. The waiter had taken her order for a steak and inquired 'and the vegetables?'

An extraordinary affair. I gave them their orders and they wanted to stay and discuss them.
The Duke of Wellington, describing his first Cabinet as Prime Minister

I've met serial killers and professional assassins and nobody scared me as much as Mrs T.
Ken Livingstone on Margaret Thatcher

Cette femme Thatcher! Elle a les yeux de Caligule, mais elle a la bouche de Marilyn Monroe.

(That woman Thatcher! She has the eyes of Caligula, but the mouth of Marilyn Monroe.)

François Mitterrand on Margaret Thatcher

In my lifetime all our problems have come from mainland Europe and all the solutions have come from the English-speaking nations of the world.

Margaret Thatcher

I wouldn't say she is open-minded on the Middle East, so much as empty-headed. She probably thinks Sinai is the plural of Sinus.

Jonathan Aitken MP on Margaret Thatcher

I wish that cow would resign.

Richard Needham MP, Northern Ireland minister, overheard on a telephone, on his Prime Minister, Margaret Thatcher

Like the deadly Upas tree, beneath whose branches nothing grows.

Denis Healey on Margaret Thatcher's deadening effect upon her Cabinet

La Pasionaria of middle-class privilege.

Denis Healey on Margaret Thatcher

Petain in petticoats.

Denis Healey on Margaret Thatcher

Rhoda the Rhino.

Denis Healey on Margaret Thatcher

The great she-elephant.
Julian Critchley on Margaret Thatcher

Jezebel.
Revd Ian Paisley on Margaret Thatcher

The Immaculate Misconception.
Norman St John-Stevas on Margaret Thatcher

Attila the Hen.
Clement Freud on Margaret Thatcher

David Owen in drag.
Rhodesia Herald on Margaret Thatcher

The trouble is that when she speaks without thinking she says what she thinks.
Norman St John Stevas on Margaret Thatcher

One of the things politics has taught me is that men are not a reasoned or reasonable sex.
Margaret Thatcher

Her Majesty does not notice what other people are wearing.
Buckingham Palace's alleged response to a request from Mrs Thatcher for advance notice of the Queen's wardrobe, so she could avoid embarrassing her by wearing the same

I wasn't lucky. I deserved it.

Margaret Thatcher, aged nine, after receiving a school prize

It's a pity that others had to lose theirs at Goose Green to prove it.

Neil Kinnock, on Question Time in 1983, responding to a heckler who had shouted 'At least she's got guts' in response to an answer about Margaret Thatcher

The self-appointed king of the gutter.

Michael Heseltine on Neil Kinnock after the above attack on Margaret Thatcher

Neil Kinnock's speeches go on for so long because he has nothing to say, so he has no way of knowing when he's finished saying it.

John Major

They never miss an opportunity to miss an opportunity.

Conor Cruise O'Brien on the Ulster Unionists

Jesus Christ, in any case, is a Name Which Makes News ... From Lord Beaverbrook's point of view, his was essentially a success story. From humble origins (though, as the son of God, he might be considered to have exalted connections) he achieved a position of outstanding power and influence. The Crucifixion was a set-back, certainly, but the Resurrection more than compensated for it. Thenceforth, the movement he

founded progressed almost as fast as the circulation of the
Daily Express ...
Malcolm Muggeridge, reviewing The Divine Propagandist, *a life of Christ by Lord Beaverbrook*

'His sentences burble from his lips ... a susurration of clichés
barely turning a leaf ... Each phrase is laced with laudanum ...
political musak, a background hum. We search in vain for the
knob to turn them off ... Put Mr Ashdown in a Labour cabinet
and he would sink gently to the bottom, leaving only silver
bubbles on the surface.
Simon Jenkins on Paddy Ashdown, in The Times

If you're calling Paddy Ashdown please leave a message after
the high moral tone.
Charles Kennedy

Paddy Ashdown is the only party leader who's a trained killer.
Although, to be fair, Mrs Thatcher was self-taught.
Charles Kennedy

A mind not so much open as permanently vulnerable to a
succession of opposing certainties.
Hugo Young on David Howell, in One of Us: Life of Margaret Thatcher

A man who could start a fight in an empty room.
Anonymous on Gerald Kaufman

He was swaggering in a predatory way towards the susceptible of this conference like a gigolo eyeing the passenger deck.
Edward Pearce on Michael Portillo, in the Guardian

Is there no beginning to your talents?
Clive Anderson to Jeffrey Archer

The prigs who attack Jeffrey Archer should bear in mind that we all, to some extent, reinvent ourselves. Jeffrey has just gone to a bit more trouble.
Barry Humphries

A numbing fusillade of platitudes ... his brain permanently on line to a fad lexicon ... Mr Blair uses abstract nouns as a wine writer uses adjectives, filling space with a frothy concoction devoid of meaning.
Simon Jenkins on Tony Blair, in The Times

With Tony you have to take the smooth with the smooth.
Anonymous senior Labour politician on his leader

Mr Blair is a man of hidden shallows.
Hugo Gurdon, the Daily Telegraph

He made particularly good toast.
Michael Gasgoigne on Tony Blair – Blair was his 'fag' at Fettes school

My advice is quit while you're behind.
Tony Blair to William Hague

Tory MPs are willing to be led, in the way that Henry VIII was
willing to be married.
Bruce Anderson

He has something of the night about him.
*Tory MP Ann Widdecombe on her former boss and Home Secretary Michael
Howard, 1997*

All the attributes of a populist except popularity.
Bruce Anderson on Michael Howard

I wouldn't vote for Ken Livingstone if he were running for
mayor of Toytown.
Arthur Scargill

You were the future once.
David Cameron to Tony Blair

@CAMPBELLCLARET: So @AIanucci OBE joins the
Establishment he claims to deride. Malcolm Tucker and I do
not approve of the honours system
@AIANUCCI: It's probably more Establishment to order your
army to march into other countries for no reason. Swings and
roundabouts
@CAMPBELLCLARET: you see, your wit a bit tired and blunt
already. Three little letters can have more impact than you
realise. Tut tut
@AIANUCCI: WMD
Exchange between Alastair Campbell and Armando Ianucci on Twitter

The trouble with Twitter, the instantness of it, is that too many tweets might make a twat.

David Cameron

The man loves West Ham too much.

Pig molester

But u still shagged a pig

You're still a twat

That's nowhere near enough, open up the fucking borders, you murderous necropigfucker. Also you fucked a dead pig.

Kermit is NOT happy

Mate, stop putting human beings in camps, and stop putting your knob in dead animals.

Responses to David Cameron's first tweet, promising extra funding for refugee camps, following allegations concerning his student antics

There is something about David Cameron that bothers me – those features of his are still waiting to turn into a face.

Clive James

UKIP is just a sort of bunch of fruitcakes and loonics and closet racists, mostly.

David Cameron

I always think he looks like somebody has put their finger up his bottom and he really rather likes it.

Anna Soubry on Nigel Farage

The Grand Hernia himself, Nigel Farage.
Camilla Long

I have read that there are some people – probably the type who are thinking of defecting to Ukip – who present themselves at A&E with barely credible injuries sustained through vacuum cleaner abuse.
Boris Johnson

Because the Ukips' deputy leader, Paul Nuttalls [sic], is so pleased to be the centre of attention he sports the perpetual expression of a baby that has just used a potty for the first time, holding up his arse muck delightedly for his parents to coo over.
Stewart Lee on Paul Nuttall

If you only read one thing this year ... then you're probably the kind of person who'll enjoy this.
Amazon review of Nigel Farage's The Purple Revolution

Ed Miliband is like a plastic bag caught in a tree. No one knows how he got up there and no one can be bothered to get him down.
Bill Bailey

You cannot make a man by standing a sheep on its hind legs. But by standing a flock of sheep in that position you can make a crowd of men.
Max Beerbohm, Zuleika Dobson

What men call social virtues, good fellowship, is commonly but the virtue of pigs in a litter, which lie in close together to keep each other warm.
Henry David Thoreau

He was always the sort of Socialist who would do anything for the workers except eat like them.
Bruce Anderson on Roy Hattersley, in the Spectator

Nouvelle cuisine was French for 'fucking hell, is that all you get?' This is Nouvelle Labour.
Rory Bremner

Being elected a Labour MP is the only job you can get that actually makes you redundant.
AA Gill

Only the future is certain, the past is always changing.
Paul Flynn on New Labour propaganda

As far as the 14th Earl is concerned, I suppose Mr Wilson, when you come to think of it, is the 14th Mr Wilson.
Sir Alec Douglas-Home, responding to Harold Wilson's sneers after renouncing his peerage as the 14th Earl of Home to become Prime Minister

The Minister of Technology flung himself into the Sixties technology with the enthusiasm (not to say the language) of a newly-enrolled Boy Scout demonstrating knot-tying to his indulgent parents.

Bernard Levin on Tony Benn

If I rescued a child from drowning, the press would no doubt headline the story 'Benn grabs child.'

Tony Benn

The last political battle is to avoid becoming a national treasure.

Tony Benn

Words cannot express my regret at the news that Anthony Wedgwood Benn has decided to retire from parliament. My regret is that he left it so late.

Gerald Kaufman MP

Cecil Parkinson, you're director of a fertilizer company. How deep is the mess you're in?

Jeremy Paxman's first question to former Conservative party chairman on the BBC's 1997 General Election results programme

John Major, Norman Lamont: I wouldn't spit in their mouths if their teeth were on fire.

Rodney Bickerstaffe of UNISON, 1992, who said this was based on a Scottish insult he learned in his youth: 'I wouldn't piss down his throat if his chest was on fire.'

Only some ghastly, dehumanised moron would want to get rid of the Routemaster bus.

Ken Livingstone, Mayor of London. (He did.)

You don't have to put up with dreadful human beings sitting alongside you.

Steven Norris MP, Minister of Transport, explaining the superiority of the motorcar over public transport

If you vote for Kinnock you're voting against Christ.

Dame Barbara Cartland explaining why British voters should not vote Labour

The Honourable Member for two tube stations.

Nicholas Fairbairn on Frank Dobson (MP for Holborn and St Pancras)

A bull in search of a china shop.

Unnamed union boss on Charles Clarke

Whenever Clare Short wrestles with her conscience, she wins.

Ben Macintyre

The man who takes the weight out of lightweight.

Bruce Anderson on Charles Kennedy

What is that fat gentleman in such a passion about?

Charles Shaw-Lefevre, as a child, hearing Charles James Fox speak in Parliament

They are gnats on an elephant's backside.
John Prescott on workers at New Labour's Millbank HQ, 1997

He loses his temper on Monday and doesn't find it again till Friday.
Anonymous civil servant about John Prescott

Mr Prescott has a mind like knitting the cat has played with.
John Prescott's college tutor

He has the face of a man who clubs baby seals.
Denis Healey on John Prescott

Like a fist fight in a hydrangea bush.
Craig Brown on buxom Dame Jill Knight wearing a floral print

Sir Eric Pickles sounds like a name a particularly eccentric old lady would give her favourite cat.
Martin Francis on Pickles' knighthood

Apart from my own name, the Transpennine Express is the greatest misnomer of all time.
Former transport minister Lord Adonis

Peter Mandelson has the insolent manner of one born to the top rung but three.
Gore Vidal

Having a conversation with Mr Mandelson was rather like

walking down stairs and missing the last step. You were uninjured but remained disconcerted.
Alan Watkins

Like Woody Allen without the jokes.
Simon Hoggart on Sir Keith Joseph

A tango dancer who's opened his legs to President Clinton.
Chinese government description of Chris Patten (last governor of Hong Kong)

There is nothing that you could say to me now that I could ever believe.
Gordon Brown to Tony Blair. Attrib.

If we can't take this lot apart in the next few years we shouldn't be in the business of politics at all.
Tony Blair handing over the premiership to Gordon Brown

An analogue politician in a digital age.
David Cameron on Gordon Brown

A tiny dot on this world.
Robert Mugabe on Gordon Brown

The House has noticed the Prime Minister's remarkable transformation in the past few weeks from Stalin to Mr Bean.
Vince Cable to Gordon Brown

He has the judgement of King Lear, the decisiveness of

Hamlet, the paranoia of Othello, and the loyalty of Brutus. But at least we've got rid of Lady Macbeth.

Bob Marshall-Andrews MP on Gordon Brown, shortly after he became Prime Minister

A Shakespearean tragedy.

Jonathan Powell, Tony Blair's chief of staff, describing Gordon Brown, to Boris Johnson, later Mayor of London. Powell denies the remark.

It doesn't matter how deep your intelligence or convictions, or how ingrained your sense of vocation and election, if you look sick when someone laughs at you, you aren't up to the job.

Howard Jacobson on Gordon Brown

Well that's a lie.

Overheard remark by Cherie Blair on hearing Gordon Brown say he had considered it a privilege to work with Tony Blair. Mrs Blair denies the remark.

A fucking disaster.

Alleged remark by John Hutton, Business Secretary, anticipating Gordon Brown's premiership

At Downing Street upon the stair
I met a man who wasn't Blair.
He wasn't Blair again today.
Oh how I wish he'd go away!

Limerick attributed to a cabinet minister (anonymous) describing Gordon Brown's occupancy of 10 Downing Street

Psychologically flawed.

A 'source close to' Prime Minister Tony Blair on his Chancellor of the Exchequer, Gordon Brown, 1998. Alastair Campbell, Blair's Press Secretary denies the attribution.

He can brighten a room just by leaving it.

Peter Lilley on Gordon Brown

John is John.

Tony Blair on John Prescott

[Tony Blair] doesn't like the full-frontal approach. It puts him off his tea.

John Prescott on Tony Blair

One of the Number Ten mekons.

John Prescott on David Miliband, the Foreign Secretary – a comparison with the big-brained, shrivelled-bodied, green alien dictator in the 1950s Eagle comic

A semi-detached member of the Cabinet.

Description of Tory politician John Biffen by Margaret Thatcher's Press Secretary, Bernard Ingham.

The sewer and not the sewerage.

John Biffen on Bernard Ingham

Silly old fucker.

Alastair Campbell on Margaret Thatcher's Press Secretary, Bernard Ingham

A big twat.
Alastair Campbell on Martin Sixsmith, a Whitehall director of communications

A desiccated calculating machine.
Aneurin Bevan, usually regarded as a jibe at Hugh Gaitskell

Nobody ever celebrated Devolution Day.
Alex Salmond

Lady Macbeth.
Boris Johnson on Nicola Sturgeon

For 10 years we in the Tory Party have become used to Papua New Guinea-style orgies of cannibalism and chief-killing, and so it is with a happy amazement that we watch as the madness engulfs the Labour Party.
Boris Johnson

I meant no insult to the people of Papua New Guinea, who I'm sure lead lives of blameless bourgeois domesticity in common with the rest of us ... I'm happy to add Papua New Guinea to my global itinerary of apology.
Boris Johnson, apologizing for the above remark

An enigma wrapped up in a whoopee cushion.
Will Self on Boris Johnson

A gurgling loaf with a sheepdog's haircut and a repertoire of Latin bum jokes.
Ian Martin on Boris Johnson

We cannot let that man inflict his security-threatening, terrorist-sympathising, Britain-hating ideology on the country we love.
David Cameron on Jeremy Corbyn

Jeremy Corbyn is the Left's Enoch Powell. His views and stances are equally repugnant ... Powell was always at pains to paint himself as someone who did not personally entertain prejudice. He was merely an interlocutor between the body politic and those that did. He did not endorse racism. But he thought it important to engage with those who held such views, to understand them, and provide an outlet for their opinions.

Jeremy Corbyn is the same. Terrorists. Anti-semites. Isil apologists. He doesn't share their views. But he offers himself as a conduit for them. So we can better understand them. Or so he says. And then off he goes, partying with those who chide us not to compare Isil with the Nazis, just as Isil are slipping lethal injections into the arms of disabled children.
Dan Hodges on Jeremy Corbyn

A man of herbivorous ways and carnivorous views.
Peter Hennessy on Jeremy Corbyn

Although you can take a nation's pulse, you can't be sure that the nation hasn't just run up a flight of stairs.
E.B. White on the science of polling

Peers

I am dead: dead, but in the Elysian fields.
Benjamin Disraeli on his move to the House of Lords. Attrib.

The House of Lords is like heaven – you want to get there some day, but not while there is any life in you.
Lord Denning, Master of the Rolls

They that hated the Bishops hated them worse than the devil, and they that loved them loved them not so well as their dinner.
Lucius Cary, 2nd Viscount Faulkland on failing to defeat a late-night Lords vote to curtail bishops' voting rights in 1641

The House of Lords is like a glass of champagne that has stood for five days.
Clement Attlee. Attrib.

Every man has a House of Lords in his own head. Fears,

prejudices, misconceptions – those are the peers, and they are hereditary.

David Lloyd George

Historical throwbacks and hillbilly inbreds.

Tony McNulty MP on hereditary peers

An ermine-lined dustbin, an up-market geriatric home with a faint smell of urine.

Austin Mitchell MP on the House of Lords

Last week, The Lord jetted in from New York to vote in support of tax credit cuts for the working poor ... The last time Webber voted was for same-sex marriage – so he loves gays but hates the poor. Anyone would think The Lord cared only about his audiences.

Bridget Christie on Andrew Lloyd Webber

TIM SAINSBURY: (Seeing Nicholas Soames in his hunting dress) Going rat-catching, Nick?
NICHOLAS SOAMES: Fuck off, you grocer: you don't tell a gentleman how to dress on a Friday.

Exchange in the Palace of Westminster between Nicholas Soames MP, grandson of Winston Churchill, and Tim Sainsbury MP of the supermarket dynasty

When I want a peerage I shall buy one like any honest man.

Alfred Harmsworth, 1st Viscount Northcliffe

Let me be thankful, God, that I am not
A Labour Leader when his life-work ends,
Who contemplates the coronet he got
By being false to principles and friends;
Who fought for forty years a desperate fight
With words that seared and stung and slew like swords,
And at the end, with victory in sight,
Ate them – a mushroom viscount in the Lords.

William Kean Seymour, Viscount Demos

Other people's opinions matter less – unless they're medical.

Baroness Trumpington on the benefits of ageing

Australian Politics

He [Joyce] looks somehow inbred with a tomato. It's not a criticism, I'm just saying, I was a little worried ... he might explode.

Johnny Depp on Barnaby Joyce MP after the latter had mocked Depp's apology for illegally importing his dogs into Australia

I think I'm turning into Johnny Depp's Hannibal Lecter, aren't I? I'm inside his head, I'm pulling little strings and pulling little levers. Long after I've forgotten about Mr Depp, he's remembering me.

Australian Deputy Prime Minister Barnaby Joyce

A feral calculator.

Paul Keating on John Hewson, 1993 Australian general election

Like being flogged with a warm lettuce.

Australian Prime Minister Paul Keating, referring to an attack by the Opposition leader, John Hewson

He's wound up like a thousand-day clock.

The then Australian Prime Minister, Paul Keating, about his Liberal Party opponent John Howard

What we have is a dead carcass, swinging in the breeze, but nobody will cut it down to replace him.

Paul Keating on John Howard

From this day onwards, Howard will wear his leadership like a crown of thorns and in parliament I will do everything to crucify him.

Paul Keating on John Howard

I am not like the Leader of the Opposition. I did not crawl out of the Cabinet room like a mangy maggot.

Paul Keating on John Howard

I was implying that the Honourable Member was like a lizard on a rock – alive but looking dead.

Paul Keating on John Howard

I suppose that the Honourable Gentleman's hair, like his intellect, will recede into the darkness.

Paul Keating on shadow treasurer Andrew Peacock

It is the first time the Honourable Gentleman has got out from under the sunlamp.

Paul Keating on Andrew Peacock

Just because you swallowed a fucking dictionary when you were about fifteen doesn't give you the right to pour a bucket of shit over the rest of us.

Paul Keating to a member of his Cabinet

What for? Then I'd be like you.

Paul Keating, to Australian Prime Minister Gough Whitlam. Whitlam had just said to him 'that was a good speech. You should go back, comrade, and get yourself an honours degree'.

He schemed, revised history ... the king of all larrikins, a coarse auto-didact with a tongue that could clip a hedge.

Conrad Black, owner of the Daily Telegraph, on former Australian Prime Minister, Paul Keating

Now, I know that there are some Aboriginal people who aren't happy with Australia Day. For them it remains Invasion Day. I think a better view is the view of Noel Pearson, who has said that Aboriginal people have much to celebrate in this country's British Heritage.

Tony Abbott

[Tony Abbott] stands for nothing. He is the Nancy Reagan of Australian politics without the astrology: say no to everything, just rancid, dripping, relentless negativity.

Defence Materiel Minister Jason Clare

Julia Gillard Kentucky Fried Quail: Small Breasts, Huge
Thighs, and a Big Red Box.

*Menu item at a Liberal National Party dinner. The menu was widely circulated
on social media and caused widespread outrage.*

(Mr Abbott) is Gina Rinehart's butler.

Former Prime Minister Julia Gillard

The Leader of the Opposition [then Malcolm Turnbull], faced
with the choice of a doberman or poodle, has gone for the
poodle.

Julia Gillard compares Tony Abbott and Christopher Pyne

Anyone who has chosen to remain deliberately barren ...
they've got no idea about what life's about.

Senator Bill Heffernan discussing Julia Gillard's fitness for office

American Politics

The moral character of Jefferson was repulsive. Continually puffing about liberty, equality and the degrading curse of slavery he brought his own children to the hammer and made money out of his debaucheries.

Alexander Hamilton, American politician on Thomas Jefferson, third President of the USA

DEPEW: I hope if it's a girl Mr Taft will name it for his charming wife.

TAFT: If it is a girl, I shall, of course, name it for my lovely helpmate of many years. And if it is a boy, I shall claim the father's prerogative and name it Junior. But if, as I suspect, it is only a bag of wind, I shall name it Chauncey Depew.

William Howard Taft, before his election as President, and Chauncey Depew

He looked at me as if I was a side dish he hadn't ordered.

Ring Lardner Jr. on President William Howard Taft

You pride yourself upon an animal faculty, in respect of which the slave is your equal and the jackass infinitely your superior.

John Randolph to fellow-Congressman Tristram Burges, in reply to the latter's claim he was impotent

A real Centaur: part man, part horse's ass.

Dean Acheson on President Johnson

President Robbins was so well adjusted to his environment that sometimes you could not tell which was the environment and which was President Robbins.

Randall Jarrell

Why, if a man were to call my dog McKinley, and the brute failed to resent to the death the damning insult, I'd drown it.

William Cowper Brann on William McKinley

Reader, suppose you were an idiot; and suppose you were a member of Congress; but I repeat myself.

Mark Twain

'Do you pray for the senators, Dr Hale?' 'No, I look at the senators and I pray for the country.'

Edward Everett Hale

Six inches deep – and six miles wide at the mouth.

Popular jibe comparing William Jennings Byron, American populist party's presidential candidate (known as The Boy Orator of the Platte), with the River Platte

The policeman and the trashman call me Alice. You cannot.
Alice Roosevelt Longworth, when Senator Joseph McCarthy called her Alice

The meanest kind of bawling and blowing office-holders,
office-seekers, pimps, malignants, conspirators, murderers,
fancy-men, custom-house clerks, contractors, kept-editors,
spaniels well-train'd to carry and fetch, jobbers, infidels,
dis-unionists, terrorists, mail-riflers, slave-catchers, pushers
of slavery, creatures of the President, creatures of would-be
Presidents, spies, bribers, compromisers, lobbyers, spongers,
ruin'd sports, expell'd gamblers, policy-backers, monte-
dealers, duellists, carriers of conceal'd weapons, deaf men,
pimpled men, scarr'd inside with vile disease, gaudy outside
with gold chains made from other people's money and
harlots' money twisted together; crawling, serpentine men,
the lousy combinings and born freedom-sellers of the earth.
Walt Whitman on a Democratic National Convention of the 1850s

A large shaggy dog, just unchained, scouring the beaches of
the world and baying at the moon.
Robert Louis Stevenson on Walt Whitman

A man of taste, arrived from Mars, would take one look at the
convention floor and leave forever, convinced he had seen one
of the drearier squats of Hell ... a cigar-smoking, stale-aired,
slack-jawed, butt-littered, foul, bleak, hardworking,
bureaucratic death gas of language and faces ... lawyers,
judges, ward heelers, mafiosos, Southern goons and grandees,

grand old ladies, trade unionists and finks; of pompous words and long pauses which lie like a leaden pain over fever.

Norman Mailer *on the Democratic National Convention of* 1960

My dear McClellan: If you don't want to use the army I should like to borrow it for a while. Yours respectfully, A. Lincoln

Abraham Lincoln *to General McClellan, accused of inactivity in the American Civil War*

Filthy Story-Teller, Despot, Liar, Thief, Braggart, Buffoon, Usurper, Monster, Ignoramus Abe, Old Scoundrel, Perjurer, Robber, Swindler, Tyrant, Field-Butcher, Land-Pirate.

Harper's Weekly *on Abraham Lincoln*

God damn you god damn old hellfiered god damned soul to hell god damn you and god damn your god damned family's god damned hellfiered god damned soul to hell and good damnation god damn them and god damn your god damned friends to hell.

Peter Muggins, *American citizen, in a letter to President Abraham Lincoln*

He is not known except as a slang-whanging stump-speaker of which all parties are ashamed.

The Albany Atlas and Argus *on the Gettysburg Address,* 1863

A horrid looking wretch he is, sooty and scoundrelly in aspect, a cross between the nutmeg dealer, the horse swapper, and the

night man, a creature fit evidently for petty treason, small stratagems and all sorts of spoils.
Charleston Mercury on Lincoln 1863

Lincoln is the leanest, lankest, most ungainly mass of legs and arms and hatchet face ever strung on a single frame. He has most unwarrantably abused the privilege, which all politicians have, of being ugly.
Houston Telegraph on Lincoln, 1863

... the small intellect, growing smaller ... [the Republicans] take up a fourth-rate lecturer who cannot speak good grammar and who ... delivers hackneyed, illiterate compositions.
New York Herald on Lincoln, 1860 election

Anything more dull and commonplace it wouldn't be easy to reproduce.
The Times on President Lincoln's Gettysburg Address, 1863

His argument is as thin as the homeopathic soup that was made by boiling the shadow of a pigeon that had been starved to death.
Abraham Lincoln on Stephen A. Douglas

Deformed Sir, The Ugly Club in full meeting have elected you an honorary member of the Hood-Favored Fraternity. Prince Harry was lean, Falstaff was fat. Thersites was hunchbacked, and Slowkenlengus was renowned for the eminent miscalculation which Nature had made in the length of the

nose; but it remained for you to unite all species of deformity and stand forth as The Prince of Ugly Fellows.
Anonymous letter to Abraham Lincoln

If I were two-faced, would I be wearing this one?
Abraham Lincoln

His speeches leave the impression of an army of pompous phrases moving over the landscape in search of an idea. Sometimes these meandering words would actually capture a straggling thought and bear it triumphantly, a prisoner in their midst, until it died of servitude and overwork.
Senator William McAdoo on Warren Harding, US President

He writes the worst English that I have ever encountered. It reminds me of a string of wet sponges; it reminds me of tattered washing on the line; it reminds me of stale bean soup, of college yells, of dogs barking idiotically through endless nights. It is so bad that a sort of grandeur creeps into it. It drags itself out of the dark abysm of pish and crawls insanely up the topmost pinnacle of posh. It is rumble and bumble. It is flap and doodle. It is balder and dash.
H.L. Mencken on Warren Harding

The only man, woman or child who wrote a simple declarative sentence with seven grammatical errors is dead.
E.E. Cummings on hearing of Warren Harding's death

He had a bungalow mind.
Woodrow Wilson on Warren G. Harding, his successor as President

He's thin, boys. He's thin as piss on a hot rock.
Senator William E. Jenner on W. Averell Harriman, Governor of New York

A Byzantine logothete.
Theodore Roosevelt on Woodrow Wilson

A taste for charming and cultivated friends and a tendency to
bathe frequently causes in them the deepest suspicion.
Theodore Roosevelt on members of the 'Free Silver' populist movement

Thomas E. Dewey is just about the nastiest little man I've ever
known. He struts sitting down.
Mrs Clarence Dykstra

How can they tell?
Dorothy Parker on being told that Calvin Coolidge was dead

Democracy is that system of government under which the
people, having 35,717,342 native-born adult whites to choose
from, including thousands who are handsome and many of
whom are wise, pick out a Coolidge to be head of state.
H.L. Mencken on Calvin Coolidge

Hoover, if elected, will do one thing that is almost

incomprehensible to the human mind: he will make a great
man out of Coolidge.

Clarence Darrow during the 1928 American presidential campaign

His attachment to those of his friends whom he could make
useful to himself was thoroughgoing and exemplary.

John Quincy Adams on Thomas Jefferson

That dark designing sordid ambitious vain proud arrogant and
vindictive knave.

General Charles Lee on George Washington

Not worth a pitcherful of warm piss.

*John Nance Garner, FDR's vice-president, on the importance of his position.
The quote is often amended to 'warm spit' and often misattributed.*

All the president is is a glorified public relations man who
spends his time flattering, kissing and kicking people to get
them to do what they are supposed to do anyway.

Harry S. Truman

He'll sit right here and he'll say do this, do that! And nothing
will happen! Poor Ike – it won't be a bit like the Army.

Harry S. Truman on Dwight D. Eisenhower

As an intellectual he bestowed upon the games of golf and
bridge all the enthusiasm and perseverance that he withheld
from books and ideas.

Emmet John Hughes on Dwight D. Eisenhower

An intellectual is a man who takes more words than necessary
to tell more than he knows.
Dwight D. Eisenhower

I guess it proves that in America anyone can be President.
Gerald Ford on his appointment

When his library burned down it destroyed both books. Dole
hadn't finished colouring in the second.
Jack Kemp on Bob Dole

When he was a quarterback he played without a helmet.
Dole on Kemp

Bob says he offers real leadership – he's right, backwards not
forwards.
Kemp on Dole

The candidate of pain, austerity and sacrifice.
Kemp on Dole

It is the greatest honour of my life to have been asked to run by
the greatest American hero.
Kemp, accepting Dole's invitation to be his vice-presidential running-mate

You don't want to get in a wrestling match with a pig. You both
get dirty, and the pig likes it.
Bob Dole

Always be sincere, whether you mean it or not.
Charles Percy, US Senator

Mothers all want their sons to grow up to be President but they don't want them to become politicians in the process.
John F. Kennedy

The enviably attractive nephew who sings an Irish ballad for the company and then winsomely disappears before the table-clearing and dishwashing begin.
Lyndon B. Johnson on John F. Kennedy

Lyndon acts like there was never going to be a tomorrow.
Lady Bird Johnson on her husband

Johnson's instinct for power is as primordial as a salmon's going upstream to spawn.
Theodore H. White

I'd much rather have that fellow inside my tent pissing out than outside my tent pissing in.
Lyndon B. Johnson, explaining why he retained J. Edgar Hoover at the FBI

Trust him as much as you would trust a rattlesnake with a silencer on its rattle.
Dean Acheson on J. Edgar Hoover, head of the FBI

The most notorious liar in America.
J. Edgar Hoover on Martin Luther King

Nixon is the kind of politician who would cut down a
redwood tree and then mount the stump to make a speech for
conservation.

Adlai Stevenson on Richard Nixon. Attrib.

Richard Nixon is a no-good lying bastard. He can lie out of
both sides of his mouth at the same time and if he ever caught
himself telling the truth he'd lie just to keep his hand in.

Harry S. Truman

Richard Nixon was an evil man – evil in a way that only those
who believe in the physical reality of the Devil can understand
it. He was utterly without ethics or morals or any bedrock
sense of decency. Nobody trusted him – except maybe the
Stalinist Chinese, and honest historians will remember him
mainly as a rat who kept scrambling to get back on the ship.

Hunter S. Thompson on Richard Nixon

Richard Nixon is a pubic hair in the teeth of America.

Graffiti on Richard Nixon

The Republicans are a party that says government doesn't
work – and then get elected and prove it.

P.J. O'Rourke

Gerry Ford is so dumb that he can't fart and chew gum at the
same time.

Lyndon B. Johnson on Gerald Ford (often misquoted)

He's so dumb he couldn't tip shit out of a boot if the instructions were written on the heel.
Lyndon Johnson on Gerald Ford

He looks like the guy in a science fiction movie who is the first to see the Creature.
David Frye on Gerald Ford

I love all my children, but some of them I don't like.
Lillian Carter, mother of Jimmy Carter

A triumph of the embalmer's art.
Gore Vidal on Ronald Reagan

He doesn't make snap decisions but he doesn't overthink either.
Nancy Reagan on her husband

If the President's penis is straight, it is the only thing about his administration that is.
Mark Steyn on rumours of an intimate nature concerning Bill Clinton

He is the bride at every wedding and the corpse at every funeral he attends.
Todd Purdum on Bill Clinton, post-presidency

I have difficulty in looking humble for extended periods of time.
Henry Kissinger

I am being frank about myself in this book. I tell of my first
mistake on page 850.
Henry Kissinger

Satire died the day they gave Henry Kissinger the Nobel Peace
Prize. There were no jokes left after that.
Tom Lehrer

A joke that doesn't make you laugh about someone you don't
know told by a man who went to Oxford.
AA Gill on satire

I think I speak for everyone when I say what a shame it is that
only one of these guys can lose.
David Letterman on the 2000 Presidential election campaign between George
W. Bush and Al Gore

I am Al Gore and I used to be the next President of the United
States.
Al Gore, to an audience of students

Al Gore is an old person's idea of what a young person should
be.
Michael Kinsey

The start of spring, otherwise known to Al Gore as proof of
global warming.
Bill Clinton

He struggles to exude authority. He furrows his brow, trying to look more sagacious, but he ends up looking as if he has indigestion. Appearing confused at his own speech, he seems like a first-grade actor in a production of *James and the Giant Peach*. Are his blinks Morse code for 'Oh, man, don't let that teleprompter break'?
Maureen Dowd of George W. Bush

That's like saying the veterinarian and the taxidermist are in the same business because either way you get your dog back.
Joseph Lieberman on the suggestion that he shared many of the views of George W. Bush

George Bush is not Hitler. He would be if he fucking applied himself.
Margaret Cho

George Bush doesn't care about black people.
Kanye West, going off script at a Hurricane Katrina benefit concert

The progressive approach to policy which directly addresses the effects of white supremacy is simple – talk about class and hope no one notices.
Ta-Nehisi Coates

I was a black boy at the height of the crack era, which meant that my instructors pitched education as the border between those who would prosper in America, and those who would be

fed to the great hydra of prison, teenage pregnancy and murder.
Ta-Nehisi Coates

Candidates without ideas hiring consultants without convictions to run campaigns without content.
President Gerald Ford talking about a US Presidential race

Too few have the courage of my convictions.
Robert M. Hutchins (Margaret Thatcher made a similar remark about her Cabinet)

Cheer up, only one of them can win.
Bumper sticker in the US Election 1992

She's every American's ex-wife.
P.J. O'Rourke on Hillary Clinton

A congenital liar.
William Safire on Hillary Clinton

If I want to knock a story off the front page, I just change my hairstyle.
Hillary Rodham Clinton

A goddamned fool he was on television talking about mortgages, and it was quite clear he didn't know what a mortgage is. His head rattles as he walks.
Gore Vidal on John McCain

I think her strategy is more or less insane ... I'd always rather liked her. She's a perfectly able lawyer ... But this long campaign, this daily search for the grail, has driven her crazy.

Gore Vidal on Hillary Clinton's 2008 campaign for the Democratic Presidential nomination

It's the sort of thing parents might chant encouragingly to a child slow on the potty-training.

Christopher Hitchens on Barack Obama's campaign slogan of 'Yes we can'

They never open their mouths without subtracting from the sum of human knowledge.

Thomas Reed, Speaker of the House of Representatives on members of Congress

Arianna Huffington is unattractive, both inside and out. I fully understand why her former husband left her for a man – he made a good decision.

Donald Trump

You know, it really doesn't matter what the media write as long as you've got a young, and beautiful, piece of ass.

Donald Trump

One of the key problems today is that politics is such a disgrace. Good people don't go into government.

Donald Trump

When Mexico sends its people, they're not sending their best ... They are sending people that have lots of problems, and

they are bringing those problems to us. They are bringing
drugs. They're bringing crime. They're rapists, and some, I
assume, are good people.
Donald Trump

Mr Trump is a misogynist, a racist and a xenophobe. He
glories in his own ignorance and inconsistency. Truth is
whatever he finds convenient. His policy ideas are ludicrous,
where they are not horrifying. Yet his attitudes and ideas are
less disturbing than his character: he is a narcissist, bully and
spreader of conspiracy theories. It is frightening to consider
how such a man would use the powers at the disposal of the
president.
Martin Wolf in the Financial Times

We'll burn that bridge when we come to it.
Euan Ferguson's suggested campaign slogan for Donald Trump

Faced with the prospect of voting for either Donald Trump
or Hillary Clinton, Mary Anne Noland of Richmond chose,
instead to pass into the eternal love of God on Sunday, May 15
2016, at the age of 68.
Obituary in the Richmond Times-Dispatch

On some great and glorious day, the plain folks of the land will
reach their heart's desire at last, and the White House will be
adorned with a moron.
H.L. Mencken

No one is prouder to put this birth certificate matter to rest than the Donald. And that's because he can finally get back to the issues that matter, like: did we fake the moon landing? What really happened in Roswell? And where are Biggie and Tupac?

Barack Obama on producing his certificate, whose authenticity Donald Trump had publicly called into doubt

Facts, evidence, reason, logic, an understanding of science – these are good things. These are qualities you want in people making policy ... In politics and in life, ignorance is not a virtue. It's not cool to not know what you're talking about. That's not keeping it real, or telling it like it is. That's not challenging political correctness. That's just not knowing what you're talking about.

Barack Obama

Scratch any American and underneath you'll find an isolationist.

Dean Rusk

A few decades ago we had Johnny Cash, Bob Hope and Steve Jobs. Now we have no cash, no hope and no jobs. Please don't let Kevin Bacon die.

Bill Murray

Politics in Europe and Beyond

I wonder what he meant by that.
Prince Metternich on the death of scheming statesman Talleyrand

This going into Europe will not turn out to be the thrilling mutual exchange supposed. It is more like nine middle-aged couples with failing marriages meeting in a darkened bedroom in a Brussels hotel for a Group Grope.
E.P. Thompson on the EEC, in the Sunday Times, 1975

Up Yours Delors!
Sun headline, attacking the President of the European Commission, Jaques Delors

I was my best successor but I decided not to succeed myself.
Pierre Trudeau on his decision not to seek another term as Canadian Prime Minister

A political leader worthy of assassination.
Irving Layton on Pierre Trudeau

A man who looks as if he has two flies fucking in his mouth.
Boris Yeltsin on his adviser Sergei Filatov

He has missed a wonderful opportunity to keep his mouth shut.
Jacques Chirac on Ariel Sharon

Israel's dark id.
Tony Judt on Ariel Sharon

I understand why he has to do this – to prove he's a man. He's afraid of his own weakness. Russia has nothing, no successful politics or economy. All they have is this.
Angela Merkel, after Vladimir Putin brought a dog to a press conference, knowing she had a fear of them

An unfuckable lard-arse.
Silvio Berlusconi on Angela Merkel

What is his name? It's someone with a tan. Barack Obama!
Silvio Berlusconi

Better to like women than to be gay.
Silvio Berlusconi

In twenty years of politics, I have never insulted anyone.
Silvio Berlusconi

You won the elections, but I won the count.
Anastasio Somoza, dictator of Nicaragua

Why the fuss over the Burmese elections? They said it was a general election – and the generals were elected.
Ray Rayner

War

Of the love or hatred God has for the English, I know nothing, but I do know that they will all be thrown out of France, except those who die there.

Joan of Arc

War is the national industry of Prussia.

Honoré Gabriel Riqueti, comte de Mirabeau. Attrib.

When God wants to punish a nation, he makes them invade Afghanistan.

Afghan saying

It's God's responsibility to forgive Bin Laden ... it's our responsibility to arrange the meeting.

Slogan on a US marine's bumper sticker

If you're not at the table, you're on the menu.

US diplomat Charles W. Freeman

Military intelligence is a contradiction in terms.
Groucho Marx

Military justice is to justice, as military music is to music.
Groucho Marx

War is God's way of teaching Americans geography.
Ambrose Bierce

They've got to draw in their horns and stop their aggression,
or we're going to bomb them back into the Stone Age.
Curtis E. LeMay

War hath no fury like a non-combatant.
C.E. Montague, Disenchantment

But when we open our dykes, the waters are 10ft deep.
Queen Wilhelmina replying to a boast by Wilhelm II that all his guardsmen were 7ft tall

Götterdämmerung without the gods.
Dwight Macdonald on the nuclear bombing of Hiroshima and Nagasaki

It's easy to be brave from a distance.
Aesop

Peace: in international affairs, a period of cheating between
two periods of fighting.
Ambrose Bierce

If I were fierce, and bald, and short of breath,
I'd live with scarlet Majors at the base,
And speed glum heroes up to the line of death.
You'd see me with my puffy petulant face,
Guzzling and gulping in the best hotel,
Reading the Roll of Honour. 'Poor young chap,'
I'd say – 'I used to know his father well;
Yes, we've lost heavily in this last scrap.'
And when the war is done and youth stone dead,
I'd toddle safely home and die – in bed.

Siegfried Sassoon, Counter-Attack, *'Base Details'*

To save your world you asked this man to die:
Would this man, could he see you now, ask why?

W.H. Auden, Epitaph for an Unknown Soldier

This war, like the next war, is a war to end war.

David Lloyd George on the First World War

Patriots always talk of dying for their country, and never of
killing for their country.

Bertrand Russell

A soldier is a man whose business it is to kill those who
never offended him, and who are the innocent martyrs of
other men's iniquities. Whatever may become of the abstract
question of the justifiableness of war, it seems impossible that
the soldier should not be a depraved and unnatural thing.

William Godwin

Seven months ago I could give a single command and 541,000 people would immediately obey it. Today I can't get a plumber to come to my house.
H. Norman Schwarzkopf III, Commander of US forces in the Gulf War

Lions led by donkeys.
Max Hoffmann on the British army in the First World War

Suez – a smash and grab raid that was all smash and no grab.
Harold Nicolson

Restraint? Why are you so concerned with saving their lives? The whole idea is to kill the bastards. At the end of the war if there are two Americans and one Russian left alive, we win.
US General Thomas Power, Head of Strategic Air Command

Standing at the head of his troops, his drawn salary in his hand.
Henry Labouchère on the Duke of Clarence

The scum of the earth.
Duke of Wellington on the British army

These boys have fought for four years. They deserve their fun.
Joseph Stalin on reports of the mass rape of German women by Russian soldiers

Marijuana smokers, drug addicts, long-hairs, homosexuals and unionists.
General Augusto Pinochet, describing the West German army

This man is depriving a village somewhere of an idiot.
Extract from Royal Navy and Marines Fitness Report, 1997

He never commanded more than ten men in his life – and he ate three of them.
General Weston on Adolphus Greely being made a general. Much of his life had been spent as an Arctic explorer.

He's a war hero because he was captured. I like people that weren't captured.
Donald Trump on John McCain

He would kill his own mother just so that he could use her skin to make a drum to beat his own praises.
Margot Asquith on Winston Churchill

If Kitchener was not a great man, he was, at least, a great poster.
Margot Asquith

In defeat unbeatable; in victory unbearable.
Winston Churchill on Viscount Montgomery

Don't talk to me about naval tradition. It's nothing but rum, sodomy, and the lash.
Winston Churchill

The British soldier can stand up to anything except the British War Office.

George Bernard Shaw

One to mislead the public, another to mislead the Cabinet, and the third to mislead itself.

Herbert Asquith, explaining why the War Office kept three sets of figures

You can't say civilization don't advance, however, for in every war they kill you a new way.

Will Rogers, Autobiography

What have we acquired? What, but a bleak and gloomy solitude, an island thrown aside from human use, stormy in winter and barren in the summer; an island which not even the Southern savages have dignified with habitation; where a garrison must be kept in a state that contemplates with envy the exiles of Siberia; of which the expense will be perpetual and the use only occasional; and which, if fortune smiles upon our labours, may become a nest of smugglers in peace, and in war the refuge of future buccaneers.

Samuel Johnson on the Falkland Islands

The Falklands thing was a fight between two bald men over a comb.

Jorge Luis Borges on the Falklands War

To all the Libyan people, the Libyan land belongs to you. Those who are trying to take it away from you are outsiders, they are

mercenaries. They are dogs. They are spies for France and
Britain. They are all germs and rats.
Libyan dictator Colonel Gaddafi, having been driven out of Tripoli

Who cares about a little terrorist in Afghanistan?
*Paul Wolfowitz, Deputy Defense Secretary on concerns about al-Qaeda (April
2001)*

Imperialist running dogs.
Approved Chinese term for Americans in print and on radio

They present themselves to the public as superheroes, but
away from the camera are a bit pathetic in many ways: street
kids drunk on ideology and power. In France we have a saying
– stupid and evil. I found them more stupid than evil. That is
not to understate the murderous potential of stupidity.
Nicolas Hénin, French journalist and former ISIS hostage on his former captors

Maybe it would have been better if neither of us had been born.
Napoléon Bonaparte, looking at the tomb of Jean-Jacques Rousseau

Empire

A crew of pirates are driven by a storm they know not whither;
at length a boy discovers land from the topmast; they go on
shore to rob and plunder; they see a harmless people, are
entertained with kindness; they give the country a new name;
they take formal possession of it for their king; they set up a
rotten plank or a stone for a memorial; they murder two or
three dozen natives; bring away a couple more by force for a
sample; return home and get their pardon. Here commences
a new dominion acquired with a title by divine right. Ships
are sent with the first opportunity; the natives driven out or
destroyed; their princes tortured to discover their gold; a
free licence given to all acts of inhumanity and lust, the earth
reeking with the blood of its inhabitants; and this execrable
crew of butchers, employed in so pious an expedition, is a
modern colony, sent to convert and civilize an idolatrous and
barbarous people!

Jonathan Swift, Gulliver's Travels. *'Gulliver on the English system of
colonizing'*

Civilized men arrive in the Pacific, armed with alcohol, syphilis, trousers and the Bible.
Havelock Ellis

The West won the world not by the superiority of its ideas or values or religion (to which few members of other civilisations were converted) but rather by its superiority in applying organised violence. Westerners often forget this fact; non-Westerners never do.
Samuel Huntingdon

Columbus was not a learned man, but an ignorant. He was not an honourable man, but a professional pirate ... To the harmless and hospitable peoples among whom he came he was a terror and a curse ...
Ambrose Bierce on Christopher Columbus

I admire him, I frankly confess it; and when his time comes I shall buy a piece of the rope for a keepsake.
Mark Twain on Cecil Rhodes

It is nauseating to see Mr Gandhi, a seditious Middle Temple lawyer, now posing as a fakir of a type well known in the East, striding half naked up the steps of the Viceregal Palace.
Winston Churchill on Mahatma Gandhi

I think it would be a good idea.
Mahatma Gandhi on being asked his view of Western civilization. Attrib.

A nagging desire to rule the world, or at least to tell it how to behave, is embedded in the genes of every British politician.
Simon Jenkins

[He] speaks like a Buddha and thinks like a serpent ... His soul is possessed by British colonialism. Nothing can distract him from his perfidy ... The truth has come to light ... Chris Patten will stand condemned down the ages.
Wen Wei Po, the Communist-run newspaper in Hong Kong on Chris Patten, the Governor

Journalism

I always turn to the sports section first. The sports page
records people's accomplishments; the front page has nothing
but man's failures.

Earl Warren on journalism

Journalism largely consists of saying 'Lord Jones is Dead' to
people who never knew that Lord Jones was alive.

G.K. Chesterton

Journalism consists in buying white paper at two cents a
pound and selling it for ten cents a pound.

Cyril Connolly

News is what a chap who doesn't care much about anything
wants to read. And it's only news until he's read it. After that
it's dead.

Evelyn Waugh, Scoop

They are only ten.
Lord Northcliffe, notice to remind staff on his newspaper of the mental age of readers

A single sentence will suffice for modern man: he fornicated and read the papers.
Albert Camus, The Fall

A journalist is a person who works harder than any other lazy person in the world.
Anonymous

Facing the press is more difficult than bathing a leper.
Mother Teresa

Bye! I won't miss you.
Cherie Blair, leaving Downing Street for the last time, to the attendant press corps

I have spent half my life trying to get away from journalism, but I am still mired in it – a low trade and a habit worse than heroin, a strange seedy world full of misfits and drunkards and failures.
Hunter S. Thompson

Sometimes I suspect most of the media commentariat are suffering from Munchausen syndrome.
Rebekah Brooks

A journalist is a reporter out of a job.
Mark Twain

All newspaper opinion-writers ever do is come down from the
hills after the battle is over, and bayonet the wounded.
Adage

The ordinary is the proper domain of the artist. The
extraordinary can safely be left to journalists.
James Joyce

A foreign correspondent is someone who flies around from
hotel to hotel and thinks that the most interesting thing about
any story is the fact that he has arrived to cover it.
Tom Stoppard, Night and Day

A drink-soaked former Trotskyist popinjay.
George Galloway MP on Christopher Hitchens

Ba'athist, short-arse, sub-Leninist, Eastend carpet-bagger.
Christopher Hitchens on George Galloway

Made natural history by metamorphosing from a butterfly to a
slug.
George Galloway MP on Christopher Hitchens

How unwise and incautious it is for such a hideous person
to resort to personal remarks. Unkind nature, which could
have made a perfectly good butt out of his face, has spoiled

the whole effect by taking an asshole and studding it with ill-brushed fangs.
Christopher Hitchens on George Galloway

Ready to fight to the last drop of other people's blood.
George Galloway on Christopher Hitchens

This is not just a matter of which of us can be the rudest, because I already conceded that to Mr Galloway. Or which of us can be the most cerebral, because he already conceded that to me.
Christopher Hitchens on George Galloway

Every journalist who is not too stupid or too full of himself to notice what is going on knows that what he does is morally indefensible. He is a kind of confidence man, preying on people's vanity, ignorance, or loneliness, gaining their trust and betraying them without remorse.
Janet Malcolm

The way I had it is all gone now. The bars are gone, the drinkers, gone. There remain the smartest, healthiest newspeople in the history of the business. And they are so boring that they kill the business right in front of you.
Jimmy Breslin

You cannot hope to bribe or twist,
Thank God! the British journalist.
But, seeing what the man will do

Unbribed, there's no occasion to.
Humbert Wolfe

To a newspaperman, a human being is an item with skin wrapped around it.
Fred Allen

Once a newspaper touches a story, the facts are lost forever, even to the protagonists.
Norman Mailer

I hesitate to say what the functions of the modern journalist may be, but I imagine that they do not exclude the intelligent anticipation of facts before they occur.
Lord Curzon

Trying to determine what is going on in the world by reading newspapers is like trying to tell the time by watching the second hand of a clock.
Ben Hecht

A newspaper is a device unable to distinguish between a bicycle accident and the collapse of civilization.
George Bernard Shaw

The government of bullies, tempered by editors.
Ralph Waldo Emerson on democracy

Some editors are failed writers, but so are most writers.
T.S. Eliot

What the proprietorship of these papers is aiming at is power, and power without responsibility – the prerogative of the harlot throughout the ages.
Stanley Baldwin on press barons Lord Rothermere and Beaverbrook

Good God, that's done it. He's lost us the tarts' vote.
The 10th Duke of Devonshire on Stanley Baldwin's attack on newspaper proprietors. Attrib.

There are moments when we in the British press can show extraordinary sensitivity: these moments usually coincide with the death of a proprietor, or a proprietor's wife.
Craig Brown

The press is the enemy.
Richard Nixon

Politicians who complain about the media are like ships' captains who complain about the sea.
Enoch Powell

The freedom of the press works in such a way that there is not much freedom from it.
Grace Kelly

All the faults of the age come from Christianity and
Journalism.
Frank Harris

Christianity, of course, but why journalism?
Arthur James Balfour in reply

Frank Harris has been invited to all the great houses in
England once.
Oscar Wilde

You lying BBC; you're photographing things that aren't
happening.
Belfast woman to a BBC cameraman

To press journalists, television is like a mendacious, boastful
cousin who keeps turning up at family parties with a prettier
girl and a more powerful motor that you rather hope will end
up in a ditch.
Allison Pearson, Evening Standard

An editor is one who separates the wheat from the chaff and
prints the chaff.
Adlai Stevenson

Getting information from the internet is like getting a glass of
water from Niagara.
Arthur C. Clarke

The most truthful part of a newspaper is the advertisements.
Thomas Jefferson

It's amazing that the amount of news that happens in the
world every day always just exactly fits the newspaper.
Jerry Seinfeld

It's a wonder none of them crash-landed on the magazine.
Private Eye, responding to the editor of Punch's *comment that 'jokes winged
back and forth between the men and women'*

The Times is speechless and takes three columns to express its
speechlessness.
Winston Churchill on Irish Home Rule

When it is said of a man that he didn't suffer fools gladly, it
means he was an intolerant old brute. When it is said of an old
lady that she was lively and vivacious, it means she was usually
plastered.
Anthony Howard on the obituarist's code

If I see 'upcoming' in the paper one more time, I will be
downcoming and someone will be outgoing.
Unnamed editor of The Wall Street Journal

Unreconstructed wankers.
Tony Blair's description of the Scottish media, 1997

No one ever went broke underestimating the taste of the American public.

H.L. Mencken

Every item should make our readers hate someone or something, or fear something or someone, a little bit more.

Instruction to a young journalist joining the Daily Mail's Wicked Whispers diary column

By office boys for office boys.

Lord Salisbury on the Daily Mail

If a person is not talented enough to be a novelist, not smart enough to be a lawyer, and his hands are too shaky to perform operations, he becomes a journalist.

Norman Mailer

People who are drawn to journalism are usually people who, because of their cynicism or emotional detachment or reserve or whatever, are incapable of being anything but witnesses to events. Something prevents them from becoming involved, committed, and allows them to remain separate.

Nora Ephron

It's great to be with Bill Buckley, because you don't have to think. He takes a position and you automatically take the opposite one and you know you're right.

John Kenneth Galbraith on William F. Buckley, Jr., right-wing editor of the National Review

Price of *Herald* three cents daily. Five cents Sunday. Bennett.

Telegram from James Gordon Bennett, American newspaper owner and editor, to William Randolph Hearst, when Hearst, who was trying to buy his paper, asked for a price

I have just seen your submission to the Press Complaints Commission. For sheer, pathetic, childish, toys-out-of-the-pram crap, it's hard to beat. Tantrums and tiaras, darlings? Stick them where the sun don't shine.

Piers Morgan in a letter to Sir Elton John's lawyer

I think we fell out when you said 'I think' and I said 'I don't give a fuck what you think'.

Kelvin MacKenzie, former editor of the Sun, to a marketing man at the latter's leaving party

Has there ever been a more confusing face? With an expression half-bovine and half sheep-like he stares out of the screen in such a way as to leave us all uncertain whether he wants to cut our throats or lick our boots.

Peregrine Worsthorne on Sunday Times editor Andrew Neil, in the Sunday Telegraph

That is a bit rich coming from a man who looks like a sexually confused, ageing hairdresser: the Teasy Weasy of Fleet Street ...

Richard Littlejohn, in the Sun, on Peregrine Worsthorne after the latter's attack on Andrew Neil

Rock journalism is people who can't write, interviewing people who can't talk, for people who can't read.
Frank Zappa

A columnist is a person with weak opinions, strongly held.
Adage, adapted

This dodipoule, this didopper ... why, thou arrant butter whoe, thou coteueane & scrattop of scoldes, will thou never leave affecting a dead Carcasse ... a wispe, a wispe, rippe, rippe, you kitchen-stuff wrangler!
Thomas Nashe, a 16th-century pamphleteer and novelist, on Gabriel Harvey, a contemporary writer. The pair conducted a feud so furious that in 1599 the Archbishop of Canterbury ordered all their works to be burned.

One fact, one generalisation, and one very slight inaccuracy.
Hugo Wortham, editor of the Daily Telegraph's 'Peterborough' column, on the ideal contents of a successful diary column item

Writers, Publishers and Critics

Times are bad. Children no longer obey their parents, and everyone is writing a book.
Marcus Tullius Cicero

A writer is someone for whom writing is harder than it is for other people.
Thomas Mann

A bottle full of tapeworms trying to feed on each other.
Ernest Hemingway on writers

Writers, like teeth, are divided into incisors and grinders.
Walter Bagehot

Thank you for the manuscript; I shall lose no time in reading it.
Benjamin Disraeli's standard reply to authors who sent him unsolicited copies of their books

Great editors do not discover nor produce great authors; great authors create and produce great publishers.
John Farrar

I object to publishers: the one service they have done me is to teach me to do without them. They combine commercial rascality with artistic touchiness and pettiness, without being either good businessmen or fine judges of literature. All that is necessary in the production of a book is an author and a bookseller, without any intermediate parasite.
George Bernard Shaw

The secret to creativity is knowing how to hide your sources.
Adage

When I split an infinitive, god damn it, I split it so it stays split.
Raymond Chandler, letter to his British publisher

As repressed sadists are supposed to become policemen or butchers, so those with irrational fear of life become publishers.
Cyril Connolly

Every author, however modest, keeps an outrageous vanity chained like a madman within the padded cell of his breast.
Logan Pearsall Smith

Authors are easy to get on with – if you're fond of children.
Michael Joseph, publisher

A great author, notwithstanding his Dictionary is imperfect, his Rambler pompous, his learning common, his ideas vulgar, his Irene a child of mediocrity, his genius worldly, his politics narrow and his religion bigoted.
Robert Potter, a critic, on Samuel Johnson

Chuang Tzu was born in the 4th century before Christ. The publication of this book in English, two thousand years after his death, is obviously premature.
Now-forgotten critic

Plato is a bore.
Friedrich Nietzsche

The more I read him, the less I wonder that they poisoned him.
Thomas Babington Macaulay on Socrates

A crawling and disgusting parasite, a base scoundrel, and pander to unnatural passions.
William Cobbett on Virgil

Every man with a belly full of the classics is an enemy of the human race.
Henry Miller

A gentleman need not know Latin, but he should at least have forgotten it.
Brander Matthews. Attrib.

The classics are only primitive literature. They belong in the same class as primitive machinery and primitive music and primitive medicine.
Stephen Leacock, Homer and Humbug

Twitter is unspeakably irritating ... It's like writing a novel without the letter 'P'... It's the ultimate irresponsible medium.
Portentous American novelist Jonathan Franzen

Lighten up, Franzo.
India Knight, tweeting in response

Jeff Bezos of Amazon may not be the antichrist, but he surely looks like one of the four horsemen.
Jonathan Franzen

Google is not a synonym for research.
Dan Brown, author of The Da Vinci Code

Calling Jeffrey Archer's fictional characters cardboard is an insult to the British packaging industry.
Peter Preston

Googling yourself is like opening the door to a room full of people telling you how shit you are.
Armando Iannucci's fictional MP Peter Mannion, in The Thick of It

All the universities and all the old writers put together are less talented than my arsehole.

Theophrastus Bombastus von Hohenheim, known as Paracelsus, German alchemist and physician, to his critics

Critics are like eunuchs in a harem: they know how it's done, they've seen it done every day, but they're unable to do it themselves.

Brendan Behan

Most critics are educated beyond their intelligence.

Critic Kenneth Tynan

The thankless task of drowning other people's kittens.

Cyril Connolly on book reviewing

I will hate you till the day I die and wish you nothing but ill will in every career move you make. I will be watching with interest and schadenfreude.

Alain de Botton, to a critic who gave his book a bad review

Donkeyosities, egotistical earthworms, hogwashing hooligans, critic cads, random hacks of illiteration, talent wipers of wormy order, the gas-bag section, poking hounds, poisonous apes, maggotty numbskulls, evil-minded snapshots of spleen and, worst of all, the mushroom class of idiots.

Amanda Malvina Fitzalan Anna Margaret McLelland McKittrick Ros, an unsuccessful writer, on her critics

I am sure I have only slightly less high an opinion of
Matthew's literary ability than he does himself.
Alan Lomberg, this book's editor's English teacher in Swaziland, in a school report

The little shit Parris, with his perma-smirk.
Alastair Campbell, Tony Blair's former press secretary, on the editor of this book

The thinking man's Matthew Parris.
John Patten on Simon Hoggart, Guardian parliamentary sketchwriter

Critics! appall'd I venture on the name,
Those cut-throat bandits in the path of fame.
Robert Burns

Thou eunuch of language ... thou pimp of gender ...
murderous accoucheur of infant learning ... thou pickle-
herring in the puppet show of nonsense.
Robert Burns on a critic

If you imagine a Scotch commercial traveller in a Scotch
commercial hotel leaning on the bar and calling the barmaid
'Dearie' then you will know the keynote of Burns's verse.
A.E. Housman on Robert Burns

Descended from a long line of maiden aunts.
A fellow don (anon) on A.E. Housman

A louse in the locks of literature.
Tennyson on Churton Collins, a critic

The difference between genuine poetry and the poetry of
Dryden, Pope, and all their school, is briefly this: their poetry
is conceived and composed in their wits, genuine poetry is
conceived and composed in the soul.
Matthew Arnold

What is Conrad but the wreck of Stevenson floating about in
the slipsop of Henry James?
George Moore on Joseph Conrad

... an umbrella left behind at a picnic.
George Moore on W.B. Yeats

That vague formless obscene face.
Oscar Wilde on George Moore

Henry James writes fiction as if it were a painful duty.
Oscar Wilde

He hangs poised for the right word while the wheels of life go
round.
Description of Henry James by his cousin

The dullest Briton of them all.
Henry James on Anthony Trollope

Trollope! Did anyone bear a name that predicted a style more Trollopy?

George Moore on Anthony Trollope

A name is just a name ... Somewhere in Las Vegas there's probably a male prostitute called John Updike.

Salman Rushdie, after Updike criticised his choice of names for his characters

It's not that he 'bites off more than he can chew' but he chews more than he bites off.

Clover Adams on Henry James

A church lit but without a congregation to distract you, with every church light and line focused on the high altar. And on the altar, very reverently placed, intensely there, is a dead kitten, an eggshell, a bit of string.

H.G. Wells on a book by Henry James

Henry James had turned his back on one of the great events in the world's history, the rise of the United States, in order to report tittle-tattle at tea parties in English country houses.

W. Somerset Maugham on Henry James

I doubt that the infant monster has any more to give.

Henry James on Rudyard Kipling

Poor Henry James! He's spending eternity walking round and round a stately park and the fence is just too high for him to

peep over and he's just too far away to hear what the countess
is saying.
W. Somerset Maugham

Henry James has a mind so fine that no idea could violate it.
T.S. Eliot. Attrib.

How unpleasant it is to meet Mr Eliot!
With his features of clerical cut,
And his brow so grim
And his mouth so prim
And his conversation, so nicely
Restricted to What Precisely
And If and Perhaps and But.
T.S. Eliot on himself

Mr Eliot is at times an excellent poet and has arrived at the
supreme Eminence among English critics largely through
disguising himself as a corpse.
Ezra Pound on T.S. Eliot

To me Pound remains the exquisite showman minus the show.
Ben Hecht on Ezra Pound

Jane Austen's books, too, are absent from this library. Just that
one omission alone would make a fairly good library out of a
library that hadn't a book in it.
Mark Twain

A hack writer who would not have been considered fourth rate in Europe, who tried out a few of the old proven 'sure-fire' literacy skeletons with sufficient local colour to intrigue the superficial and the lazy.

William Faulkner on Mark Twain

I have discovered that our great favourite, Miss Austen, is my countryman ... with whom Mama, before her marriage, was acquainted. Mama says that she was then the prettiest, silliest, most affected, husband-hunting butterfly she ever remembers.

Mary Russell Mitford on Jane Austen, letter to a friend

I think I may boast myself to be, with all possible vanity, the most unlearned and uninformed female who ever dared be an authoress.

Jane Austen on herself

I found out in the first two pages that it was a woman's writing – she supposed that in making a door, you last of all put in the panels!

Thomas Carlyle on Adam Bede by George Eliot

I wish her characters would talk a little less like the heroes and heroines of police reports.

George Eliot on Jane Eyre by Charlotte Brontë

George Eliot had the heart of Sappho; but the face, with the

long proboscis, the protruding teeth of the Apocalyptic horse,
betrayed animality.

George Meredith on George Eliot

All the faults of *Jane Eyre* are magnified a thousandfold, and the
only consolation which we have in reflecting upon it is that it
will never be generally read.

*James Lorimer on Wuthering Heights by Emily Brontë, in the North British
Review*

Oh really. What is she reading?

*Dame Edith Evans to a friend who said Nancy Mitford was borrowing her villa
in France to finish a book*

A woman who writes a book commits two sins; she increases
the number of books, and decreases the number of women.

Alphonse Karr

One of the surest signs of his genius is that women dislike his
books.

George Orwell on Joseph Conrad

He would not blow his nose without moralizing on conditions
in the handkerchief industry.

Cyril Connolly on George Orwell

I cannot abide Conrad's souvenir shop style and bottled ships
and necklaces of romanticist clichés.

Vladimir Nabokov on Joseph Conrad

One could always baffle Conrad by saying 'humour'. It was one of our damned English tricks he had never learned to tackle.

H.G. Wells on Joseph Conrad

Analysing humour is like dissecting a frog. Few people are interested and the frog dies of it.

E.B. White

One must have a heart of stone to read the death of little Nell without laughing.

Oscar Wilde on Charles Dickens's Old Curiosity Shop

Of Dickens's style it is impossible to speak praise. It is jerky, ungrammatical and created by himself in defiance of the rules. No young novelist should ever dare to imitate the style of Dickens.

Anthony Trollope on Charles Dickens

It was not he who fathered that trite little whimsy about characters getting out of hand, it is as old as the quills, although of course, one sympathizes with his people if they try to wriggle out of that trip to India or wherever he takes them. My characters are all galley-slaves.

Vladimir Nabokov on E.M. Forster, The Paris Review Interviews

He is limp and damp and milder than the breath of a cow.

Virginia Woolf on E.M. Forster

We are nauseated by the sight of trivial personalities decomposing in the eternity of print.
Virginia Woolf

I am fairly unrepentant about her poetry. I really think that three quarters of it is gibberish. However, I must crush down these thoughts, otherwise the dove of peace will shit on me.
Noël Coward on Dame Edith Sitwell

Mr Lawrence looked like a plaster gnome on a stone toadstool in some suburban garden ... he looked as if he had just returned from spending an uncomfortable night in a very dark cave.
Dame Edith Sitwell on D.H. Lawrence

My god, what a clumsy 'olla putrida' James Joyce is! Nothing but old fags and cabbage-stumps of quotations from the Bible and the rest, stewed in the juice of deliberate, journalistic dirty-mindedness.
D.H. Lawrence on Ulysses by James Joyce

The work of a queasy undergraduate scratching his pimples.
Virginia Woolf on Ulysses by James Joyce

She has been a peculiar kind of snob without really belonging to a social group with whom to be snobbish.
Edmund Wilson on Virginia Woolf

We have met too late. You are too old for me to have any effect on you.

James Joyce on meeting W.B. Yeats

Wanting to meet an author because you like his books is like wanting to meet a duck because you like pâté.

Margaret Atwood

The quick brown fox jumps over the lazy dog. How fucking difficult is that? It's the sentence that bestrides the fucking book I reviewed for you. It is the sentence I wrote first in my fucking review. It is 35 fucking letters long, which is why I wrote that it was. And so some useless cunt sub-editor decides to change it to 'jumps over a lazy dog'. Can you fucking count? Can you see that that makes it a 33 letter sentence? So it looks as if I can't count, and the cunting author of the book, poor Mr Dunn, cannot count. The whole bastard book turns on the sentence being as I wrote it, and that is exactly 35 letters long. Why do you meddle? What do you think you achieve with that kind of dumb-witted smart arsery? Why do you change things you do not understand without consulting? Why do you believe you know best when you know fuck all, jack shit? That is as bad as editing can be. Fuck. I hope you're proud. It will be small relief for the author that nobody reads your poxy magazine. Never ever ask me to write something for you. And don't pay me. I'd rather take 400 quid for assassinating a crack whore's only child in a revenge killing for a busted drug deal –

my integrity would be less compromised. Jesus fucking wept. I don't know what else to say.

British columnist Giles Coren in a memo to the editor of his paper's review-and-listings section when he noticed that a word had been changed in his review of a novel by Mark Dunn

The number one book of the ages was written by a committee, and it was called The Bible.

Louis B. Mayer, to a writer who complained of excessive editing

Why don't you write books people can read?

Mrs Nora Joyce to her husband, James

An essentially private man who wished his total indifference to public notice to be universally recognised.

Tom Stoppard on James Joyce

He had a genius for backing into the limelight.

Lowell Thomas, biographer of T.E. Lawrence

They are rather out of touch with reality; by reality I mean shops like Selfridges, and motor buses, and the Daily Express.

T.E. Lawrence on expatriate authors living in Paris

A bore and a bounder and a prig. He was intoxicated with his own youth, and loathed any milieu which he couldn't dominate. Certainly he had none of a gentleman's instincts, strutting about Peace Conferences in Arab dress.

Sir Henry Channon on T.E. Lawrence

A novelist who writes nothing for 10 years finds his reputation rising. Because I keep on producing books they say there must be something wrong with this fellow.
J.B. Priestley

At the age of 50 Priestley will be saying, why don't the highbrows admire me? It isn't true that I only write for money. He will be enormously rich; but there will be that thorn in his shoe – or so I hope.
Virginia Woolf on J.B. Priestley

It seems that Dr Leavis gave a lecture at Nottingham University on 'Literature in My Time' and declared that apart from D.H. Lawrence there had been no literature in his time. He knocked hell out of everybody, and no doubt had all the Lucky Jims rolling down the aisles. Like Groucho Marx on another academic occasion, whatever it was he was against it. Virginia Woolf was a 'slender talent'; Lytton Strachey 'irresponsible and unscrupulous'; W.H. Auden 'the career type', fixed at 'the undergraduate stage'; Spender 'no talent whatsoever'; Day-Lewis 'Book Society author'; the whole age 'dismal', and outlook 'very poor'. By the time Dr Leavis caught his train back to Cambridge, there was hardly anything left to read in Nottingham. I have not the pleasure of the doctor's acquaintance – he was up at Cambridge just after me – but I have a vague but impressive vision of him, pale and glittering-eyed, shining with integrity, marching out of Downing to close whole departments of libraries, to snatch books out of people's hands, to proclaim the bitter truth that nobody writes

anything worth reading. There is Lawrence; there is Leavis on
Lawrence; perhaps a disciple, Jones, is writing something – let
us say, Jones on Leavis on Lawrence, after that, nothing.
J.B. Priestley on F.R. Leavis

He is important not because he leads to Mr J.B. Priestley
but because he leads to Jane Austen, to appreciate whose
distinction is to feel that life isn't long enough to permit of
one's giving much time to Fielding or any to Mr Priestley.
F.R. Leavis on Fielding

It is sad to see Milton's great lines bobbing up and down in
the sandy desert of Dr Leavis's mind with the grace of a fleet of
weary camels.
Edith Sitwell on F.R. Leavis, Aspects of Modern Poetry

Then Edith Sitwell appeared, her nose longer than an
anteater's, and read some of her absurd stuff.
Lytton Strachey, An evening at Arnold Bennett's House

I do not want Miss Mannin's feelings to be hurt by the fact that
I have never heard of her. At the moment I am debarred from
the pleasures of putting her in her place by the fact she has not
got one.
Edith Sitwell on Ethel Mannin

So you've been reviewing Edith Sitwell's last piece of virgin
dung, have you? Isn't she a poisonous thing of a woman, lying

concealing, flipping, plagiarizing, misquoting, and being as clever a crooked literacy publicist as ever.
Dylan Thomas on Edith Sitwell

He was a detestable man. Men pressed money on him, and women their bodies. Dylan took both with equal contempt. His great pleasure was to humiliate people.
A.J.P. Taylor on Dylan Thomas

Somebody's boring me. I think it's me.
Dylan Thomas after talking continuously for some time

You have but two topics, yourself and me, and I'm sick of both.
Samuel Johnson on James Boswell

E.M. Forster never gets any further than warming the teapot. He's a rare fine hand at that. Feel this teapot. Is it not beautifully warm? Yes, but there ain't going to be no tea.
Katherine Mansfield on E.M. Forster

I loathe you. You revolt me stewing in your consumption.
D.H. Lawrence to Katherine Mansfield

Good reviews make your heart swell. Bad reviews are like seeing your daughter heckled during the Nativity play.
Mark Haddon

Like a piece of litmus paper he has always been quick to take
the colour of the times.
The Observer *on Aldous Huxley*

You could tell by his conversation which volume of the
Encyclopaedia Britannica he'd been reading. One day it would be
Alps, Andes and Apennines, and the next it would be the
Himalayas and the Hippocratic Oath.
Bertrand Russell on Aldous Huxley

The stupid person's idea of a clever person.
Elizabeth Bowen writing in the Spectator, *on Aldous Huxley*

Your manuscript is both good and original; but the part that
is good is not original, and the part that is original is not good.
Samuel Johnson to an author

I hate a fellow whom pride, or cowardice, or laziness drives
into a corner, and who does nothing when he is there but sit
and growl; let him come out as I do, and bark.
Samuel Johnson

There is no arguing with Johnson; for when his pistol misses
fire, he knocks you down with the butt end of it.
Oliver Goldsmith on Samuel Johnson

Curse the blasted, jelly-boned swines, the slimy, the belly-
wriggling invertebrates, the miserable sodding rotters, the
flaming sods, the snivelling, dribbling, dithering, palsied,

pulseless lot that make up England. They've got white of egg in their veins, and their spunk is that watery it's a marvel they can breed. Why, why, why, was I born an Englishman!

D.H. Lawrence after a publisher rejected his manuscript of Sons and Lovers

I like to write when I feel spiteful: it's like having a good sneeze.

D.H. Lawrence, review of Art-Nonsense *by Eric Gill, in the* Phoenix

He's impossible. He's pathetic and preposterous. He writes like a sick man.

Gertrude Stein on D.H. Lawrence

I am only one, only one, only one. Only one being, one at the same time. Not two, not three, only one. Only one life to live, only sixty minutes in one hour. Only one pair of eyes. Only one brain. Only one being. Being only one, having only one pair of eyes, having only one time, having only one life, I cannot read your MS three or four times. Not even one time. Only one look, only one look is enough. Hardly one copy would sell here. Hardly one. Hardly one.

A.J. Fifield, rejecting a manuscript by Gertrude Stein

Gertrude Stein's prose is a cold, black suet-pudding. We can represent it as a cold suet-roll of fabulously reptilian length. Cut it at any point, it is ... the same heavy, sticky, opaque mass all through, and all along.

Percy Wyndham Lewis

... a flabby lemon and pink giant, who hung his mouth open as though he were an animal at the zoo inviting buns – especially when the ladies were present.

Wyndham Lewis on Ford Madox Ford

I do not think I have ever seen a nastier-looking man ... Under the black hat, when I had first seen them, the eyes had been those of an unsuccessful rapist.

Ernest Hemingway on Percy Wyndham Lewis

He has never been known to use a word that might send a man to a dictionary.

William Faulkner on Ernest Hemingway

Poor Faulkner. Does he really think emotions come from big words?

Ernest Hemingway on William Faulkner

If my books had been any worse I should not have been invited to Hollywood, and if they had been any better I should not have come.

Raymond Chandler

Another damned, thick, square book! Always scribble, scribble, scribble! Eh! Mr Gibbon?

William, Duke of Gloucester, later George III, to Edward Gibbon

Gibbon's style is detestable; but it is not the worst thing about him.
Samuel Taylor Coleridge on Edward Gibbon

Gibbon is an ugly, affected, disgusting fellow, and poisons our literary club for me. I class him among infidel wasps and enormous snakes.
James Boswell on Edward Gibbon

That he was a coxcomb and a bore, weak, vain, pushing, curious, garrulous, was obvious to all who were acquainted with him. That he could not reason, that he had no wit, no humour, no eloquence, is apparent from his writings. Nature had made him a slave and an idolater. His mind resembled those creepers which the botanists call parasites and which can subsist only by clinging round the stems and imbibing the juices of stronger plants.

Servile and impertinent, shallow and pedantic, a bigot and a sot, bloated with family pride, and eternally blustering about the dignity of a born gentleman, yet stooping to be a tablebearer, an eavesdropper, a common butt in the taverns of London ... Everything which another man would have hidden, everything the publication of which would have made another man hang himself, was a matter of exaltation to his weak and diseased mind.
Thomas Babington Macaulay on James Boswell

I wish I was as cocksure of anything as Tom Macaulay is of everything.

Lord Melbourne on Thomas Babington Macaulay

You know, when I am gone you will be sorry you never heard me speak.

Sydney Smith to Thomas Babington Macaulay, a non-stop talker

CONCERNED LADY: Oo poor 'ickle fing, did oo hurt oo's 'ickle finger then?
MACAULAY, AGED 4: Thank you, Madam, but the agony has somewhat abated.

Thomas Babington Macaulay, quoted in Wanda Orton's biography

Rogers is not very well .... Don't you know he has produced a couplet? When he is delivered of a couplet, with infinite labour and pain, he takes to his bed, has straw laid down, the knocker tied up, expects his friends to call and make enquiries, and the answer at the door invariably is 'Mr Rogers and his little couplet are as well as can be expected.' When he produces an Alexandrine he keeps to his bed a day longer.

Sydney Smith on Samuel Rogers

Reading Proust is like bathing in someone else's dirty water.

Alexander Woollcott on Marcel Proust. Attrib.

The majority of husbands remind me of an orang-utan trying to play the violin.

Honoré de Balzac

A fat little flabby person with the face of a baker, the clothes of a cobbler, the size of a barrelmaker, the manners of a stocking salesman and the dress of an innkeeper.

Victor de Balabin on Honoré de Balzac, Diary

Everywhere I go I'm asked if university stifles writers. My opinion is that they don't stifle enough of them.

Flannery O'Connor

This is not a novel to be tossed aside lightly. It should be thrown with great force.

Dorothy Parker on Benito Mussolini's L'Amante del Cardinale, Claudia Particella

'That's a very good idea, Piglet,' said Pooh. 'We'll practise it now as we go along. But it's no good going home to practise it, because it's a special Outdoor Song Which Has To Be Sung In The Snow.'

'Are you sure?' asked Piglet anxiously.

'Well, you'll see, Piglet, when you listen. Because this is how it begins. The more it Snows-tiddely-pom-'

'Tiddely what?' said Piglet. (He took, as you might say, the words out of your correspondent's mouth.)

'Pom!' said Pooh. 'I put it in to make it hummy.'

And it is that word 'hummy', my darlings, that marks the first place in 'The House at Pooh Corner' at which Tonstant Weader Fwowed up.

Dorothy Parker on The house at Pooh Corner by A.A. Milne, Constant Reader review in the New Yorker

Oh for the hour of Herod.
Anthony Hope Hawkins on Peter Pan by J.M. Barrie

Nothing but a pack of lies.
Damon Runyon on Alice in Wonderland by Lewis Carroll

Every word she writes is a lie, including 'and' and 'the'.
Mary McCarthy on Lillian Hellman. Hellman responded with a $2.25 million lawsuit

From the moment I picked up your book until I laid it down I was convulsed with laughter. Someday I intend reading it.
Grouch Marx on Dawn Ginsbergh's Revenge by Sidney J. Perelman

To see him fumbling with our rich and delicate language is to experience all the horror of seeing a Sèvres vase in the hands of a chimpanzee.
Evelyn Waugh on Sir Stephen Spender

Mr Waugh, I always feel, is an antique in search of a period, a snob in search of a class, perhaps even a mystic in search of a beatific vision.
Malcolm Muggeridge on Evelyn Waugh

Insects sting, not from malice, but because they want to live. It is the same with critics – they desire our blood, not our pain.
Friedrich Nietzsche

In the 'About the Author' note ... we are told 'Roy Blount, Jr is a novelist. Now.' This makes sense only if the errant 'w' at the end of the last word is omitted. Apart from this bit of inadvertent humour, *First Hubby* is flawlessly lame.

L.S. Klepp *on First Hubby by Roy Blount, Jr, in Entertainment Weekly*

The covers of this book are too far apart.

Ambrose Bierce, *review*

Book reviewers can be divided into batchers (who review several books at a time), betchers ('betcher I could have written it better'), bitchers, botchers and butchers.

Paul Jennings

Asking a working writer what he thinks about critics is like asking a lamppost what he feels about dogs.

Christopher Hampton

They point to an elephant and say that 'that is a terrible rhinoceros'.

Ford Madox Ford *on literary critics*

like a person who has put on full armour and attacked a hot fudge Sunday.

Kurt Vonnegut *on critics who rage against novels*

There are three rules for writing a novel. Unfortunately, nobody knows what they are.

W. Somerset Maugham

The ratio of literacy to illiteracy is constant but nowadays the illiterates can read and write.
Alberto Moravia

Read over your compositions, and wherever you meet with a passage which you think is particularly fine, strike it out.
Samuel Johnson, *recalling the advice of a college tutor*

A vain, silly transparent coxcomb without either solid talents or a solid nature.
J.G. Lockhart on Samuel Pepys

It is only fair to Allen Ginsberg to remark on the utter lack of decorum of any kind in his dreadful little volume. Howl is meant to be a noun, but I can't help taking it as an imperative.
John Hollander on Howl by Allen Ginsberg, in the Partisan Review

The face to launch a thousand dredgers.
Jack de Manio on Glenda Jackson in Women in Love

That face that lunched a thousand shits.
Anonymous, *of the conviviality of the (Greek-born) Arianna Stassinopoulos (now Huffington)*

So boring you fall asleep halfway through her name.
Alan Bennett on Arianna Stassinopoulos, in the Observer

Reading is a pernicious habit. It destroys all originality of sentiment.
Thomas Hobbes

That's not writing, it's typing.
Truman Capote on James A. Michener

You can type this shit, George, but you can't say it.
Harrison Ford to George Lucas after reading the script for Star Wars

Having to read a footnote resembles having to go downstairs to answer the doorbell while in the middle of making love.
Noël Coward

Beckett was early commandeered by Enthusiasts whose object is always to quarantine their heroes. Under their influence, critics dwindle into a priesthood, readers vanish into a congregation, and art freezes into a sacrament that can never be questioned.
Robert Robinson on Samuel Beckett's enthusiasts

I love it when you talk like that. It reminds me of how much we lost when the grammar schools went comprehensive.
Ann Leslie on Robert Robinson, who had been talking for some time

Sir Walter Scott, when all is said and done, is an inspired butler.
William Hazlitt

He could not think up to the height of his own towering style.

G.K. Chesterton on Tennyson

Hardy became a sort of village atheist brooding and
blaspheming over the village idiot.

G.K. Chesterton on Thomas Hardy

Chesterton is like a vile scum on a pond ... All his slop – it is
really modern Catholicism to a great extent, the never taking
a hedge straight, the mumbo-jumbo of superstition dodging
behind clumsy fun and paradox ... I believe he creates a milieu
in which art is impossible. He and his kind.

Ezra Pound on G.K. Chesterton

Where were you fellows when the paper was blank?

Fred Allen to editors who heavily edited one of his scripts

February 1755
My Lord
I have been lately informed by the proprietor of The World
that two papers in which my dictionary is recommended to the
Public were written by your Lordship. To be so distinguished is
an honour which, being very little accustomed to favours from
the Great, I know not well how to receive, or in what terms to
acknowledge.

When upon some slight encouragement I first visited your
Lordship I was overpowered like the rest of Mankind by the
enchantment of your address, and could not forbear to wish
that I might boast myself Le Vainqueur du Vainqueur de la

Terre, that I might obtain that regard for which I saw the world contending, but I found my attendance so little encouraged, that neither pride nor modesty would suffer me to continue it. When I had once addressed your Lordship in public, I had exhausted all the art of pleasing which a retired and uncourtly Scholar can possess. I had done all that I could, and no Man is well pleased to have his all neglected, be it ever so little. Seven years, My Lord, have now passed since I waited in your outward Rooms or was repulsed from your Door, during which time I have been pushing on my work through difficulties of which it is useless to complain, and have brought it at last to the verge of Publication without one Act of assistance, one word of encouragement, or one smile of favour. Such treatment I did not expect, for I never had a Patron before ...

Is not a Patron, My Lord, one who looks with unconcern on a Man struggling for Life in the water and when he has reached ground encumbers him with help? The notice which you have been pleased to take of my Labours, had it been early, had been kind; but it was delayed till I am indifferent and cannot enjoy it, till I am solitary and cannot impart it, till I am known and do not want it.

I hope it is no very cynical asperity not to confess obligation where no benefit has been received, or to be unwilling that the Public should consider me as owing that to a Patron, which Providence has enabled me to do for myself.

Having carried on my work thus far with so little obligation to any Favourer of Learning I shall not be disappointed though I should conclude it, if less be possible, with less, for I have

been long wakened from that Dream of hope, in which I once boasted myself with so much exaltation, My lord, Your Lordship's Most humble Obedient Servant, Sam: Johnson
Samuel Johnson to Lord Chesterfield

PATRON: n.s. One who countenances, supports or protects. Commonly a wretch who supports with insolence, and is paid with flattery.
Samuel Johnson, Dictionary of the English Language

Very nice, though there are dull stretches.
Antoine de Rivarol on a two-line poem

Chaucer, notwithstanding the praises bestowed upon him, I think obscene and contemptible; he owes his celebrity merely to his antiquity.
Lord Byron on Geoffrey Chaucer. Attrib.

A hyena that wrote poetry in tombs.
Friedrich Nietzsche on Dante

A Methodist parson in Bedlam.
Horace Walpole on Dante

Dr Donne's verses are like the Peace of God, for they pass all understanding.
James I on John Donne

His verse ... is the beads without the string.

Gerard Manley Hopkins on Robert Browning

He has plenty of music in him, but he cannot get it out.

Lord Tennyson on Robert Browning

Our language sunk under him.

Joseph Addison on John Milton

Thomas Gray walks as if he had fouled his small-clothes and looks as if he smelt it.

Christopher Smart

There are two ways of disliking poetry. One is to dislike it. The other is to read Pope.

Oscar Wilde on Alexander Pope

In science you want to say something nobody ever knew before, in words everyone can understand. In poetry, you are bound to say something everyone knows already in words that nobody can understand.

Mathematician Paul Dirac

Most people ignore most poetry because most poetry ignores most people.

Adrian Mitchell

The truth is like poetry. And most people fucking hate poetry.

Overheard in a Washington DC bar by author Michael Lewis

My favourite poem is the one that starts 'Thirty days hath
September' because it actually tells you something.
Groucho Marx

Great Wits are sure to Madness near alli'd
And thin Partitions do their Bounds divide ...
John Dryden on the Earl of Shaftesbury, Absalom and Achitophel

His imagination resembled the wings of an ostrich. It enabled
him to run, though not to soar.
Thomas Babington Macaulay on John Dryden

Who is this Pope I hear so much about? I cannot discover what
is his merit. Why will my subjects not write in prose?
George II on Alexander Pope

Damn with faint praise, assent with civil leer,
And without sneering, teach the rest to sneer;
Willing to wound, and yet afraid to strike,
Just hint a fault, and hesitate dislike;
Alike reserved to blame, or to commend,
A tim'rous foe, and a suspicious friend ...
Alexander Pope on Joseph Addison, Epistle to Dr Arbuthnot

Steele might become a reasonably good writer if he would
pay a little attention to grammar, learn something about the
propriety and disposition of words and incidentally, get some
information on the subject he intends to handle.
Jonathan Swift on Richard Steele

A monster, gibbering shrieks and gnashing imprecations against mankind – tearing down all shreds of modesty, past all sense of manliness and shame: filthy in word, filthy in thought, furious, raging, obscene.
William Thackeray on Jonathan Swift

Thackeray settled like a meat-fly on whatever one had got for dinner; and made one sick of it.
John Ruskin on William Thackeray

Here are Jonny Keats' piss-a-bed poetry, and three novels by God knows whom … No more Keats, I entreat: flay him alive; if some of you don't I must skin him myself: there is no bearing the drivelling idiotism of the Mankin.
Lord Byron on John Keats

A mere sodomite and a perfect leper.
Ralph Waldo Emerson on Algernon Swinburne

Such writing is a sort of mental masturbation … a bedlam vision produced by raw pork and opium.
Lord Byron on John Keats, letter to John Murray

The world is rid of Lord Byron, but the deadly slime of his touch still remains.
John Constable (the artist) on news of Byron's death

A tadpole of the Lakes.
Lord Byron on John Keats

A denaturalized being who, having exhausted every species of sensual gratification, and drained the cup of sin to its bitterest dregs, is resolved to show that he is no longer human, even in his frailties, but a cool, unconcerned fiend.
John Styles on Lord Byron

Mad, bad, and dangerous to know.
Lady Caroline Lamb on Lord Byron

A man must serve his time to every trade
Save censure –critics all are ready made.
Lord Byron, English Bards and Scotch Reviewers

Byron! – he would be all forgotten today if he had lived to be a florid old gentleman with iron-grey whiskers, writing very long, very able letters to *The Times* about the Repeal of the Corn Laws.
Max Beerbohm on Lord Byron

Here is Miss Seward with six tomes of the most disgusting trash, sailing over Styx with a Foolscap over her periwig as complacent as can be – Of all Bitches dead or alive a scribbling woman is the most canine.
Lord Byron on Anna Seward

A system in which the two greatest commandments were to hate your neighbour and to love your neighbour's wife.
Thomas Babington Macaulay on Byron's poetry

Shelley is a poor creature, who has said or done nothing worth a serious man being at the trouble of remembering ... Poor soul, he has always seemed to me an extremely weak creature; a poor, thin, spasmodic, hectic, shrill and pallid being ... The very voice of him, shrill, shrieky, to my ear has too much of the ghost.

Thomas Carlyle on Percy Bysshe Shelley

The same old sausage, fizzing and sputtering in its own grease.

Henry James on Thomas Carlyle

A lewd vegetarian.

Charles Kingsley on Percy Bysshe Shelley

Walt Whitman is as unacquainted with art as a hog with mathematics.

London Critic on Walt Whitman

Longfellow is to poetry what the barrel-organ is to music.

Van Wyck Brooks on Henry Wadsworth Longfellow

A bell with a wooden tongue.

Ralph Waldo Emerson on William Wordsworth

Two voices there are: one is of the deep;
It learns the storm-cloud's thunderous melody ...
And one is of an old half-witted sheep
Which bleats articulate monotony ...

And, Wordsworth, both are thine.
James Kenneth Stephen on William Wordsworth

Wordsworth went to the Lakes, but he never was a lake poet.
He found in stones the sermons he had already put there.
Oscar Wilde on William Wordsworth

Dark, limber verses stuft with lakeside sedges,
And propt with rotten stakes from rotten hedges.
Walter Savage Landor on William Wordsworth

Never did I see such apparatus got ready for thinking, and so
little thought. He mounts scaffolding, pulleys, and tackle,
gathers all the tools in the neighbourhood with labour, with
noise, demonstration, precept, abuse, and sets – three bricks.
Thomas Carlyle on Samuel Taylor Coleridge

Carlyle is a poet to whom nature has denied the faculty of
verse.
Alfred Lord Tennyson on Thomas Carlyle, letter to W.E. Gladstone

A dirty man with opium-glazed eyes and rat-taily hair.
Lady Frederick Cavendish on Alfred Lord Tennyson

Twin miracles of mascara, her eyes looked like the corpses of
two small crows that had crashed into a chalk cliff.
Clive James on Barbara Cartland

English Literature's performing flea.
Seán O'Casey on P.G. Wodehouse

Reading him is like wading through glue.
Alfred Lord Tennyson on Ben Jonson

There was little about melancholia that he didn't know; there was little else that he did.
W.H. Auden on Alfred Lord Tennyson

A fly would break its legs walking across his face.
Anonymous on W.H. Auden

My face looks like a wedding cake that has been left out in the rain.
W.H. Auden on himself

The higher water mark, so to speak, of Socialist literature is W.H. Auden, a sort of gutless Kipling.
George Orwell, The Road to Wigan Pier

He is all ice and wooden-faced acrobatics.
Wyndham Lewis on W.H. Auden

He is all blood, dirt and sucked sugar stick.
W.B. Yeats on Wilfred Owen

By appointment: Teddy Bear to the Nation.
Alan Bell on John Betjeman, in The Times

All right, then, I'll say it: Dante makes me sick.
Félix Lope de Vego y Carpio after being told he was about to die

Cusk herself seems extraordinary – a brittle little dominatrix
and peerless narcissist who exploits her husband and her
marriage with relish ... acres of poetic whimsy and vague
literary blah, a needy, neurotic mandolin solo of reflections on
child sacrifice and asides about drains.
Camilla Long

I know nothing of Parris's social background ... [but] whatever
his social origins the general style of his letter with its
illiterate, petulant, self-righteous tone, is the voice of the new,
'classless' Conservatism ... jumping up everywhere nowadays,
usually from the lower middle class. Frequently they have very
unattractive moustaches.
Auberon Waugh in April 1979 on the editor of this book

One thing is certain, Parris will never be heard of again.
Frank Johnson, April 1979

Fuck off Parris, you talentless bastard.
*Anonymous note found, by chance, apparently slipped quite randomly into the
pages of one of the editor's books in his bookshelves*

Art

The finest collection of frames I ever saw.

Scientist and inventor Sir Humphrey Davy, asked his opinion of Paris art galleries. Attrib.

If people only knew as much about painting as I do, they would never buy my pictures.

Sir Edwin Henry Landseer to W.P. Frith

Art is the unceasing effort to compete with the beauty of flowers – and never succeeding.

Marc Chagall

If Botticelli were alive today he'd be working for *Vogue*.

Peter Ustinov

Tracey Emin's bed is art because it's made by an artist, and yours isn't, because it isn't.

AA Gill

Cold, mechanical, conceptual bullshit.
Kim Howells MP, Culture Minister, on the Turner Prize

Pretentious, self-indulgent, craftless tat.
Ivan Massow on modern art while Chairman of the Institute of Contemporary Arts

They say Rothko killed himself because he met the people who bought his art.
Adrian Searle

Skill without imagination is craftsmanship and gives us many useful objects such as wickerwork picnic baskets. Imagination without skill gives us modern art.
Tom Stoppard

Mrs Balinger is one of those ladies who pursue Culture in bands, as though it were dangerous to meet it alone.
Edith Wharton, novelist

Art today is institutionalised narcissism, a conspiracy between creators and curators to make poor people feel stupid.
Stephen Bayley

He bores me. He ought to have stuck to his flying machines.
Pierre-Auguste Renoir on Leonardo da Vinci

Degas is nothing but a peeping Tom, behind the coulisses,

and among the dressing-rooms of the ballet dancers, noting only travesties of fallen debased womanhood.
Pamphlet published by The Churchman

The English public takes no interest in a work of art until it is told that the work in question is immoral.
Oscar Wilde

The kind of people who always go on about whether a thing is in good taste invariably have very bad taste.
Joe Orton

The masses' bad taste is rooted more deeply in reality than the intellectuals' good taste.
Bertolt Brecht

In the art world, 'tasteful' is probably a bigger insult than 'tasteless'.
Grayson Perry

He will never be anything but a dauber.
Titian on Tintoretto

Daubaway Weirdsley.
Punch on Aubrey Beardsley, British artist

Rembrandt is not to be compared in the painting of character with our extraordinarily gifted English artist, Mr Rippingille.
John Hunt, 19th-century art critic, on Rembrandt

I doubt that art needed Ruskin any more than a moving train
needs one of its passengers to shove it.

Tom Stoppard on John Ruskin, in The Times Literary Supplement

I don't mind. I have gloves on.

*Mark Twain after running his hand over a Whistler painting, which caused the
artist to exclaim: 'Don't touch that, Can't you see, it isn't dry yet.'*

Well, not bad, but there are decidedly too many of them,
and they are not very well arranged. I would have done it
differently.

*James Whistler when asked if he agreed that the stars were especially beautiful
one night*

Perhaps not, but then you can't call yourself a great work of
nature.

*James Whistler after a sitter complained that his portrait was not a great work
of art*

The explanation is quite simple. I wished to be near my
mother.

*James Whistler after a snob asked him why he had been born in such an
unfashionable place as Lowell, Massachusetts*

I cannot tell you that, madam. Heaven has granted me no
offspring.

James Whistler when asked if he thought genius hereditary

Mr Whistler has always spelt art with a capital 'I'.
Oscar Wilde on James Whistler

My dear Whistler, you leave your pictures in such a sketchy, unfinished state. Why don't you ever finish them?
Frederic Leighton, British painter, on James Whistler

My dear Leighton, why do you ever begin yours?
James Whistler's riposte to Frederic Leighton

Like a carbuncle on the face of an old and valued friend.
Charles, Prince of Wales, 1986, on a proposed extension to the National Gallery

A pot of paint has been thrown in the public's face.
Variously believed to have been said by John Ruskin about Whistler's painting Nocturne in Black and Gold: The Falling Rocker, *or by Camille Mauclair about Jean Puy's* Stroll under the Pines

Mr Lewis' pictures appeared to have been painted by a mailed fist in a cotton glove.
Dame Edith Sitwell on Wyndham Lewis

It resembles a tortoise-shell cat having a fit in a plate of tomatoes.
Mark Twain on J.M.W. Turner's The Slave Ship

It makes me look as if I were straining at a stool.
Winston Churchill on his portrait by Graham Sutherland

If my husband would ever meet a woman on the street who looked like the woman in his paintings, he would fall over in a dead faint.

Mrs Pablo Picasso on her husband's paintings

His pictures seem to resemble, not pictures, but a sample book of patterns of linoleum.

Cyril Asquith on Paul Klee

A decorator tainted with insanity.

Kenyon Cox on Paul Gauguin

The only genius with an IQ of 60.

Gore Vidal on Andy Warhol

Inspiration is for amateurs. I just get to work.

American artist Chuck Close

How can I take an interest in my work when I don't like it?

Francis Bacon

I stick to my business, which is art. Suggest you stick to yours, which is butchery.

Jacob Epstein to Nikita Khrushchev after he made what was described as a 'vigorous' observation about Epstein's work

Music

Listening to a record is like going to bed with Marilyn Monroe's photograph.
Otto Klemperer

I can't stand to sing the same song the same way two nights in succession, let alone two years or ten years. If you can, then it ain't music, it's close-order drill or exercise or yodeling or something, not music.
Billie Holiday

Of all the bulls that live, this hath the greatest ass's ears.
Elizabeth I on the musician John Bull

Those people on the stage are making such a noise I can't hear a word you're saying.
Henry Taylor Parker, American music critic, rebuking some members of an audience who were talking near him

I like your Opera. One day I think I'll set it to music.
Richard Wagner to a young composer, also attributed to Ludwig van Beethoven

Wagner has beautiful moments but awful quarter hours.
Gioachino Rossini on Richard Wagner

After Rossini dies, who will there be to promote his music?
Richard Wagner on Gioachino Rossini

... This din of brasses, tin pans and kettles, this Chinese or Caribbean clatter with wood sticks and ear-cutting scalping knives ... Heartless sterility, obliteration of all melody, all tonal charm, all music ... This revelling in the destruction of all tonal essence, raging satanic fury in the orchestra, this diabolic, lewd caterwauling, scandal-mongering, gun-toting music, with an orchestral accompaniment slapping you in the face ...
J.L. Klein on Richard Wagner

Don't trouble yourself to play further. I much prefer the second.
Gioachino Rossini to a would-be composer who had just played the first of two works from which he wished Rossini to choose the better

Rossini would have been a great composer if his teacher had spanked him enough on the backside.
Ludwig van Beethoven on Gioachino Rossini

When I composed that, I was conscious of being inspired by

God Almighty. Do you think I can consider your puny little fiddle when He speaks to me?

Ludwig van Beethoven in reply to a complaint by a violinist that a passage was unplayable

All Bach's last movements are like the running of a sewing-machine.

Arnold Bax on Johann Sebastian Bach

The audience seemed rather disappointed; they expected the ocean, something big, something colossal, but they were served instead with some agitated water in a saucer.

Louis Scheider on La Mer by Claude Debussy

I like the bit about quarter to eleven.

Erik Satie on 'From dawn to noon on the sea' from La Mer by Claude Debussy

Little pink bonbons stuffed with snow.

Claude Debussy on Edvard Grieg

Too many pieces of music finish too long after the end.

Igor Stravinsky

Gaudy musical harlotry, savage and incoherent bellowings.

Boston Gazette on Franz Liszt

Composition indeed! Decomposition is the proper word for such hateful fungi!

The Dramatic and Musical World on Franz Liszt, 1855

I had another dream the other day about music critics. They were small and rodent-like with padlocked ears, as if they had stepped out of a painting by Goya.
Igor Stravinsky, in the Evening Standard

I can compare *Le Carnaval Romain* by Berlioz to nothing but the caperings and gibberings of a big baboon, over-excited by a dose of alcoholic stimulus.
George Templeton Strong on Hector Berlioz, Diary

A Tub of Pork and Beer.
Hector Berlioz on George Frideric Handel

If there is anyone here whom I have not insulted, I beg his pardon.
Johannes Brahms on leaving a gathering of friends

Brahms is just like Tennyson, an extraordinary musician with the brains of a third-rate village policeman.
George Bernard Shaw on Johannes Brahms

The scoundrel Brahms. What a giftless bastard! It annoys me that this self-inflated mediocrity is hailed as a genius. Chaotic and absolutely empty dried-up stuff.
Pyotr Tchaikovsky on Johannes Brahms, Diary

Music that stinks to the ear.
Eduard Hanslick on Tchaikovsky

I nearly trod in some once.

Sir Thomas Beecham on Stockhausen

Listening to the Fifth Symphony of Ralph Vaughan Williams is like staring at a cow for forty-five minutes.

Aaron Copland

Critics are misbegotten abortions.

Ralph Vaughan Williams on music critics

You know whatta you do when you shit? Singing, it's the same thing, only up!

Enrico Caruso

The only time you want to see 100 gypsies on your doorstep.

Publicity by Mole Valley District Council, for a Romany orchestra's visit to Surrey

It is quite untrue that the English people don't appreciate music. They may not understand it but they absolutely love the noise it makes.

Sir Thomas Beecham

I had not realized that the Arabs were so musical.

Sir Thomas Beecham on hearing that a concert by Malcolm Sargent in Tel Aviv had been interrupted by the sound of gunfire directed at the concert hall

The musical equivalent of St Pancras station.

Sir Thomas Beecham on Edward Elgar's Symphony in A Flat

Like playing a birdcage with a toasting fork.
Sir Thomas Beecham on the harpsichord

A glorified bandmaster.
Sir Thomas Beecham on Arturo Toscanini

Madame, there you sit with that magnificent instrument
between your legs, and all you can do is scratch it!
Arturo Toscanini to a woman cellist; also attributed to Sir Thomas Beecham

If you will make a point of singing 'All we, like sheep, have
gone astray' with a little less satisfaction, we shall meet the
aesthetical as well as the theological requirements.
Sir Thomas Beecham to a choir

Brass bands are all very well in their place – outdoors and
several miles away.
Sir Thomas Beecham. Attrib.

Jazz is the only form of music that the musicians seem to be
enjoying more than the audience.
Adage

There are two golden rules for an orchestra: start together and
finish together. The public doesn't give a damn what goes on
in between.
Sir Thomas Beecham

Dominoes.

George Bernard Shaw to the conductor of a palm-court orchestra in a restaurant, who had asked what he would like the orchestra to play

One should try everything once, except incest and folk-dancing.

Arnold Bax

Music written by dead guys.

Nigel Kennedy on classical music

Nothing thrills a classical music crowd more than a new piece of music that doesn't make them physically ill.

Joe Queenan

When Jack Benny plays the violin it sounds as if the strings are still in the cat.

Fred Allen

George Melly you're a repulsive sweaty faced lout singing love songs. Why your past it. Hang your gun up. And all your dirty jokes leave them to real comedians. You have a mouth like a ducks ass. Have you only one suit and shabby at that. And your dirty suggestive songs. Somebody ought to tell you. You dirty minded oaf. You're a load of rubbish.

Anonymous letter, as spelt, to George Melly

His approach to the microphone is that of an accused man pleading with a hostile jury.
Kenneth Tynan on Frankie Lane

Miss Truman is a unique American phenomenon with a pleasant voice, of little size and fair quality ... There are few moments during her recital when one can relax and feel confident she will make her goal, which is the end of the song.
Paul Hume on the singer Margaret Truman, in the Washington Post

I have just read your lousy review buried in the back pages of the paper. You sound like a frustrated old man who never made a success, an eight-ulcer man on a four-ulcer job, and all four ulcers working. I have never met you, but if I do you'll need a new nose and plenty of beefsteak and perhaps a supporter below.
Harry S. Truman replying to a review of Truman's daughter's recital in the Washington Post

Frank Sinatra is a singer who comes along once in a lifetime ... why did he have to come along in my lifetime?
Bing Crosby

I always knew Frank would end up with a boy.
Ava Gardner on Sinatra's marriage to Mia Farrow

Mr Jones is, in the words of his own hit, not unusual ... at least

not as a singer; as a sex symbol he is nothing short of inexplicable.
Sheridan Morley, in Punch

Do you gargle with pebbles?
Prince Philip to Tom Jones, after a Royal Variety show

He sang like a hinge.
Ethel Merman on Cole Porter

If white bread could sing it would sing like Olivia Newton-John.
Anonymous review

For years I've been vaguely aware of [pop star] Michael Bolton's existence, just as I'd been vaguely aware that there was an Ebola virus in Africa. Horrible tragedies, yes, but they had nothing to do with me.
Joe Queenan

I don't like country music, but I don't mean to denigrate those who do. And for the people who like country music, denigrate means 'put down'.
Bob Newhart

The Beatles are not merely awful, I would consider it sacrilegious to say anything less than that they are godawful. They are so unbelievably horrible, so appallingly unmusical, so dogmatically insensitive to the magic of the art, that they

qualify as crowned heads of anti-music, even as the imposter popes went down in history as 'anti-popes'.
William F. Buckley, Jr.

Their lyrics are unrecognisable as the Queen's English.
Edward Heath on The Beatles

Europe is not just about free trade and single currencies, it's about building a continent fit for Sir Edward Heath to conduct the European Community Youth Orchestra in the Ode to Joy.
Mark Steyn, the Daily Telegraph

He's not even the best drummer in The Beatles.
John Lennon, when asked whether Ringo Starr was the best drummer in the world. Attrib.

John Lennon ain't no revolutionary. He's a fucking idiot, man.
Todd Rundgren, in an interview with Melody Maker in 1974

I guess we're all looking for attention Rodd [sic], do you really think I don't know how to get it, without revolution? I could dye my hair green and pink for a start!
John Lennon, in a letter of reply to the same magazine, titled AN OPENED LETTUCE TO SODD RUNTLESTUNTLE

This man has child-bearing lips.
Joan Rivers on Mick Jagger

Surely nothing could be that funny.
George Melly when told the wrinkles on Mick Jagger's face were laughter lines

You have Van Gogh's ear for music.
Billy Wilder to Cliff Osmond. Attrib.

Among certain more affluent hippies Bowie is apparently
the symbol of a kind of thrilling extremism, a life-style
(the word is for once permissible) characterised by sexual
omnivorousness, lavish use of stimulants – particularly
cocaine, very much an elitist drug, being both expensive and
galvanising – self-parodied narcissism, and a glamorously
early death. To dignify this unhappy outlook with such a term
as nihilist would, of course, be absurd ... [Bowie] is unlikely to
last long as a cult.
Martin Amis on David Bowie in 1973

Wood Green shopping centre has been committed to vinyl.
The New Musical Express on the pop group Five Star

The 'Mode' make very dubious puffing noises as though they
were blowing up a paddling pool.
Smash Hits on Depeche Mode

He has an attractive voice and a highly unattractive bottom. In
his concert performances he now spends more time wagging
the latter than exercising the former.
Clive James on Rod Stewart

Her voice sounded like an eagle being goosed.
Ralph Novak on Yoko Ono, in People

I remember when pop music meant jerking off to pictures
of Marc Bolan and duffing up Bay City Rollers' fans in lunch
breaks. Being 13 was never as vapid as this. If it had been, we
would all be traffic wardens by now.
Melody Maker on the pop group Bros

They are the Hollow Men. They are electronic lice.
Anthony Burgess on disc jockeys, in Punch

Bambi with testosterone.
Owen Gleiberman on Prince, in Entertainment Weekly

Michael Jackson's album was called *Bad* because there wasn't
enough room on the sleeve for Pathetic.
Prince

If you're horrible to me, I'm going to write a song about it, and
you won't like it. That's how I operate.
Taylor Swift

I don't want a wig that looks like a wig; I want one that could
pass for a weave.
Nicki Minaj

All that money, and he's still got hair like a fucking dinner lady.

Boy George on Elton John

I never liked the sound of my own voice. Till it made me rich.

James Blunt responding to criticism of his music

What can you say about five women whose principal distinguishing characteristic is that they have different names?

Roger Ebert on the Spice Girls

If you can imagine a soothing blend of jojoba oils, vanilla, and WD40 being poured into both ear holes simultaneously, then you will have only been able to scratch the surface of the feast of pleasure that is Katie And Pete's 'A Whole New World' Album. I also found the case very useful for replacing a tile that had been missing in my bathroom for the past two and a half years.

R.C. Murray, Amazon Review of Katie Price and her then husband Peter Andre's A Whole New World

Liam Gallagher, the younger of the Oasis brothers, has the kind of eyes in which the pupils are half-hidden under the eyelids; as if the eyes had stopped between floors.

Alan Bennett

A man with a fork in a world of soup.

Noel Gallagher on Liam Gallagher

Zorro on doughnuts.
Noel Gallagher on musician Jack White

What has he done to me? Nothing. He's just somebody I'd like to hang.
Noel Gallagher on Robbie Williams

With people in the world such as Jamie Oliver and Clarissa Dickson-Wright there isn't much hope for animals.
Morrissey, a vegetarian, on chefs Jamie Oliver and the late Clarissa Dickson-Wright

It's the refuge for the mentally deficient. It's made by dull people for dull people.
Morrissey on dance music

The fire in the belly is essential, otherwise you become Michael Bublé – famous and meaningless.
Morrissey on passion

He referred to me as an 'insufferable puffed-up prat'. This is a bit rich coming from a man who actually married his own mother.
Morrissey on daytime TV host Richard Madeley

St Mary's Secondary Modern School on Renton Road in Stretford may indeed be secondary, but it is not modern.
Morrissey on his school

What's the difference between God and Bono? God doesn't wander down Grafton Street thinking he's Bono.
Louis Walsh

There are probably more annoying things than being hectored about African development by a wealthy Irish rock star in a cowboy hat, but I can't think of them at the moment.
Paul Theroux on Bono

If I don't win, the award show loses credibility.
Kanye West

You've had three hairstyles, what's next for your career?
Zach Galifianakis to Justin Bieber

Your bus leaves in ten minutes ... be under it.
John Cooper Clarke in response to a heckler

You couldn't get a fan if you were hangin' from the ceiling.
Nicki Minaj

Next time someone offers a penny for your thoughts – sell.
Peter Kay putdown to heckler

My apartment is too nice to listen to rap in.
Kanye West

Theatre, Film and Television

When your grandmother's swinging from a tree, it's really hard to care about best documentary foreign short.

Chris Rock on the historical lack of participation in the Oscars by black people, while presenting the Oscars

Mummy, what is that lady for?

Child at a matinee performance by Hermione Gingold

She was good at playing abstract confusion in the same way that a midget is good at being short ...

Clive James on Marilyn Monroe

I watched *The Music Lovers*. One can't really blame Tchaikovsky for preferring boys. Anyone might become a homosexualist who had once seen Glenda Jackson naked.

Auberon Waugh in Private Eye

I invariably miss most of the lines in the last act of an Ibsen play; I always have my fingers in my ears waiting for the loud retort that means the heroine has just Passed On.

Dorothy Parker on Henrik Ibsen

A bargain basement Bette Davis, whose lightest touch as a comedienne would stun a horse.

Time on Susan Hayward

What exactly is on your mind – if you'll excuse the exaggeration?

Inquiry by David Letterman

[A] vamp who destroys families and sucks on husbands like a praying mantis.

Il Tempo on Elizabeth Taylor

Overweight, overbosomed, overpaid and under-talented, she set the acting profession back a decade.

David Susskind on Elizabeth Taylor in Cleopatra

Miss Taylor is monotony in a slit skirt, a pre-Christian Elizabeth Arden with sequinned eyelids and occasions constantly too large for her.

New Statesman on Elizabeth Taylor in Cleopatra

Just how garish her commonplace accent, squeakily shrill voice, and the childish petulance with which she delivers her

lines are, my pen is neither scratchy nor leaky enough to
convey.
John Simon on Elizabeth Taylor's Kate, The Taming of the Shrew

Elizabeth Taylor has more chins than the Chinese telephone
directory.
Joan Rivers

... An incipient double chin, legs too short, and she has a
slight pot belly.
Richard Burton on Elizabeth Taylor

In general, Mr Burton resembles a stuffed cabbage.
*Harry Medved and Randy Dreyfuss on Richard Burton in 'The Assassination of
Trotsky,' The Fifty Worst Films of All Time*

She cannot change her face, which is that of a worried
hamster.
*Review of Prunella Scales playing all six female parts in Anatole France by
David Tylden-Wright*

Like acting with two and a half tons of condemned veal.
Coral Browne on a leading man

He has taken to ambling across our stages in a spectral,
shell-shocked manner, choosing odd moments to jump and
frisk, like a man through whom an electric current is being
intermittently passed.
Kenneth Tynan on Ralph Richardson in The White Carnation

Tony Britton's habit of curling his lip villainously and so relentlessly gives one the impression that he had it permanently waved.

Plays and Players *on Tony Britton in* A Woman of No Importance *by Oscar Wilde*

A bore is starred.

Village Voice *review of* A Star is Born *starring Barbra Streisand*

She looks like a cross between an aardvark and an albino rat surmounted by a platinum-coated horse bun.

John Simon *on Barbra Streisand*

A woman whose face looked as if it had been made of sugar and someone had licked it.

George Bernard Shaw *on Isadora Duncan*

Marie Osmond is so pure, not even Moses could part her knees.

Joan Rivers

You should never say bad things about the dead, you should only say good ... Joan Crawford is dead. Good.

Bette Davis

There's a kind of flowering dullness about her, a boredom in rowdy bloom.

Joyce Haber *on Julie Andrews*

She needs open-heart surgery, and they should go in through her feet.

Julie Andrews on Joyce Haber

It's a new low for actresses when you have to wonder what's between her ears instead of her legs.

Katharine Hepburn on Sharon Stone

I like a drink as much as the next man. Unless the next man is Mel Gibson.

Ricky Gervais, introducing Gibson onstage at the Golden Globes

Literally, physically, she has a very big mouth ... I was aware of a faint echo when I was kissing her.

Hugh Grant on Julia Roberts

I thought I told you to wait in the car.

Tallulah Bankhead, when greeted by a former admirer after many years. Attrib.

She was always a star, but only intermittently a good actress.

Brendan Gill on Tallulah Bankhead, in The Times

Systematically invading her own privacy she was the first of the modern personalities.

Lee Israel on Tallulah Bankhead

I'm as pure as the driven slush.

Tallulah Bankhead

The T is silent, as in Harlow.

Lady Margot Asquith, explaining that her name should not be pronounced 'Margot'. The reference is to Jean Harlow.

This was Doris Day's first picture; before she became a virgin.

Oscar Levant on Doris Day in Romance on the High Seas

Guido Nadzo was Nadzo Guido.

Brooks Atkinson on Valentino look-alike Guido Nadzo

Not content to stop the show, she merely slowed it down.

Anonymous, of Elaine Paige

It is greatly to Mrs Patrick Campbell's credit that, bad as the play was, her acting was worse. It was a masterpiece of failure.

George Bernard Shaw on Mrs Patrick Campbell

When you were a little boy, somebody ought to have said 'hush' just once.

Mrs Patrick Campbell to George Bernard Shaw

GEORGE BERNARD SHAW: I am enclosing two tickets to the first night of my new play. Bring a friend ... if you have one.
WINSTON CHURCHILL: Cannot possibly attend first night, will attend second ... if there is one.

Exchange between George Bernard Shaw and Winston Churchill, sometimes attributed to correspondence between Randolph Churchill and Noël Coward

She was so dramatic she stabbed the potatoes at dinner.
The Reverend Sydney Smith on Sarah Siddons, a melodramatic actress

Do you know how they are going to decide the Shakespeare-Bacon dispute? They are going to dig up Shakespeare and dig up Bacon; they are going to set their coffins side by side, and they are going to get Tree to recite *Hamlet* to them. And the one who turns in his coffin will be the author of the play.
W.S. Gilbert on Herbert Beerbohm Tree

At the end, when the whale has lured Harris north with a come-hither flick of its tail, Miss Rampling is caught in the ice floes, leaping from one to t'other and clad in thigh boots, homespun poncho and a turban, as if she expected David Bailey to surface and photograph her for *Vogue*'s Arctic number.
Alexander Walker on Charlotte Rampling in Orca the Killer Whale, *in the Evening Standard*

Dame Anna Neagle was game enough to have a little stab at the Charleston, and was wildly and sympathetically applauded by admirers who plainly felt any gesture more extravagant than holding a hand above her head – as though hailing a cab, or conceivably signalling for help – was a grave imposition upon a Lady of her advanced years.
Kenneth Hurren reviewing No, No, Nanette, *in the Spectator*

A plumber's idea of Cleopatra.
W.C. Fields on Mae West

She has a face that belongs to the sea and the wind, with large rocking-horse nostrils and teeth that you just know bite an apple every day.

Cecil Beaton on Katharine Hepburn

Katharine Hepburn ran the whole gamut of emotions from A to B.

Dorothy Parker reviewing The Lake *by Dorothy Massingham and Murray MacDonald*

I have knocked everything but the knees of the chorus girls, and nature has anticipated me there.

Percy Hammond, critic, on a musical

It's like getting a prize from the snipers because they have missed you.

Michael Caine on winning an award from the London Film Critics Circle

Insecurity, commonly regarded as a weakness in normal people, is the basic tool of an actor's trade.

Miranda Richardson

Remember, it's not who you know – it's whom.

Joan Rivers

An actor's a guy who, if you ain't talking about him, ain't listening.

Marlon Brando

You can pick out actors by the glazed look that comes into their eyes when the conversation wanders away from themselves.
Michael Wilding

Actors should be treated like cattle.
Alfred Hitchcock

Theatre actors look down on film actors, who look down on TV actors. Thank God for reality shows or we wouldn't have anybody to look down on.
George Clooney

George Clooney always looks like he's in an advert for George Clooney.
Geoff Dyer

Acting is the most minor of gifts ... after all, Shirley Temple could do it at the age of four.
Katharine Hepburn

Directors are people too short to be actors.
Josh Greenfield on film directors

He was once Slightly in Peter Pan, and has been wholly in Peter Pan ever since.
Kenneth Tynan on Noël Coward. Attrib.

He was his own greatest invention.
John Osborne on Noël Coward

Television? Television is for being on, dear boy, not for watching.
Noël Coward

Two things should be cut – the second act and the child's throat.
Noël Coward on a dull play with an annoying child star

If they'd stuffed the child's head up the horse's arse, they would have solved two problems at once.
Noël Coward on a performance starring a child and a horse, which defecated on stage

Not just an artist, but a critic, too!
Sir Thomas Beecham, during a performance when a horse on stage defecated

He's the kind of man who thinks Mea Culpa is an Italian starlet.
Brian Viner on the impresario Lord Grade

The reason why so many people turned up at Louis Mayer's funeral was because they wanted to make sure he was dead.
Sam Goldwyn

Give the public what they want to see and they'll come out for it.

Anonymous on the crowds at the funeral of Hollywood mogul Harry Cohn

What critics call dirty in our movies they call lusty in foreign films.

Billy Wilder

Monica Lewinsky has agreed to host a new Fox reality show called Mr. Personality. Lewinsky says this way, when people ask her the most degrading thing she's ever done, she'll have a new answer.

Tina Fey

Television? No good will come of this device. The word is half Greek and half Latin.

C.P. Scott

Television is a medium of entertainment which permits millions of people to listen to the same joke at the same time, and yet remain lonesome.

T.S. Eliot, in the New York Post

If a tree falls in a forest and there is no one to record the event on YouTube, does it still make a sound?

E. Jane Dickinson

Swearing on television is now like Muzak in a lift: an ambient

noise that is pumped routinely into the atmosphere without any particular purpose.
Jenny McCartney

TV is an invention that permits you to be entertained in your living-room by people you wouldn't have in your home.
David Frost

I once saved David Frost from drowning.
Peter Cook, asked if he had any regrets in his life

The bubonic plagiarist.
Peter Cook on Sir David Frost

He rose without trace.
Kitty Muggeridge on the career of David Frost

I'm afraid I'm watching television that night.
Peter Cook, invited by David Frost to dinner with Prince Andrew and Sarah Ferguson

Looking at the past by digging holes in the ground is like making a cookery programme exclusively by examining the washing up.
AA Gill on TV archaeology programmes

We are drowning our youngsters in violence, cynicism and sadism ... The grandchildren of the kids who used to weep because the Little Match Girl froze to death now feel cheated

if she isn't slugged, raped and thrown into a Bessemer
converter.
Jenkin Lloyd Jones

You know, I go to the theatre to be entertained ... I don't want
to see plays about rape, sodomy and drug addiction ... I can
get all that at home.
Peter Cook, caption to cartoon in the Observer

Popular Stage – playes ... are sinfull, heathenish, lewde,
ungodly Spectacles, and most pernicious Corruptions;
condemned in all ages, as intolerable Mischiefes to Churches,
to Republickes, to the manners, mindes and soules of men.
And that the Profession of Play-poets, of Stage-players;
together with the penning, acting, and frequenting of
Stage-players, are unlawful, infamous, and misbeseeming
Christians.
William Prynne, 17th-century critic

It had only one fault. It was kind of lousy.
James Thurber on a play

I saw it at a disadvantage – the curtain was up.
Walter Winchell on a show starring Earl Carroll

I've had a perfectly wonderful evening. But this wasn't it.
Groucho Marx

The play was a great success, but the audience was a disaster.
Oscar Wilde

What a tiresome affected sod.
Noël Coward on Oscar Wilde

Busy yourselves with that, you damned walruses, while the rest of us proceed with the play.
John Barrymore, throwing a fish into the stalls of a coughing audience

I would just like to mention Robert Houdini who in the eighteenth century invented the vanishing bird-cage trick and the theatre matinee. May he rot and perish. Good afternoon.
Orson Welles, addressing the audience at the end of a matinee performance

I've seen more excitement at the opening of an umbrella.
Earl Wilson, reviewing a play

If you love *The War of the Worlds* then crank up the volume at home. Don't waste your money on this.
Ann Treneman on a 2016 production of The War of the Worlds

The touring production of *Five Guys Named Moe* ... performed a bluesey, doleful number with so little feeling that I suspect the only cotton their ancestors ever picked was out of an Anadin bottle.
Victor Lewis-Smith, newspaper critic, 1994

There was laughter at the back of the theatre, leading to the belief that someone was telling jokes back there.

George S. Kaufman on a Broadway comedy

Darling, they've absolutely ruined your perfectly dreadful play.

Tallulah Bankhead to Tennessee Williams after seeing the film version of Orpheus Descending, *entitled* The Fugitive Kind

There is enough Irish comedy to make us wish Cromwell had done a more thorough job.

James Agee on Fort Apache

A film so awe-inspiringly wooden that it is basically a fire risk.

Peter Bradshaw on Grace of Monaco

I hated this movie. Hated hated hated hated hated this movie. Hated it. Hated every simpering stupid vacant audience-insulting moment of it. Hated the sensibility that thought anyone would like it. Hated the implied insult to the audience by its belief that anyone would be entertained by it.

Roger Ebert on North

To call it an anticlimax would be an insult not just to climaxes but to prefixes.

Roger Ebert on the end of The Village

No.

Leonard Maltin's complete review of Isn't It Romantic?

Very well then: I say Never.
George Jean Nathan on Tonight or Never

Transported to a surreal landscape, a young girl kills the first person she meets and then teams up with three strangers to kill again.
Rick Polito's synopsis of The Wizard of Oz

There were no wolves in the movie.
Amazon user Joe Watson on The Wolf of Wall Street

Too many monsters.
Amazon user Joe A. Gonzales on Monsters, Inc.

My friend Carl told me to watch this. Carl is no longer my friend.
Amazon user M.W. Malone on The Expendables 2

I don't know what's happening. I bought this movie to have something happened.
Amazon user Eric Majewski on The Happening

How many times must Willy be freed before he's freed?
Amazon user pauljolly65 on Free Willy: Escape from Pirate's Cove, *the fourth film in the series.*

Hunger isn't a game.
Amazon user Ryan Galaska on The Hunger Games

If Peter O'Toole was any prettier they'd have to call it Florence of Arabia.

Noël Coward on O'Toole's T.E. Lawrence in the film Lawrence of Arabia

As synthetic and padded as the transvestite's cleavage.

Frank Rich, 'The Butcher of Broadway', on La Cage aux Folles, in the New York Times

It is not true that Andrew Lloyd Webber and I are no longer speaking to each other. I saw his last show. At least I hope it was his last show.

Sir Tim Rice

There is less in this than meets the eye.

Tallulah Bankhead on the revival of a play by Maurice Maeterlinck

It can probably be said that Pinter raised to a new level of acceptability the kind of play in which the audience not only has no precise idea of what is going on, but seriously doubts whether the author has, either.

Kenneth Hurren on The Birthday Party by Harold Pinter, in the Mail on Sunday

A theatrical whore of the first quality.

Peter Hall on Bertolt Brecht

Shakespeare, Madam, is obscene, and, thank God, we are sufficiently advanced to have found it out.

Frances Trollope on William Shakespeare

Crude, immoral, vulgar and senseless.

Leo Tolstoy on William Shakespeare

One of the greatest geniuses that ever existed, Shakespeare undoubtedly wanted taste.

Horace Walpole on William Shakespeare

This enormous dunghill.

Voltaire on William Shakespeare

We can say of Shakespeare that never has a man turned so little knowledge to such great account.

T.S. Eliot on William Shakespeare

Pale, marmoreal Eliot was there last week, like a chapped office boy on a high stool, with a cold in his head.

Virginia Woolf on T.S. Eliot

I have tried lately to read Shakespeare, and found it so intolerably dull that it nauseated me.

Charles Darwin on William Shakespeare

A sycophant, a flatterer, a breaker of marriage vows, a whining and inconstant person.

Elizabeth Forsyth on William Shakespeare

Shakespeare never had six lines together without a fault.

Perhaps you may find seven, but this does not refute my general assertion.

Samuel Johnson on William Shakespeare

A strange, horrible business, but I suppose good enough for Shakespeare's day.

Queen Victoria giving her opinion of King Lear

When I read Shakespeare
I am struck with wonder
that such trivial people
should muse and thunder
in such lovely language.

D.H. Lawrence

The intensity of my impatience with him occasionally reaches such a pitch, that it would positively be a relief to me to dig him up and throw stones at him.

George Bernard Shaw on William Shakespeare, Dramatic Opinions and Essays

George too Shaw to be good.

Dylan Thomas on George Bernard Shaw

The way Bernard Shaw believes in himself is very refreshing in these atheistic days when so many people believe in no God at all.

Israel Zangwill on George Bernard Shaw

He is an old bore; even the grave yawns for him.

Herbert Beerbohm Tree on Israel Zangwill

He is the true Elizabethan blank-verse beast, itching to frighten other people with the superstitious terrors and cruelties in which he does not himself believe, and wallowing in blood, violence, muscularity of expression and strenuous animal passion as only literary men do when they become thoroughly depraved by solitary work, sedentary cowardice, and starvation of the sympathetic centres. It is not surprising to learn that Marlowe was stabbed in a tavern brawl: what would be utterly unbelievable would be his having succeeded in stabbing anyone else.

George Bernard Shaw on Christopher Marlowe, Dramatic Opinions and Essays

The first man to have cut a swathe through the theatre and left it strewn with virgins.

Frank Harris on George Bernard Shaw

Dramatized stench.

A review of George Bernard Shaw's Mrs Warren's Profession

He hasn't an enemy in the world, and none of his friends like him.

Oscar Wilde on George Bernard Shaw

Oscar Wilde's talent seems to me to be essentially rootless, something growing in a glass on a little water.

George Moore, novelist

He was over-dressed, pompous, snobbish, sentimental and vain. But he had an undeniable flair for the possibilities of commercial theatre.

Evelyn Waugh on Oscar Wilde

I really enjoy only his stage directions ... He uses the English language like a truncheon.

Max Beerbohm on George Bernard Shaw

Mr Shaw is (I suspect) the only man on earth who has never written any poetry.

G.K. Chesterton on George Bernard Shaw

He writes like a Pakistani who has learned English when he was twelve years old in order to become a chartered accountant.

John Osborne on George Bernard Shaw in the Manchester Guardian

There are no human beings in *Major Barbara*; only animated points of view.

William Archer on Major Barbara by George Bernard Shaw, World

More than once, I found myself asking: 'Is this homage or just horseshit?' In many instances I couldn't decide, concluding that it must be both. Surely no one makes a movie this bad by accident?

Mark Kermode on Grace of Monaco

Doctors and Psychologists

It seems a commonly received idea among men and even among women themselves that it requires nothing but a disappointment in love, the want of an object, a general disgust, or incapacity for other things, to turn a woman into a good nurse. This reminds one of the parish where a stupid old man was set to be schoolmaster because he was 'past keeping the pigs'.

Florence Nightingale

If they do no other good they do at least this, that they prepare their patients early for death, undermining little by little and cutting off their enjoyment of life.

Michel de Montaigne on physicans who prescribe diets

The art of medicine consists in amusing the patient while nature cures the disease.

Voltaire

Throw physic to the dogs; I'll none of it.
William Shakespeare, Macbeth

I find medicine is the best of all trades because whether you do any good or not you still get your money.
Molière

When a lot of remedies are suggested for a disease, that means it cannot be cured.
Anton Chekhov, The Cherry Orchard

Despite all our toils and progress, the art of medicine still falls somewhere between trout casting and spook writing.
Ben Hecht

Nobody can read Freud without realizing he was the scientific equivalent of another nuisance, George Bernard Shaw.
Robert M. Hutchins on Sigmund Freud

Anyone who pays to see a psychiatrist needs their head looking at.
Woody Allen

A psychiatrist is a fellow who asks you a lot of expensive questions your wife asks for nothing.
Joey Adams

Instead of wishing to see more doctors made by women joining what there are, I wish to see as few doctors, male or female, as possible. For, mark you, the women have made no improvement – they have only tried to be men and they have only succeeded in being third-rate men.

Florence Nightingale

If the human brain were simple enough to understand we'd be too simple to understand it.

Emerson Pugh

I've frequently observed that people who believe in a sixth sense are usually deficient in the other five.

Victor Lewis-Smith

A successful parent is one who raises a child who grows up and is able to pay for his or her own psychoanalysis.

Nora Ephron

He was meddling too much in my private life.

Tennessee Williams on why he had given up visiting his psychoanalyst

Actually I loathed the Viennese quack.

Vladimir Nabokov on Sigmund Freud

I'm a fucking doctor.

R.D. Laing's last reported words after suffering a heart attack in public. As people gathered round the spot someone said 'Get a doctor.'

Law and Lawyers

The first thing we do, let's kill all lawyers.
William Shakespeare, Henry VI, part 2

Ninety-nine per cent of lawyers give the rest a bad name.
Steven Wright

This is a British murder inquiry and some degree of justice must be seen to be more or less done.
Tom Stoppard, Jumpers

The basic test of a decent police force is that it should catch more criminals than it employs.
Robert Mark, ex-Police Commissioner

The majestic egalitarianism of the law, which forbids rich and poor people alike to sleep under bridges, to beg in the streets, and to steal bread.
Anatole France, The Red Lily

The law-courts of England are open to all men, like the doors of the Ritz Hotel.
Charles, Lord Darling

Laws are like sausages: if you like them, don't watch them being made.
Otto von Bismarck

The scandalous part of most scandals is often not the law-breaking but the law itself.
Michael Kinsley

The one great principle of English law is to make business for itself.
Charles Dickens

A lawyer is never entirely comfortable with a friendly divorce, any more than a good mortician wants to finish his job and then have the patient sit up on the table.
Jean Kerr

Lawyers, not poets, are the unacknowledged legislators of mankind.
Columnist Simon Carr

I have come to regard the law-courts not as a cathedral but rather as a casino.
Richard Ingrams, in the Guardian

A jury consists of 12 persons chosen to decide who has the better lawyer.
Robert Maxwell

Laws are like spiders' webs: if some poor weak creature comes up against them it is caught; but a bigger one can break through and get away.
Solon, an Athenian statesman

When I hear any man talk of an unalterable law, the only effect it produces on me is to convince me that he is an unalterable fool.
Sydney Smith

I do not care to speak ill of any man behind his back, but I believe the gentleman is an attorney.
Samuel Johnson

A qadi [judge] who, when two parties part in peace,
Rekindles their dispute with binding words.
Indifferent to this world and its luxuries, he seems,
But in secret, he wouldn't say no to camel dung.
Oh, people, pause and hark
To the charming qualities of our qadi,
A homosexual, drunkard, fornicator, and takes bribes,
A tell-tale liar whose judgements follow his whims.
Ibn Ayas on Ibn al-Naqib, the Egyptian Chief Justice, Mameluke era (1250–1517)

My definition of utter waste is a coachload of lawyers going over a cliff, with three empty seats.

Lamar Hunt on the increasing problems of litigation in the American National Football League

PRISONER (in the dock after being sentenced to be hanged): My Lord, spare me: I am a product of my upbringing.
JUDGE: So am I! Send him down.

YOUNG BARRISTER: My lord, my unfortunate client ... my lord, my unfortunate client ... my lord, my ... my ...
LORD ELLENBOROUGH: Go on, sir, go on. As far as you have proceeded hitherto, the court is entirely in agreement with you.

Lord Ellenborough

JUDGE: Counselor, are you trying to show contempt for this court?
LAWYER: No, your Honour, I'm trying to conceal it.

Possibly not, m'Lud, but you are much better informed.

F.E. Smith to a judge who failed to understand one of the barrister's legal speeches. The judge had told Smith: 'I have listened to you, Mr Smith, but I am none the wiser.'

He lied like an eye-witness.

Russian proverb

George Jeffreys pointed his stick at one of the rebels hauled

before him in the famous 'bloody assizes' saying: 'There is a rogue at the end of my cane.' 'At which end. My Lord?' retorted the man.
Anonymous

LORD SANDWICH: You will die either on the gallows, or of the pox.
WILKES: That must depend on whether I embrace your lordship's principles or your mistress.
John Wilkes; sometimes attributed to Samuel Foote

I have forgotten more law than you ever knew, but allow me to say, I have not forgotten much.
Judge John Maynard, replying to Judge Jeffrey's assertion that he was so old he had forgotten the law

I can't take my chauffeur everywhere.
Derek Laud, Conservative candidate, explaining a drink-driving charge

CONVICTED CRIMINAL: As God is my judge – I am innocent.
MR JUSTICE BIRKETT: He isn't; I am, and you're not!
Sir Norman Birkett

[It is reported that] after a ten year stand off, Lord Longford is again visiting the Moors murderer Ian Brady. Thank goodness, a nation will sleep more soundly for knowing that, at last, this revolting psychopath is being properly punished.
Simon Heffer

The difference is that we Europeans accept we've all got to die of something or other. Americans think death is a calamity for which you can sue somebody.
Jonathan Miller

From every treetop some wild woods songster will carol his mating song, butterflies will sport in the sunshine, the busy bee will hum happy as it pursues its accustomed vocation. The gentle breeze will tease the tassels of the wild grasses, and all nature, José Manuel Miguel Xavier Gonzales, will be glad but you. You won't be here to enjoy it because I command the sheriff or some other officer of this country to lead you out to some remote spot, swing you by the neck from the knotting bough of a sturdy oak, and let you hang until you are dead. And then, José Manuel Miguel Xavier Gonzales, I further command that such officer or officers retire quickly from your dangling corpse, that vultures may descend from the heavens upon your filthy body until nothing shall remain but bare, bleached bones of a cold-blooded, copper-coloured, blood-thirsty, throat-cutting, chilli-eating, sheep-herding, murdering son-of-a-bitch.
Transcript from US District Court, New Mexico Territory, 1881, USA v. Gonzales

You are a low-down, depraved son-of-a-bitch. There were only seven Democrats in Hinsdale County, and you ate five of them.
US trial judge sentencing Alferd [sic] Packer for cannibalism, 1874

Here comes counsel for the other side.
Sydney Smith as the lawyer Lord Brougham arrived at a performance of The Messiah

Business and Economics

Advertising is the rattling of a stick inside a swill bucket.
George Orwell

Ours is the age of substitutes: instead of language we have
jargons; instead of principles, slogans; and instead of genuine
ideas, bright suggestions.
Eric Bentley

People of the same trade seldom meet together but the
conversation ends in a conspiracy against the public, or in
some diversion to raise prices.
Adam Smith, The Wealth of Nations

Economics is extremely useful as a form of employment for
economists.
John Kenneth Galbraith

An economist is someone who can't see something working in practice without asking whether it would work in theory.
Walter Wolfgang Heller, advisor to President Kennedy

An economist is a man who states the obvious in terms of the incomprehensible.
Alfred A. Knopf

An economist is an expert who will know tomorrow why the things he predicted yesterday didn't happen today.
Laurence J. Peter

Economists have predicted nine out of the last five recessions.
Paul Samuelson

Making a speech on economics is a lot like pissing down your leg. It seems hot to you, but it never does to anyone else.
Lyndon B. Johnson

Economic forecasters were invented to make weather forecasters look good.
Irwin Stelzer

Why did nobody notice it?
Queen Elizabeth II to LSE Professor Luis Garicano asking how economists missed the global crash of 2008

Making predictions is difficult, especially about the future.
Sam Goldwyn

Sell a man a fish, he eats for a day. Teach a man how to fish, you ruin a wonderful business opportunity.
Sometimes attributed to Karl Marx

A fool and his money get a lot of publicity.
Al Bernstein

If you would know what the Lord God thinks of money, you only have to look at those to whom He gives it.
Maurice Baring

There is plenty of affordable housing. It is simply occupied by the wrong people. The problem in New York is not high rents but low income.
John Gilbert III, President, New York Landlords' Association

It is a social experience for most people. They want to meet the people in the queue.
David Mills, Chief Executive of the Post Office, defending Post Office queues, 2004

Overseas aid is a transfer of money from poor people in rich countries to rich people in poor countries.
Peter Bauer

A bank is a place that will lend you money if you can prove that you don't need it.
Bob Hope

Never take financial advice from anyone in a tie.
Nassim Nicholas Taleb

The salary of the chief executive of a large corporation is not a market award for achievement. It is frequently in the nature of a warm personal gesture by the individual to himself.
John Kenneth Galbraith, Annals of an Abiding Liberal

In any successful enterprise there must be an uneven number of directors and three is too many.
Giovanni Agnelli, founder of Fiat

It's easy to become a millionaire – start out as a billionaire, then buy an airline.
Richard Branson

The worst imaginable world would be one in which the leading expert in each field had total control over it.
Friedrich Hayek

Finding a businessman interested in the arts is like finding chicken shit in the chicken salad.
Alice Neel

Studying the science of yesteryear one comes upon such interesting notions as gravity, electricity, and the roundness of the earth – while an examination of more recent phenomena shows a strong trend towards spray cheese, stretch denim and the Moog synthesizer.

Fran Lebowitz

I am going into space in a vehicle comprising three million parts – each supplied by the lowest bidder.

Anonymous American astronaut

Sport

When it comes to sports I am not particularly interested. Generally speaking, I look upon them as dangerous and tiring activities performed by people with whom I share nothing except the right to trial by jury.
Fran Lebowitz

I told him, 'Son, what is it with you? Is it ignorance or apathy?' He said 'Coach, I don't know and I don't care.'
Frank Layden

I wanted to have a career in sports when I was young, but I had to give it up. I'm only six feet tall, so I couldn't play basketball. I'm only 190 pounds, so I couldn't play football. And I have 20-20 vision, so I couldn't be a referee.
Jay Leno

It is remarkable that a fist-gnawingly dire England performance still has the power to shock, when in some ways this one had all the exquisite unpredictability of Norman

Wisdom approaching a banana skin in the immediate vicinity of a swimming pool ... The England shirt is the precise opposite of a superhero costume, turning men with extraordinary abilities into mild-mannered guys next door.
Marina Hyde on the England football team

You can't see as well as these fucking flowers – and they're fucking plastic.
John McEnroe to a line judge at the US Open, 1980

A man whose chief ambition is to show his bravery in hunting foxes. A term of reproach used of country gentlemen.
Dr Johnson's dictionary entry for 'Foxhunting'

They came to see me bat, not to see you bowl.
W.G. Grace, refusing to leave the crease after being bowled first ball. Attrib.

Which of you bastards called this bastard a bastard?
Vic Richardson, the Australian cricket team's vice-captain, after Douglas Jardine complained that one of the team had called him a 'Pommy bastard' on the field

Don't bother shutting it, son, you won't be out there long enough.
Fred Trueman, to a new Australian batsman as he closed the gate leaving the Pavilion at Lords

A corpse with pads on.
Ian Wooldridge on Australian cricket captain Bill Lawry

The only fellow I've met who fell in love with himself at a young age and has remained faithful ever since.

Dennis Lillee on Geoff Boycott

You have done for Australian cricket what the Boston Strangler did for door-to-door salesmen.

Telegram sent to Geoff Boycott

ROD MARSH: So how's your wife and my kids?
IAN BOTHAM: The wife's fine – the kids are retarded.

Exchange between Australian wicketkeeper Rod Marsh and England all-rounder Ian Botham

MARK WAUGH: Fuck me, look who it is. Mate, what are you doing out here? There's no way you're good enough to play for England.
JAMES ORMOND: Maybe not, but at least I'm the best player in my family.

Exchange between Australian cricketer Mark Waugh, whose brother Steve was also in the team, and England newbie James Ormond

Sure, I know where the press room is – I just look for where they throw the dog meat.

Martina Navratilova

Would you like me to bowl a piano and see if you can play that?

Mervyn Hughes to Graham Gooch

If you turn the bat over you'll get the instructions, mate.

Merv Hughes to Robin Smith

WARNE: I've been waiting two years for another chance at you.

CULLINAN: Looks like you spent it eating.

Exchange between Daryll Cullinan and Shane Warne as the former came out to bat.

The only sport in which spectators burn as many calories as players (more if they are moderately restless).

Bill Bryson on cricket

An ineffectual attempt to put an elusive ball into an obscure hole with implements ill-adapted to the purpose.

Woodrow Wilson on golf

Cricket – a game which the English, not being a spiritual people, have invented in order to give themselves some conception of eternity.

Lord Mancroft

This is great. When does it start?

Groucho Marx, watching a cricket match at Lord's

Oh God, if there be cricket in heaven, let there also be rain.

Alec Douglas Home

If defensive linemen's IQs were 5 points lower, they'd be geraniums.
Russ Francis on American football

Football is a game for trained apes.
Edward Abbey on American football

I looked in the mirror one day and I said to my wife 'How many great coaches do you think there are?' She said 'One less than you think.'
Joe Paterno

Whoever said, 'It's not whether you win or lose that counts', probably lost.
Martina Navratilova

Most football players are temperamental. That's 90 per cent temper and 10 per cent mental.
Doug Plank on American football

American football makes Rugby look like a Tupperware party.
Sue Lawley

I'd run over my own mother to win the Super Bowl.
Joe Jacoby

To win, I'd run over Joe's mom, too.
Matt Millen

We can't run. We can't pass. We can't stop the run. We can't stop the pass. We can't kick. Other than that, we're just not a very good football team right now.
Bruce Coslet

Baseball is like a church. Many attend, few understand.
Leo Durocher

I never question the integrity of an umpire. Their eyesight, yes.
Leo Durocher

I have discovered in 20 years of moving around a ball park that the knowledge of the game is usually in inverse proportion to the price of the seats.
Bill Veeck

There are three types of baseball players: those who make it happen, those who watch it happen and those who wonder what happens.
Tommy Lasorda

We don't need referees in basketball, but it gives the white guys something to do.
Charles Barkley

I am often mentioned in the same sentence as Michael Jordan. You know, 'That Scott Hastings, he's no Michael Jordan.'
Scott Hastings

In my prime I could have handled Michael Jordan. Of course, he would be only 12 years old.

Jerry Sloan

A computer once beat me at chess, but it was no match for me at kick boxing.

Emo Philips

Never fight ugly people – they have nothing to lose.

Wayne Kelly

Prize fighters can sometimes read and write when they start – but they can't when they finish.

Martin H. Fischer

Boxing is just show business with blood.

Frank Bruno

Me and Jake LaMotta grew up in the same neighbourhood. You wanna know how popular Jake was? When he played hide and seek, nobody ever looked for LaMotta.

Rocky Graziano

I'll beat him so bad he'll need a shoehorn to put his hat on.

Muhammad Ali

I've seen George Foreman shadow boxing, and the shadow won.

Muhammad Ali

Sure there's been injuries and deaths in boxing, but none of them serious.
Alan Minter

Lie down so I can recognise you.
Willie Pep

Anglers think they are divining some primeval natural force by outwitting a fish, a creature that never even got out of the evolutionary starting gate.
Rich Hall

It has always been my conviction that any man who pits his intelligence against a fish and loses has it coming.
John Steinbeck

Fishing is boring, unless you catch an actual fish, and then it is disgusting.
Dave Barry

There he stands, draped in more equipment than a telephone lineman, trying to outwit an organism with a brain no bigger than a breadcrumb, and getting licked in the process.
Paul O'Neil on fishermen

I used to like fishing because I thought it had some larger significance. Now I like fishing because it's the only thing I can think of that probably doesn't.
John Gierach

I'm the best. I just haven't played yet.

Muhammad Ali on golf

Golf combines two favourite American pastimes: taking long walks and hitting things with a stick.

P.J. O'Rourke

Man blames fate for other accidents but feels personally responsible for a hole in one.

Martha Beckman

Although golf was originally restricted to wealthy, overweight Protestants, today it's open to anybody who owns hideous clothing.

Dave Barry

Golf is the only sport where a white man can dress like a black pimp and get away with it.

Robin Williams

The only decent people I ever saw at the racecourse were horses.

James Joyce

If you remove the gambling, where is the fun in watching a load of horses being whipped by midgets?

Ian O'Doherty

A major rugby tour by the British Isles to New Zealand is a cross between a medieval crusade and a prep-school outing.
John Hopkins

We've lost seven of our last eight matches. Only team that we've beaten was Western Samoa. Good job we didn't play the whole of Samoa.
Gareth Davies

I'd like to thank the press from the heart of my bottom.
Nick Easter

Rugby football is a game I can't claim absolutely to understand in all its niceties, if you know what I mean. I can follow the broad, general principles, of course. I mean to say, I know that the main scheme is to work the ball down the field somehow and deposit it over the line at the other end and that, in order to squelch this programme, each side is allowed to put in a certain amount of assault and battery and do things to its fellow man which, if done elsewhere, would result in 14 days without the option, coupled with some strong remarks from the Bench.
P.G. Wodehouse

Rugby is a good occasion for keeping 30 bullies far from the centre of the city.
Oscar Wilde

In football everything is complicated by the presence of the opposite team.
Jean-Paul Sartre

Football is a simple game; twenty-two men chase a ball for ninety minutes and at the end, the Germans win.
Gary Lineker

I wouldn't say I was the best manager in the business. But I was in the top one.
Brian Clough

They say Rome wasn't built in a day, but I wasn't on that particular job.
Brian Clough

We talk about it for twenty minutes and then we decide I was right.
Brian Clough

Beckham? His wife can't sing and his barber can't cut hair.
Brian Clough

Ah yes, Frank Sinatra. He met me once, you know?
Brian Clough

When I go, God's going to have to give up his favourite chair.
Brian Clough

It's a huge honour to wear number seven at Liverpool. I think about the legends: Dalglish, Keegan, and that Australian guy.

Luis Suárez

A virgin.

Peter Crouch, when asked what he would be if he weren't a footballer

I hope I don't come across as bitter and twisted, but that man can rot in hell for all I care.

Roy Keane on Ireland manager Mick McCarthy

Mick, you're a liar ... you're a fucking wanker. I didn't rate you as a player, I don't rate you as a manager, and I don't rate you as a person. You're a fucking wanker and you can stick your World Cup up your arse. The only reason I have any dealings with you is that somehow you are the manager of my country! You can stick it up your bollocks.

Roy Keane to Mick McCarthy, before being sent home from the 2002 World Cup in disgrace

I did want to nail him and let him know what was happening. I wanted to hurt him and stand over him and go: 'Take that, you cunt.' I don't regret that. But I had no wish to injure him.

Keane on Alf-Inge Haaland, whom he tackled violently and injured in revenge for an incident years earlier. Haaland eventually retired from complications relating to the injury.

At the end of the day they need to get behind the team. Away from home our fans are fantastic, I'd call them the hardcore fans. But at home they have a few drinks and probably the prawn sandwiches, and they don't realise what's going on out on the pitch. I don't think some of the people who come to Old Trafford can spell 'football', never mind understand it.

Roy Keane on the fans of the club he played for, Manchester United

Fuck off back to France, you French motherfucker.

Alleged words of Crystal Palace fan Matthew Simmons to Eric Cantona, as Cantona walked off the pitch. Cantona responded with a flying kung-fu kick, for which he was later charged with assault and banned from football for 8 months.

He's six foot something, fit as a flea, good looking – he's got to have something wrong with him. Hopefully he's hung like a hamster – that would make us all feel better. Having said that, my missus has got a pet hamster at home, and his cock's massive.

Blackpool manager Ian Holloway on Cristiano Ronaldo

I write like a two-year-old and I can't spell. I can't work a computer. I don't even know what an email is. I've never sent a fax or a text message. I'm the most disorganised person in the world. I can't even fill in the team-sheet.

Harry Redknapp on himself

Do you think I would enter into a contract with that mob? Absolutely no chance. I would not sell them a virus.

Sir Alex Ferguson, in December 2008, on the sale of Cristiano Ronaldo to Real Madrid. Ronaldo was sold the following summer for £80m.

I think he is one of these people who is a voyeur. He likes to watch other people. There are some guys who, when they are at home, have a big telescope to see what happens in other families. He speaks, speaks, speaks about Chelsea.

Chelsea manager José Mourinho on Arsenal manager Arsène Wenger

If Everton were playing at the bottom of the garden, I'd pull the curtains.

Bill Shankly

Football is a simple game, complicated by idiots.

Bill Shankly

Football is war minus the shooting.

George Orwell

Football is popular because stupidity is popular.

Jorge Luis Borges

The politics of Fifa, they make me nostalgic for the Middle East.

Henry Kissinger

Runners run because they love running. Joggers jog because they love cake.

Stuart Heritage

Cycling releases a chemical that makes you feel utterly smug and superior for the rest of the day.
Mark Steel

I can't play bridge. I don't play tennis. All those things that people learn, and I admire, there hasn't seemed time for. But what there is time for is looking out the window.
Alice Munro

Celebrity

The main advantage of being famous is that when you bore people at dinner parties they think it is their fault.
Henry Kissinger

Being famous is like having dementia. Everyone knows who you are, but you don't know who they are.
Michael Douglas

Anyone enquiring: 'Do you know who I am?' is effectively asking: 'Do you know who I was?'
Marina Hyde

Celebrity is just obscurity biding its time.
Carrie Fisher

Beware the celebrity who refers to himself in the third person.
Jemima Khan on Julian Assange

When I read the lives of celebrities in our newspapers I sometimes wish we had a Freedom From Information Act.
Theodore Dalrymple

I'd rather have a rectal examination on live TV by a fellow with cold hands than have a Facebook page.
George Clooney

Malibu is the only place in the world where you can lie on the sand and look at the stars – or vice versa.
Joan Rivers

To people making mean comments about my G[olden] G[lobe] pics, I mos def cried about it on that private jet on my way to my dream job last night. #JK
Gabourey Sidibe, actress, on Twitter

I don't care what you think about me. I don't think about you at all.
Coco Chanel

A whole family of women who take the faces they were born with as a light suggestion.
Amy Schumer on the Kardashians

When someone asks me, 'What do you do?' under my breath I want to say, 'Ask my fucking bank account what I do.'
Kim Kardashian

You know why she's the most Googled person? Because she was Googling herself.
Khloe Kardashian on her sister Kim

If Kim wants us to see a part of her we've never seen, she's gonna have to swallow the camera.
Bette Midler on Kim Kardashian, after the latter had tweeted a nude selfie

A walking X-ray.
Oscar Levant on Audrey Hepburn

A vacuum with nipples.
Otto Preminger on Marilyn Monroe

It's like kissing Hitler.
Tony Curtis on kissing Marilyn Monroe

Her body has gone to her head.
Barbara Stanwyck on Marilyn Monroe

Like a condom full of walnuts.
Clive James on Arnold Schwarzenegger

He has turned alarmingly blond – he's gone past platinum, he must be into plutonium; his hair is coordinated with his teeth.
Pauline Kael on Robert Redford

His skin looks like a child's sandpit after heavy rain.
Lynn Barber on Robert Redford

His ears make him look like a taxi-cab with both doors open.
Howard Hughes on Clark Gable

If you say 'Hiya, Clark, how are you?' he's stuck for an answer.
Ava Gardner on Clark Gable

A face unclouded by thought.
Lillian Hellman on Norma Shearer

Jeremy Clarkson is like Marmite. Disgusting.
Peter Serafinowicz

What is she peddling, anyway? Sex repeal?
Mae West on Twiggy

She looks like she combs her hair with an egg-beater.
Louella Parsons on Joan Collins

In real life, Keaton believes in God. But she also believes that
the radio works because there are tiny people inside it.
Woody Allen on Diane Keaton

I'd rather have a cup of tea than go to bed with someone – any
day.
Boy George

That big blob ... too bad there's not a closet big enough for
him to hide in.
Rupert Everett on Boy George

Boy George is all England needs: another queen who can't dress.
Joan Rivers

@PIERSMORGAN: I currently air in 200 countries/territories – how you getting on? #SmallPondMinnow
@GARYLINEKER: I think the 2 world cups I played in probably edged that
Exchange between Piers Morgan and Gary Lineker on Twitter

What a monumental twat this man is.
Jeremy Clarkson on Piers Morgan

Being called a 'monumental twat' by a pot-bellied pig @JeremyClarkson who wants nurses executed is the purest definition of irony.
Piers Morgan responding to Jeremy Clarkson

Ghastly simpering thespian toad.
Piers Morgan on Rupert Everett

The definition of countryside is the murder of Piers Morgan.
Stephen Fry

Basically a slug.
Tony Blair on Piers Morgan

If name-dropping were an Olympic sport, Yentob would be suspected of doping.
Henry Mance on Alan Yentob

The shit hits the fan.
Headline suggested by Kenneth Tynan after Rex Harrison punched an autograph hunter

Food and Drink

I will not eat oysters. I want my food dead, not sick and wounded.
Woody Allen

Cheese – milk's leap towards immortality.
Clifton Fadiman

Only the dull are brilliant at breakfast.
Oscar Wilde

Custard is a detestable substance produced by a malevolent conspiracy of the hen, the cow and the cook.
Ambrose Bierce

Cauliflower is nothing but cabbage with a college education.
Mark Twain

The national dish of America is menus.
Robert Robertson

American society is pyramid-shaped: the further down you go,
the wider people grow.
Craig Brown, the Daily Telegraph

My mother was a good recreational cook, but what she
basically believed about cooking was that if you worked hard
and prospered, someone else would do it for you.
Nora Ephron

Life is too short for platonic love affairs or savoury desserts.
Food writer Josh Ozersky

Avoid any restaurant where a waiter arrives with a handful of
knives and forks just as you reach the punchline of your best
story and says: 'which of you is having the fish?'
John Mortimer

We are living in a world today where lemonade is made
from artificial flavors and furniture polish is made from real
lemons.
Alfred E. Newman

Fish is the only food considered spoiled once it smells like
what it is.
P.J. O'Rourke

It was the food! Don't touch the food!
*Last words of Richard Harris, actor, spoken to fellow hotel guests, as he was
wheeled through the foyer by paramedics*

Going to Starbucks for coffee is like going to prison for sex. You know you're going to get it, but it's going to be rough.
Adam Hills

I have always preferred the old-fashioned term 'drunkard'. Alcoholic makes it sound like an achievement, and alcoholism a branch of knowledge.
Timothy Mo

Someone I don't like who drinks almost as much as I do.
Dylan Thomas on alcoholics

I'm on a whisky diet. Last week I lost three days.
Tommy Cooper

Nothing good ever happens in a blackout. I've never woken up and been like, 'What is this Pilates mat doing out?'
Amy Schumer on heavy drinking

I tried to drown my sorrows, but the bastards learnt how to swim.
Frida Kahlo

There have been two great accidents in my life. One was the trolley, and the other was Diego. Diego was by far the worst.
Frida Kahlo who had suffered horrific injuries when her bus hit a trolley. Later she married Diego Rivera.

One of the disadvantages of wine is that it makes a man mistake thoughts for words.
Samuel Johnson

Seduction is often difficult to distinguish from rape. In seduction, the rapist often bothers to buy a bottle of wine.
Andrea Dworkin

The trouble with the world is that everybody in it is three drinks behind.
Humphrey Bogart

Las Vegas is the only place I know where money really talks – it says 'Goodbye'.
Frank Sinatra

Cocaine is terrific if you want to hang out with people you don't know very well and play ping pong all night. It's bad for almost everything else.
Amy Poehler

Cocaine is God's way of telling you you are making too much money.
Robin Williams

Drugs have taught a generation of American kids the metric system.
P.J. O'Rourke

Women and Men

Woman was God's second mistake.
Friedrich Nietzsche

When God made man, she was only testing.
Graffiti in ladies' lavatory, London W11

'O Grandson of Conn, O Cormac,' said Carbre, 'how do you
    distinguish women?'
'Not hard to tell,' said Cormac. 'I distinguish them, but I make
    no difference among them.'
They are crabbed as constant companions
haughty when visited,
lewd when neglected ...
stubborn in a quarrel,
not to be trusted with a secret ...
boisterous in their jealousy ...
lustful in bed ...
Better to whip than to humour them ...
better to scourge than to gladden them ...

They are waves that drown you,
they are fires that burn you ...
they are moths for sticking to one,
they are serpents for cunning ...
The Instructions of King Cormac MacAirt

To what purpose is it for women to make vows, when men
have so many millions of ways to make them break them?
And when sweet words, fair promises, tempting, flattering,
swearing, lying will not serve to beguile the poor soul, then
with rough handling, violence and plain strength of arms they
are, or have been heretofore, rather made prisoners to lust's
thieves than wives and companions to faithful honest lovers.
*The Law's Resolutions of Woman's Rights, published 1632 but probably
written in the 1580s*

God created Adam, lord of all living creatures, but Eve spoiled
it all.
Martin Luther

All men are rapists and that's all they are. They rape us with
their eyes, their laws and their cocks.
Marilyn French

The male is by nature superior, and the female inferior: the
one rules and the other is ruled.
Aristotle, Politics, I.5

A good part – and definitely the most fun part – of being a

feminist is about frightening men ... Of course, there's a lot
more to feminism ... but scaring the shit out of the scumbags
is an amusing and necessary part because, sadly, a good many
men still respect nothing but strength.

Julie Burchill, in Time Out

Nature intended women to be our slaves ... they are our
property; we are not theirs. They belong to us, just as a tree
that bears fruit belongs to a gardener. What a mad idea to
demand equality for women! ... Women are nothing but
machines for producing children.

Napoléon Bonaparte

The male function is to produce sperm. We now have sperm
banks.

Valerie Solanas, in S.C.U.M. Manifesto

Marie Stopes was living with him, an arrangement which I
would have thought would satisfy any woman's craving for
birth control.

Muriel Spark on Lord Douglas and the campaigner for contraception, Marie
Stopes

It's a pity it was not her parents, rather than her, who thought
of birth control.

Muriel Spark on Marie Stopes

Feminism is the radical notion that women are people.

Marie Shear

I myself have never been able to find out precisely what feminism is: I only know that people call me a feminist whenever I express sentiments that differentiate me from a doormat.

Rebecca West

When a woman inclines to learning there is usually something wrong with her sex apparatus.

Friedrich Nietzsche

Interviewer: People think you are very hostile to men.
Andrea Dworkin: I am.
Interviewer: Doesn't that worry you?
Andrea Dworkin: From what you said, it worries them.
Men are rewarded for learning the practice of violence in virtually any sphere of activity by money, admiration, recognition, respect, and the genuflection of others honoring their sacred and proven masculinity.

Andrea Dworkin

I would venture to guess that Anon, who wrote so many poems without signing them, was often a woman.

Virginia Woolf, A Room of One's Own

A very little wit is valued in a woman; as we are pleased with a few words spoken plain by a parrot.

Jonathan Swift, Thoughts on Various Subjects

Sir, a woman's preaching is like a dog's walking upon his hinder legs. It is not done well; but you are surprised to find it done at all.
Samuel Johnson

I have always been amazed that women are allowed to enter churches. What sort of conversations can they have with God?
Charles Baudelaire

We have no desire to say anything that might tend to encourage women to embark on accountancy, for although women might make excellent book-keepers, there is much in accountancy proper that is, we think, unsuitable for them.
English Institute of Chartered Accountants, in the Accountant (1912)

Do you know why God withheld the sense of humour from women? That we may love you instead of laugh at you.
Mrs Patrick Campbell, an actress, to a man

An ego like a raging tooth.
W.B. Yeats on Mrs Patrick Campbell

All women are little balls of fluff in the eyes of the Creator.
Donald Pomerleau, Baltimore Police Commissioner, testifying in a sex discrimination case

What a mighty man he turns out to be! He raped ten women –

I would never have expected this from him. He surprised us all. We all envy him.

Vladimir Putin, Russian President, to visiting Israeli Prime Minister Ehud Olmert, on Israeli President Moshe Katsav

A man is in general better pleased when he has a good dinner upon his table, than when his wife talks Greek.

Samuel Johnson

These are rare attainments for a damsel, but pray tell me, can she spin?

James I, when introduced to a young girl proficient in Latin, Greek and Hebrew. Attrib.

That woman can speak eighteen languages and she can't say 'no' in one of them.

Dorothy Parker of a guest surrounded by men at one of her parties

The only place men want depth in a woman is in her cleavage.

Zsa Zsa Gabor

Beneath this stone, a lump of clay
Lies Arabella Young
Who on the 21st of May
Began to hold her tongue.

Epitaph, Hatfield, Massachusetts

A friend of mine, who is an excellent anatomist, had promised me the first opportunity to dissect a woman's tongue, and to

examine whether there may not be in it certain juices which render it so wonderfully voluble or flippant ...
Joseph Addison, in the Spectator, 1711

[Men's] slanderous tongues are so short, and the time wherein they have lavished out their words freely hath been so long, that they know we cannot catch hold of them to pull them out, and they think we will not write to reprove their lying lips.
Jane Anger, Her Protection for Women, 1589

A Preface.
To all women in general,
and gentle Reader whatsoever
Fie on the falsehood of men, whose minds go oft a-madding and whose tongues cannot so soon be wagging, but straight they fall a-tattling! Was there ever any so abused, so slandered, so railed upon, or so wickedly handled undeservedly, as are we women?
Jane Anger, Her Protection for Women, 1589

The only difference between men is the colour of their neckties.
Helen Broderick in Top Hat

A man wrapped up in himself makes a very small parcel.
John Ruskin

He has the heart of a cucumber fried in snow.
Ninon de l'Enclos, French courtesan, on the Marquis de Sévigné

The more I see of men, the more I admire dogs.
Marie de Rabutin-Chantal, Marquise de Sévigné

You will find that the woman who is really kind to dogs is always one who has failed to inspire sympathy in men.
Max Beerbohm, Zuleika Dobson

When a man's best friend is his dog, that dog has a problem.
Edward Abbey

I have ... observed, that in all ages [women] have been more careful than the men to adorn that part of the head which we generally call the outside.
Joseph Addison, in the Spectator, 1712

She looked as if she had been poured into her clothes and had forgotten to say 'when'.
P.G. Wodehouse

[She] appeared to have put on her lipstick during an earth tremor.
Bill Bryson on an elderly guest in his hotel

The only time I see a photograph of anybody who looks like me in a women's magazine is under the word 'Before'.
Sarah Millican

Take a close-up of a woman past sixty? You might as well use a picture of a relief map of Ireland!
Nancy Astor, asked for a close-up photograph. Attrib.

When I don't look like a tragic muse, I look like the smoky relic of the great Boston Fire.
Louisa May Alcott on herself

I hate those short skirts, for women's knees are like badly risen rock-cakes.
Sir Norman Hartnell

Sure, deck your lower limbs in pants;
Yours are the limbs, my sweeting.
You look divine as you advance –
Have you seen yourself retreating?
Ogden Nash

I wonder why men can get serious at all. They have this delicate long thing hanging outside their bodies, which goes up and down by its own will. First of all, having it outside your body is terribly dangerous. If I were a man I would have a fantastic castration complex to the point that I wouldn't be able to do a thing. Second, the inconsistency of it, like carrying a chance time alarm or something. If I were a man I would always be laughing at myself.
Yoko Ono on Film No.4

Viewed from the side, a woman presents an exaggerated S

bisected by an imperfectly straight line, and so she inevitably suggests a drunken dollar-mark.
H.L. Mencken

Give a man a free hand and he'll run it all over you.
Mae West

God created man with a penis and a brain, but only gave him enough blood to run one at a time.
Stephen Ambrose

For 50 years it was like being chained to an idiot.
Kingsley Amis on finally losing his sex drive

I feel as if I had escaped from a frantic and savage master.
Sophocles on being asked in old age about love

If, sir, I, possessed the power of conveying unlimited sexual attraction through the potency of my voice, I would not be reduced to accepting a miserable pittance from the BBC for interviewing a faded female in a damp basement.
Gilbert Harding, urged to be more 'sexy' interviewing Mae West

I used to be Snow White ... but I drifted.
Mae West

She's the original good time that was had by all.
Bette Davis on a starlet of her day

If I ever get hold of that hag, I'll tear every hair out of her moustache.

Tallulah Bankhead on Bette Davis

Mme de Genlis, in order to avoid the scandal of coquetry, always yielded easily.

Talleyrand

He's the kind of man who will end up dying in his own arms.

Mamie Van Doren on Warren Beatty

Madame, you must really be more careful. Suppose it had been someone else who found you like this.

Armand-Emmanuel du Plessis, Duc de Richelieu, when he discovered his wife with her lover

She's like the old line about justice – not only must be done but must be seen to be done.

John Osborne, Time Present

You were born with your legs apart. They'll send you to the grave in a Y-shaped coffin.

Joe Orton, What the Butler Saw

If the girls at a Yale weekend were laid end to end I wouldn't be a bit surprised.

Dorothy Parker

Women might be able to fake orgasms, but men can fake whole relationships.
Sharon Stone

She is chaste whom nobody has asked.
Ovid, Amores, I.8

Ladies, just a little more virginity, if you don't mind.
Herbert Beerbohm Tree, directing a group of actresses

Age cannot wither her, nor custom stale her infinite virginity.
Daniel Webster on hearing of an exchange of views about his friend Peggy Eaton's scandalous reputation

... Your virginity, your old virginity, is like one of our French wither'd pears: it looks ill, it eats drily ...
William Shakespeare, All's Well That Ends Well

Sara could commit adultery at one end and weep for her sins at the other, and enjoy both operations at once.
Joyce Cary, The Horse's Mouth

You can lead a whore to culture but you can't make her think.
Dorothy Parker, in a speech to the American Horticultural Society

Masculinity and stupidity are often indistinguishable.
H.L. Mencken, In Defence of Women

A woman is only a woman,
But a good cigar is a smoke.
Rudyard Kipling; later used by Groucho Marx

There she goes, not with a wimp but a banker.
Paul Desmond on seeing a former girlfriend with a suited man in the street

A woman's place is in the wrong.
James Thurber

Men are nicotine-stained, beer-besmirched, whisky-greased,
red-eyed devils.
Carry Nation

Men's men: be they gentle or simple, they're very much of a
muchness.
George Eliot, Daniel Deronda

Macho isn't mucho.
Zsa Zsa Gabor

I've never found brawn appealing. If I went out with Macho
Man I think I'd have a permanent headache. Kind of 'You
Tarzan – Mi-graine'.
Overheard on a bus

Whatever women do they must do twice as well as men to be
thought half as good. Luckily, this is not difficult.
Charlotte Whitton

The five worst infirmities that afflict the female are indocility, discontent, slander, jealously, and silliness.
Confucian Marriage Manual

Women want mediocre men, and men are working to be as mediocre as possible.
Margaret Mead

Men are stupid, and they like big tits.
Marilyn Monroe's advice to Joan Rivers

Some people think having large breasts makes a woman stupid. Actually, it's the opposite. A woman having large breasts makes a man stupid.
Rita Rudner

If there is anything more boring to me than the problems of big-busted women, it is the problems of beautiful women.
Nora Ephron

Twenty million young women rose to their feet with the cry 'we will not be dictated to' – and promptly became stenographers.
G.K. Chesterton

Why are women ... so much more interesting to men than men are to women?
Virginia Woolf, A Room of One's Own

Some pale, hueless flicker of sensitivity is in me. God, must I lose it in cooking scrambled eggs for a man?
Sylvia Plath

Once you know what women are like, men get kind of boring. I'm not trying to put them down, I mean I like some of them sometimes as people, but sexually they're dull.
Rita Mae Brown

Why did God create men? Because vibrators can't mow the lawn.
Madonna

The male is a biological accident: the Y (male) chromosome is an incomplete X (female) chromosome, that is, has an incomplete set of genes. In other words, the male is an incomplete female, a walking abortion, aborted at the chromosome stage.
Valerie Solanas, in S.C.U.M. Manifesto

Man ... is an afterthought of creation; he is simply a modification of the female.
Deborah Moggach

If they can put one man on the Moon, why not all of them?
Feminist T-shirt

Militant feminists. I take my hat off to them. They don't like that.
Milton Jones

Nobody will ever win the battle of the sexes. There's too much fraternising with the enemy.
Henry Kissinger

I will rather trust a Fleming with my butter, Parson Hugh the Welshman with my cheese, an Irishman with my aqua-vitae bottle, or a thief to walk my ambling gelding, than my wife with herself.
William Shakespeare, The Merry Wives of Windsor

Bachelors begin at thirty-six. Up till this time they are regarded as single men. Most of them are very tidy, smell of mothballs, and have an obsessional old maid's fix about one of their ashtrays being moved an inch to the right.
Jilly Cooper, Men and Super Men

Because women can do nothing except love, they've given it a ridiculous importance.
W. Somerset Maugham, The Moon and Sixpence

Just the exchange of two momentary desires and the contact of two skins.
Nicolas Chamfort on love, 1805

By the time you swear you're his,
Shivering and sighing,
And he vows his passion is Infinite, undying –
Lady, make a note of this:
One of you is lying.

Dorothy Parker, Enough Rope, 'Unfortunate Coincidence'

How alike are the groans of love to those of the dying.

Malcolm Lowry, Under the Volcano

Love may arise from a generous sentiment – namely, the liking
for prostitution; but it soon becomes corrupted by the liking
for ownership.

Charles Baudelaire

Love is a gross exaggeration of the difference between one
person and everybody else.

George Bernard Shaw

The cure for love is to be loved back.

Friedrich Nietzsche

Girls bored me – they still do. I love Mickey Mouse more than
any woman I've ever known.

Walt Disney

Madame: I was told that you took the trouble to come here to
see me three times last evening. I was not in. And, fearing lest

persistence expose you to humiliation, I am bound by the rules
of politeness to warn you that I shall never be in.

*Gustave Flaubert in a letter to Louise Colet, his former mistress. Colet scribbled
on the note 'lâche, couard et canaille' ('poltroon, coward and cur').*

There is no such thing as an ugly woman, but there is such a
thing as too little vodka.

Russian saying

Ugliness is superior to beauty because it lasts longer.

Serge Gainsbourg

Now I know the meaning of grotesque.

*Sydney Smith on seeing the wife of Dr Grote, Regius Professor of Greek, wearing
a turban*

You know that look that women get when they want to have
sex? Me neither.

Steve Martin

No longer from head to foot than from hip to hip, she is
spherical like a globe; I could find out countries in her.
In what part of her body stands for Ireland?
Marry, sir, in her buttocks; I found it out by the bogs.
Where Scotland?
I found it by the barrenness, hard in the palm of the hand.
Where France?
In her forehead, armed and reverted, making war against her
heir.

Where England?
I looked for the chalky cliffs, but I could find no whiteness in
them. But I guess it stood in her chin, by the salt rheum that
ran between France and it.
Where Spain?
Faith, I saw it not; but I felt it hot in her breath.
Where America, the Indies?
O, sir, upon her nose, all o'er embellished with rubies,
carbuncles, sapphires, declining their rich aspect to the hot
breath of Spain, who sent whole armadas of carracks to be
ballast at her nose.
Where stood Belgia, the Netherlands?
O, sir, I did not look so low.
William Shakespeare, The Comedy of Errors

Fuck-me shoes and a bird's-nest hairdo.
Germaine Greer on her fellow Guardian writer Suzanne Moore's dress and
appearance

When I first saw Moore I at last understood why Yanks call a
woman a broad.
Paul Johnson on Guardian columnist Suzanne Moore

A woman with a heavily-lived face poised unceremoniously on
top of a torso like a dressmaker's dummy.
Paul Johnson on Lynn Barber, in the Spectator

A red-haired, red-faced man of 65 seemingly in transit
between Dr Jekyll and Mr Hyde.
Peter McKay on Paul Johnson in the Sunday Times

The flashers, grabbers, bottom-pinchers, purse-snatchers,
kerb-crawlers, verbal abusers, peeping Toms and the ultimate
cowards, the ones who roam in packs, have left an indelible
impression on women's minds and – more in anger than
in fear – women are determined to evade, forestall and
undermine these invaders of our freedom.
Valerie Grove in the Evening Standard

The Queen is most anxious to enlist every one who can speak
or write to join in checking this mad, wicked folly of 'Woman's
Rights', with all its attendant horrors, on which her poor
feeble sex is bent, forgetting every sense of womanly feeling
and propriety.
Queen Victoria

No man, not even a doctor, ever gives any other definition of
what a nurse should be than this – 'devoted and obedient'.
This definition would do just as well for a porter. It might even
do for a horse. It would not do for a policeman.
Florence Nightingale

The legend of the jungle heritage and the evolution of man as
a hunting carnivore has taken root in man's mind ... He may

even believe that equal pay will do something terrible to his
gonads.
Elaine Morgan, The Descent of Woman

An open invitation to any feminist, any harridan or any rattle-
headed female with a chip on her bra strap to take action
against her employers.
Tony Marlow MP on equal-pay law

How do you know that an advance was unwanted until you've
made it?
Alan Clark MP, responding to accusations of sexual harrassment

Homosexuality is a sickness, just as are baby-rape or wanting
to become the head of General Motors. ·
Eldridge Cleaver, black Muslim, Soul on Ice, 'Notes on a Native Son'

He is the summit of sex, the pinnacle of masculine, feminine
and neuter. Everything that he, she and it can ever want. I
spoke to sad but kindly men on this newspaper who have met
every celebrity coming from America for the past thirty years.
They say that this deadly, winking, sniggering, snuggling,
chromium-plated, scent-impregnated, luminous, quivering,
giggling, fruit-flavoured, mincing, ice-covered, heap of
mother love has had the biggest reception and impact on
London since Charlie Chaplin arrived at the same station,
Waterloo, on September 12th 1921. This appalling man, and
I use the word appalling in no other than its true sense of
terrifying, has hit this country in a way that is as violent as

Churchill receiving the cheers on VE Day. He reeks of emetic language that can only make grown men long for a quiet corner, an aspidistra, a handkerchief and the old heave-ho. Without doubt he is the biggest sentimental vomit of all time. Slobbering over his Mother, winking at his brother, and counting the cash at every second, this superb piece of calculating candyfloss has an answer for every situation.

William Connor ('Cassandra') on Liberace, in the Daily Mirror. The column became the subject of a famous libel case won by the entertainer.

I became one of the stately homos of England.

Quentin Crisp, The Naked Civil Servant

A bull who would copulate only with other bulls would be sent to the knackers.

Piers Paul Read, in The Times, 1994

This sort of thing may be tolerated by the French, but we are British – thank God.

Viscount Montgomery of Alamein on the proposed relaxation of laws against homosexuality in 1965

I was too polite to ask.

Gore Vidal, asked whether his first sexual experience was homosexual or heterosexual

If Michelangelo had been a heterosexual, the Sistine Chapel would have been painted basic white and with a roller.

Rita Mae Brown

The middle age of a bugger is not to be contemplated without horror.
Virginia Woolf

She looked like Lady Chatterley above the waist and the gamekeeper below.
Cyril Connolly on Vita Sackville-West

The trouble with Ian is that he gets off with women because he can't get on with them.
Rosamond Lehmann on Ian Fleming

Online dating: the odds are good, but the goods are odd.
Anonymous online dater

Girlfriend said last night 'You treat our relationship like some kind of game!' Which unfortunately cost her 12 points and a bonus chance.
Twitter user @Pundamentalism

They are comforted by our means, they are nourished by the meats we dress; their bodies freed from diseases by our cleanliness, which otherwise would surfeit unreasonably through their own noisomeness. Without our care they lie in their beds as dogs in litter and go like lousy mackerel swimming in the heat of summer.
Jane Anger, Her Protection for Women, 1589

The fastest way to a man's heart is through his chest.
Roseanne Barr

It makes me feel masculine to tell you that I do not answer questions like this without being paid for answering them.
Lillian Hellman, when asked by Harper's Magazine *when she felt most masculine*

Many a man has been a wonder to the world, whose wife and valet have seen nothing in him that was even remarkable. Few men have been admired by their servants.
Michel de Montaigne, Essais, III

No man is a hero to his valet.
Anne-Marie Bigot de Cornuel

But that is not because the hero is no hero, but because the valet is a valet.
Friedrich Nietzsche

A fly, Sir, may sting a stately horse and make him wince; but one is but an insect, and the other is still a horse.
Samuel Johnson

Brigands demand your money or your life; women require both.
Samuel Butler. Attrib.

A woman will always sacrifice herself if you give her the opportunity. It is her favourite form of self-indulgence.

W. Somerset Maugham, The Circle

Laughter is the best medicine, though it tends not to work in the case of impotence.

Jo Brand

Marriage and Family

A sort of friendship recognized by the police.
Robert Louis Stevenson on matrimony

Marriage is a long, dull meal with pudding as the first course.
J.B. Priestley

Nothing is to me more distasteful than that entire complacency and satisfaction which beam in the countenances of a new-married couple.
Charles Lamb, Essays of Elia, 'A Bachelor's Complaint of Married People'

My first wife drove me to drink. It is the only thing I'm indebted to her for.
W.C. Fields

I call her 'my first wife' to keep her on her toes.
Clement Freud

If you want to sacrifice the admiration of many men for the criticism of one, go ahead, get married.
Katharine Hepburn

After a certain age marriage is mostly, its bitter and tender moments both, a mental game of thrust and parry played on the edge of the grave.
John Updike

It was very good of God to let Carlyle and Mrs Carlyle marry one another and so make two people miserable instead of four.
Samuel Butler on the Carlyles

To marry a man out of pity is folly; and, if you think you are going to influence the kind of fellow who has 'never had a chance, poor devil,' you are profoundly mistaken. One can only influence the strong characters in life, not the weak; and it is the height of vanity to suppose that you can make an honest man of anyone.
Margot Asquith

Whenever I date a guy, I think, is this the man I want my children to spend their weekends with?
Rita Rudner

I'm on a search for my future ex-wife.
Richie Sambora

Marriage is like a cage: one sees the birds outside desperate to get in, and those inside equally desperate to get out.

Michel de Montaigne, Essais, III

Marriage is the only adventure open to the cowardly.

Voltaire

I am unwell. Bring me a glass of brandy.

George, Prince of Wales, in 1795, on having kissed for the first time his bride-to-be Princess Caroline of Brunswick

She's been married so many times she has rice marks on her face.

Henry Youngman on Zsa Zsa Gabor

There are two tragedies in life. One is to lose your heart's desire. The other is to gain it.

George Bernard Shaw

Marriage is the assassin of love.

Aristotle Onassis

Marriages are like tornadoes. There's all this blowing and sucking at the beginning; and at the end you lose your house.

James Caan

A man in love is incomplete until he has married. Then he's finished.

Zsa Zsa Gabor

All tragedies are finish'd by death, All comedies are ended by a
marriage.
Lord Byron, Don Juan, III

Before marriage a man yearns for the woman he loves. After
marriage, the Y becomes silent.
Anonymous

A women's silly, never staid,
By many longings stirred and swayed.
If husband can't her needs supply,
Adultery's the way she'll try ...
Her lustful loins are never stilled:
By just one man she's unfulfilled.
She'll spread her legs to all the men
But, ever hungry, won't say 'When'.
Thus married women love to stray
And wish their husbands' lives away.
Since none a woman's lust can sate
I don't commend the marriage state.
'De Coniuge non Ducenda', anonymous poem on marriage, c. 1225–50. One
of the most popular anti-matrimonial satires of the late Middle Ages, surviving
in over fifty manuscripts.

As I roll back from you,
From your flabby breasts and breath,
A faint froth is our only link.
How many beaches are you?
Must I comb them all?

I'm not a wave to roll again forever,
And unlike the sea, I don't come
Every fifteen seconds.
Jim Lindsey, 'Blank Verse for a Fat Demanding Wife'

Mrs Hall of Sherbourne was brought to bed yesterday of a dead
child, some weeks before she expected, owing to a fright. I
suppose she happened to look unawares at her husband.
Jane Austen, letter

Going to marry her! Going to marry her! Impossible! You
mean, a part of her; he could not marry her all himself.
It would be a case, not of bigamy, but of trigamy; the
neighbourhood or the magistrates should interfere. There
is enough of her to furnish wives for a whole parish. One
man marry her! – it is monstrous. You might people a colony
with her; or give an assembly with her; or perhaps take your
morning walks around her, always providing there were
frequent resting places, and you are in rude health. I once was
rash enough to try walking round her before breakfast, but
only got half-way and gave it up exhausted. Or you might read
the Riot Act and disperse her; in short, you might do anything
with her but marry her.
Sydney Smith on hearing that a young man planned to marry a fat widow

What a hideous, odd-looking man Sydney Smith is. With a
mouth like an oyster and three double chins.
Mrs Brookfield on Sydney Smith

To lose a lover or even a husband or two during the course of one's life can be vexing. But to lose one's teeth is a catastrophe.
Hugh Wheeler

Here lies my wife; here let her lie!
Now she's at rest, and so am I.
John Dryden, 'Epitaph Intended for Dryden's Wife'

Men should think twice before making widowhood women's only path to power.
Gloria Steinem

Bigamy is having one husband too many. Monogamy is the same.
Anonymous, quoted in Erica Jong, Fear of Flying

Mine, or other people's?
Peggy Guggenheim on being asked on how many husbands she had had

With all my heart. Whose wife shall it be?
John Horne Tooke, replying to the suggestion that he take a wife

I give to Elizabeth Parker the sum of £50, whom, through my foolish fondness, I made my wife; and who in return has not spared, most unjustly, to accuse me of every crime regarding human nature, save highway-robbery.
Charles Parker, excerpt from will, 1785

I bequeath all my property to my wife on the condition that she remarry immediately. Then there will be at least one man to regret my death.

Heinrich Heine

Now at least I know where he is.

Queen Alexandra, to Lord Esher, shortly after the death of her husband Edward VII, noted for his string of mistresses

It should be a very happy marriage – they are both so much in love with him.

Irene Thomas

I have very little of Mr Blake's company. He is always in paradise.

Mrs Blake on her husband William

You have sent me a Flanders mare.

Henry VIII when he saw Anne of Cleves, his fourth wife, for the first time. Quoted by Tobias Smollett.

I like him and his wife. He is so ladylike, and she is such a perfect gentleman.

Sydney Smith

She is an excellent creature, but never can remember which came first, the Greeks or the Romans.

Benjamin Disraeli on his wife. Attrib.

... fools are like husbands as pilchards are to herrings; the husband's the bigger.

William Shakespeare, Twelfth Night

Twenty years of romance makes a woman look like a ruin; but twenty years of marriage makes her something like a public building.

Oscar Wilde

A wedding is just a funeral where you can smell your own flowers.

Victor Lewis-Smith

I married beneath me – all women do.

Nancy Astor

I wouldn't be caught dead marrying a woman old enough to be my wife.

Tony Curtis

There are only about 20 murders a year in London and not all are serious – some are just husbands killing their wives.

Commander G.H. Hatherhill of Scotland Yard, 1954

It's going to be very, very expensive, but it will be worth every penny.

John Cleese referring to his divorce

The three great lies of modern divorce: it was pressure of work, it's an amicable break, and there's no one else involved.
Julie Burchill

If you are afraid of loneliness, don't marry.
Anton Chekhov

Why shouldn't gay people marry? Why shouldn't they suffer like us heterosexuals do?
Dolly Parton

A man doesn't know what happiness is until he's married. By then it's too late.
Frank Sinatra

Eighty per cent of married men cheat in America. The rest cheat in Europe.
Jackie Mason

The only time my wife and I had a simultaneous orgasm was when the judge signed the divorce papers.
Woody Allen

They fuck you up, your mum and dad.
They may not mean to, but they do.
They fill you with the faults they had
And add some extra, just for you.
Philip Larkin, This Be The Verse

As a child I thought I hated everybody, but when I grew up I realised it was just children that I didn't like.
Philip Larkin

[A] sheep on LSD.
Philip Larkin, describing his appearance

Wherever my dad is now, he's looking down on me ... Not because he is dead, but because he is very condescending.
Jack Whitehall

The problem with the gene pool is that there's no lifeguard.
Sam Levenson

She got her looks from her father. He's a plastic surgeon.
Groucho Marx

A loud noise at one end and no sense of responsibility at the other.
Ronald Knox on babies

Do not leave your mother alone with your dog. The unruliness of mothers is great.
Dabi'Ibn al-harith al-Burjumi on some people who had refused to return a borrowed dog. For this piece of hija, or Arabic invective poetry, he was imprisoned.

I haven't spoken to my mother-in-law for eighteen months. I don't like to interrupt her.
Ken Dodd

Happiness is having a large, loving, caring, close-knit family in another city.
George Burns

Santa Claus has the right idea. Visit people only once a year.
Victor Borge

Friends are God's apology for relations.
Hugh Kingsmill

His mother should have thrown him away and kept the stork.
Mae West

The first half of our lives is ruined by our parents, and the second half by our children.
Clarence Darrow, US lawyer

The reason grandparents and grandchildren get along so well is that they have a common enemy.
Sam Levenson

Guilt is to motherhood as grapes are to wine.
Fay Weldon

Who has not watched a mother stroke her child's cheek or kiss in a certain way and felt a nervous shudder at the possessive outrage done to a free solitary human soul?

John Cowper Powys, The Meaning of Culture

They make pederasty an incomprehensible vice.

Brian Sewell, asked by the head of St Paul's Boys school what he thought of the pupils

Literature is mostly about having sex and not much about having children. Life is the other way round.

David Lodge

I wonder who thought of the innocence of children. It must have been a person of great originality.

Ivy Compton-Burnett

Money – the one thing that keeps us in touch with our children.

Gyles Brandreth

Men are generally more careful of the breed of their horses and dogs than of their children.

William Penn

It is no wonder that people are so horrible when they start their life as children.

Kingsley Amis

A two-year-old is kind of like having a blender, but you don't have a top for it.

Jerry Seinfeld

It is no use telling me that there are bad aunts and good aunts. At the core they are all alike. Sooner or later, out pops the cloven hoof.

P.G. *Wodehouse*, The Code of the Woosters

Age

A man who, beyond the age of 26, finds himself on a bus can count himself a failure in life.

Sometimes wrongly attrib. to Margaret Thatcher, sometimes Virginia Woolf, probably neither

From the earliest times the old have rubbed it into the young that they are wiser than they, and before the young had discovered what nonsense this was they were too old, and it profited them to carry on the imposture.

W. Somerset Maugham, Cakes and Ale

I have lived some thirty years on this planet, and I have yet to hear the first syllable of valuable or even earnest advice from my seniors.

Henry David Thoreau

You are never so stupid as when you are 17. Never. When you are eight you're not stupid. You're many things, but not stupid. But at 17 you are.

Karl Ove Knausgård

I've never understood why people consider youth a time of freedom and joy. It's probably because they've forgotten their own.

Margaret Atwood

Education is the brief interval between ignorance and arrogance.

Old adage

The young always have the same problem – how to rebel and conform at the same time. They have now solved this by defying their parents and copying one another.

Quentin Crisp, The Naked Civil Servant

Look, the intellects of our lazy youth are asleep, nor do they wake up for the exercise of a single respectable occupation; slumber and languor and, what is more disgusting than slumber and languor, the pursuit of wicked things, has invaded their spirit.

Seneca, first century BC, Controversiae, I, Introduction, on the youth of his day, tr. Amy Richlin

Youth is when you're allowed to stay up late on New Year's Eve. Middle age is when you're forced to.

Bill Vaughan

Middle age is when you're sitting at home on a Saturday night and the telephone rings and you hope it isn't for you.

Ogden Nash

Ecstasy was once the most intense pleasure. Then Wagner.
Then Poulet de Bresse. Now it's a cancelled meeting.
The Rev Richard Coles

Adulthood is when your expenditure on Christmas presents
exceeds the value of gifts you expect to receive.
Economist John Kay

Just remember, if she looks young to you / You sure look old to
her.
Paul Heaton

Whenever a man's friends begin to compliment him about
looking young, he may be sure that they think he is growing
old.
Washington Irving, Bracebridge Hall, 'Bachelors'

The three ages of man: youth, middle age, and 'You're looking
well, Enoch!'
Enoch Powell MP on being told by the editor of this book that he looked well

Most people don't grow up. Most people age.
Maya Angelou

The trouble with retirement is that you never get a day off.
College basketball coach Abe Lemons

I sometimes feel that I should carry around some sort of rectal

thermometer, with which to test the rate at which I am
becoming an old fart.
Christopher Hitchens

Being a grandfather is like getting a telegram from the
mortuary.
Martin Amis

Old Cary Grant fine. How you?
Cary Grant, replying to a telegram to his agent, asking: 'How old Cary Grant?'

She said she was approaching 40, and I couldn't help
wondering from what direction.
Bob Hope

I am just turning forty and taking my time about it.
Harold Lloyd at seventy-seven, when asked his age, in The Times

You don't look 75. You did once, though.
Barry Cryer wishing Richard Ingrams a happy birthday

Sex at age 90 is like trying to shoot pool with a rope.
George Burns

The misery of a child is interesting to a mother, the misery of a
young man is interesting to a young woman, the misery of an
old man is interesting to no one.
Victor Hugo, Les Misérables, 'Saint Denis'

Life, as it is called, is for the most of us one long
postponement.
Henry Miller

Sometimes I think that not having to worry about your hair any
more is the secret upside of death.
Nora Ephron

Poor old Daddy – just one of those sturdy old plants left over
from the Edwardian Wilderness, that can't understand why
the sun isn't shining any more.
John Osborne, Look Back in Anger

Take care of your friends, because there will come a time when
you're not much fun to be with and there is no reason to like
you except out of long-standing habit.
Garrison Keillor

Never speak ill of yourself; your friends will say enough on
that subject.
Talleyrand

Old age isn't a battle; old age is a massacre.
Philip Roth

The older you get the stronger the wind gets – and it's always
in your face.
Pablo Picasso

Ancients, Primitives and Folk Curses

Come 'ere, you fucker.
This, the earliest recorded insult I have found, dates from around 2300 BC. It is from the tomb of Ti at Saqqara, Egypt. The hieroglyph (circled) is fairly self-explanatory. Academics have rendered the insult, which one fisherman is hurling at another, as 'Come here, you copulator'.

Imanis metula es. [You're a big prick.]
Pompeii graffiti

Your arsehole is filled with blue mud.
South-east Salish (North American Indian) insult

Commictae spurca saliva lupae. [The foul saliva of a pissed-over whore.]
Catullus, XCIX, 10, tr. Amy Richlin

Your blistered crotch!
Insult from the Marquesas Islands

Lahis felat a.II. [Lahis gives blow jobs for $2.]
Pompeii graffiti

Cosmus Equitiaes magnus cinaedus et fellator est suris apertis.
[Equitias' slave Cosmus is a big queer and a cocksucker with his legs wide open.]
Pompeii graffiti

I thought (so help me Gods!) it made no difference
Whether I smelt Aemilius' mouth or arsehole,
One being no cleaner, the other no filthier.
But in fact the arsehole's cleaner and kinder.
It has no teeth. The mouth has teeth half a yard long
And gums like an ancient wagon-chassis.
Moreover, when it opens up it's like the cunt
Of a pissing mule gaping in a heat wave.
Catullus, XCVII, tr. Guy Lee

Zoile, quid solium subluto podice perdis? Spurcius ut fiat, Zoile, merge caput. [Zoilus, if you want to pollute the public bathing place, Don't stick in your arse first, stick in your face.]
Martial, II.42, tr. Richard O'Connell

If you were as narrow-arsed as you are narrow-minded, or
broad-minded as your anus is broad, you would be the most
perfect of people walking the earth.
Di'bil, from the Arabic

Sabina felas, no belle faces. [Sabina, you give blow-jobs, you don't
do good.]
*Pompeii graffiti. The original Latin, as in many of these examples from
Pompeii, is misspelt. Amy Richlin has suggested this freestyle translation.*

I am the Roman Emperor, and am above grammar.
Sigismund, when his Latin was criticized

When you rise up from a chair, Lesbia,
(I've seen it happen frequently)
You get butt-fucked by your skirt.
The damned thing catches in the narrow crack
Between those massive buns of yours,
Those ship-crunching pillars of Hercules.
You pull with your left hand, you pull with your right,
Wincing and grunting till it comes loose.
An unladylike faux pas, to say the least
Want a tip on etiquette, Lesbia?
Don't get up, and don't sit down.
Martial, XI.99, tr. Joseph Salemi

Their teeth, because of their foul food, are like the nails of a
female circumciser whose knives are too blunt.
Hassan Ibn Thabit, a contemporary of Muhammad, on the Hawazin

Villainous and loathsome screamer! Your audacity
fills the whole earth, the whole Assembly,
all taxes, all indictments, all law-courts,
you mud-churner, you who have thrown
our whole city into chaos and confusion,
you who have defeated our Athens with your shouting,
watching like the tunny-fishers from the rocks above for
shoals of tribute.

Aristophanes on the Athenian general Cleon, The Knights. *The words are
spoken by the chorus, tr. Alan H. Sommerstein.*

The language of Aristophanes reeks of his miserable quackery:
it is made up of the lowest and most miserable puns; he
doesn't even please the people, and to men of judgement and
honour he is intolerable; his arrogance is insufferable, and all
honest men detest his malice.

Plutarch on Aristophanes

His heart shall not be content in life, he shall receive no water
in the necropolis and his soul shall be destroyed for eternity.

Egyptian curse, inscription aimed at 'anyone who desecrates the tomb-chapel'

May you get fucked by a donkey! May your wife get fucked by a
donkey! May your child fuck your wife!

Egyptian legal curse, c. 950 BC

Now in the morning as he returned into the city, he hungered.
And when he saw a fig tree in the way, he came to it, and found
nothing thereon, but leaves only, and said unto it, Let no fruit

grow on thee henceforward for ever. And presently the fig tree withered away.

Jesus curses a fig tree, Matthew 21:18–19. (Note that figs were not in season.)

After this opened Job his mouth, and cursed his day. And Job spake, and said, Let the day perish wherein I was born, and the night in which it was said, There is a man child conceived. Let that day be darkness; let not God regard it from above, neither let the light shine upon it; ... let the blackness of the day terrify it. As for that night, let darkness seize upon it; let it not be joined unto the days of the year, let it not come into the number of months. Lo, let that night be solitary, let no joyful voice come therein. Let them curse it that curse the day, who are ready to raise up their mourning. Let the stars of the twilight thereof be dark; let it look for light, but have none; neither let it see the dawning of the day: Because it shut not up the doors of my mother's womb, nor hid sorrow from mine eyes. Why died I not from the womb? Why did I not give up the ghost when I came out of the belly? Why did the knees prevent me? Or why the breasts that I should suck? ... Wherefore is light given to him that is in misery, and life unto the bitter in soul; Which long for death, but it cometh not; and dig for it more than for hid treasures; Which rejoice exceedingly, and are glad, when they can find the grave?

Job cursing the day he was born, Job 3: 1–22

Cursed shalt thou be in the city, and cursed shalt thou be in the field. Cursed shall be thy basket and thy store. Cursed shall be the fruit of thy body, and the fruit of thy land, the increase

of thy kine, and the flocks of thy sheep. Cursed shalt thou be
when thou comest in, and cursed shalt thou be when thou
goest out ...
Moses' curse in Deuteronomy 28: 16–19

May the earth refuse thee her fruits and the river his waters,
may wind and breeze deny their breath. May the sun not be
warm for thee, nor Phoebe bright, may the clear stars fail thy
vision. May neither Vulcan nor the air lend thee their aid, nor
earth nor sea afford thee any path. Mayst thou wander an exile
and destitute, and haunt the doors of others, and beg a little
food with trembling mouth. May neither thy body nor thy
sick mind be free from querulous pain, may night be to thee
more grievous than day, and day than night. Mayst thou ever
be piteous, but have none to pity thee; may men and women
rejoice at thy adversity. May hatred crown thy tears, and mayst
thou be thought worthy, having borne many ills, to bear yet
more. And (what is rare) may the aspect of thy fortune, though
its wonted favour be lost, bring thee but ill-will. Mayst thou
have cause enough for death, but no means of dying; may thy
life be compelled to shun the death it prays for. May thy spirit
struggle long ere it leave thy tortured limbs, and rack thee first
with long delaying.
Ovid, Ibis, tr. J.H. Mozley

O pour out thy wrath upon the heathen who know thee not,
and upon the kingdoms who invoke not thy name; for they
have devoured Jacob and laid waste his beautiful dwelling.
Pour out thy indignation upon them and cause thy fierce anger

to overtake them. Pursue them in wrath and destroy them from under the heavens of the Lord.

Judaic curse ritually invoked at the Passover between the third and fourth cups of wine. The door to the outside must be opened for its pronouncement. Leo Abse, who referred the editor of this book to this curse, said he had been told that, at times of danger, isolation and persecution, the pronouncement of this curse upon their persecutors was a source of great comfort to Jews assembled for the Passover.

O Lord Neptune, I give you the man who has stolen the solidus and six argentioli of Muconius! Thus I give the names which took them away, whether male or female, whether boy or girl. Thus I give you, O Niskus, and to Neptune, the life, health and blood of him who has been privy to that taking-away! The mind that stole this and which has been privy to it, may you take it away! The thief who stole this, may you consume his blood and take it away, O Lord Neptune!

Curse tablet found in Hampshire. A solidus and argentioli were forms of currency.

Just as this lead cannot be seen and is buried, so may the youth, skin, life, ox, grain and wellbeing of the ones who have done me wrong be buried.

Curse found at the Gaullish hill-fort at Montfo

I turn away Eubola from Aineas.
From his face,
From his eyes,
From his mouth,

From his breasts,
From his soul,
From his belly,
From his penis,
From his anus,
From his entire body.
I turn away Eubola from Aineas.

Fourth-century BC Greek curse from Nemea, near Corinth

Whosoever breaks these oaths ... may these oaths seize him ...
Let them fetter their feet with foot fetters below and bind their
hands above. And as the gods of the oaths bound the hands
and feet of the troops of Arzawa and piled them in heaps, so
may they bind his army and pile them into heaps.

Hittite military oath, second millennium BC

This charm is to send a spirit against Mar Zutra son of Ukmay.
In the name of Qaspiel the angel of death.

I have adjured you, Infarat, the evil spirit: Go against Mar
Zutra son of Ukmay and dwell with him, in his body and his
frame, of Mar Zutra son of Ukmay and inflate his bowels like a
bow and mix within him blood and pus and sit like a bolt on his
heart and like a load on his brain and kill him after thirty days.

Go against Mar Zutra the son of Ukmay and cast him in
exhaustion upon his bed, and do not give him bread to eat and
water to drink until he shouts and neighs noise and howls;
until his children despise him and his neighbours distance
themselves from him. And cast down his strength as fails that
of a toiling ox and forty eight organs of his body and kill him

with anger and wrath and great fury ... Howl, howl! So will you cry, Mar Zutra son of Ukmay. Enter with this charm locusts fly, these oppressors.

Aramaic inscription on a 'curse-bowl'

May you forever be plagued by rail replacement bus services
May you stand on slugs in bare feet while you have a crafty cig
    on the back step
May he never be able to find the end of the sellotape with ease,
    and may it always split when he does
May you constantly forget about your tea until it is
    unpleasantly tepid
I hope you get out of bed, stand on a plug, then a piece of
    Lego, and then a rake

Some of the tweets from the hashtag '#CurseDavidCameron' following revelations about his off-shore tax arrangements

The Lord strike him with madness and blindness. May the heavens empty upon him thunderbolts and the wrath of the Omnipotent burn itself unto him in the present and future world. May the Universe light against him and the earth open to swallow him up.

Pope Clement on a now-forgotten subject

Your stinking foreskin filth.

Polynesian insult

He waddles like an Armenian bride.

Osmanli insult

A waste of skin.
Lancashire expression

As flash as a rat with a gold tooth.
Australian expression

May you croak in the faith of the Poles!
Ukrainian, regarded as an outrageous curse

You're as ugly as a salad.
Bulgarian insult

May the fleas of a thousand camels infest your armpits.
Arab curse

Careful: my knife drills your soul
listen, [name victim]
One of the wolf people
listen I'll grind your saliva into the earth
listen I'll cover your bones with black flint
listen I'll cover your bones with black feathers
listen I'll cover your bones with black rocks
Because you're going where it's empty
Black coffin out on the hill
listen the black earth will hide you, will
find you a black hut
Out where it's dark, in that country
listen I'm bringing a box for your bones
A black box

A grave with black pebbles
listen your soul's spilling out
listen it's blue.

Cherokee Indian chant designed to bring about the death of a victim, adapted by Jerome Rothenberg, Sacred Formulas of the Cherokees

May you dig up your Father by moonlight and make soup of his bones.

Fiji islands curse

Cursed by your mother's anus
Cursed by your father's testicles.

Yoruba verbal duelling, quoted by Chief Oludare Olajuba, References to Sex in Yoruba Oral Literature

I shit on the balls of your dead ones.

Spanish gypsy insult

Copulate with my Father who is dead!

Admiralty Islands' most unpardonable insult

I shit in your Mother's milk.

Spanish insult

Copulate with your wife.

Trobriand Islands' most unpardonable insult

I hope that your piles hang like a bunch of grapes.

Greek insult directed at homosexuals

I shit on your Father's nose.
Farsi (Iranian) insult

I shit on God, on the cross, and on the carpenter who made it
(and on the son of the whore who planted the pine)!
Catalan insult

May a fart be on your beard.
Farsi insult for men

May the devil damn you to the stone of dirges, or to the well
of ashes seven miles below hell; and may the devil break your
bones! And all my calamity and harm and misfortune for a year
on you!
Curse from the Cois Fharraige, west of Galway City, in Connemara

I'll stick a pig's leg up your cunt until your back-teeth rattle.
Japanese insult

A donkey's head in your cunt.
Farsi insult used by a woman to call another stupid

Your Grandmother on roller-skates.
Central American curse

Your Grandmother in trousers.
Central American curse

A plague o' both your houses!
William Shakespeare, Romeo and Juliet

For him that stealeth a Book from this Library, let it change
into a serpent in his hand and rend him. Let him be struck
with Palsy, and all his Members blasted. Let him languish in
Pain crying aloud for Mercy and let there be no sur-cease to his
Agony till he sink in Dissolution. Let Bookworms gnaw his
Entrails in token of the Worm that dieth not, and when at last
he goeth to his final Punishment, let the flames of Hell
consume him for ever and aye.
Curse Against Book Stealers, Monastery of San Pedro, Barcelona

Roger Fuckebythenavel.
*Earliest recorded use of the word 'fuck' in English – an offensive nickname for a
man outlawed in 1311*

Die, may he; Tiger, catch him, snake bite him; Steep hill, fall
down on him; Wild boar, bite him.
Curse of Toda tribe in southern India

Woe unto bloody Lichfield!
*George Fox, founder of the Quakers, after a dream in which he saw the town
engulfed in blood*

Thou cursed cock, with thy perpetual noise,
May'st thou be capon made, and lose thy voice,
Or on a dunghill may'st thou spend thy blood,
And vermin prey upon thy craven brood;

May rivals tread thy hens before thy face
Then with redoubled courage give thee chase;
May'st thou be punished for St Peter's crime,
And on Shrove Tuesday perish in thy prime;
May thy bruised carcass be some beggar's feast –
Thou first and worst disturber of man's rest.
Sir Charles Sedley on a cock at Rochester

I charm thy life
From the weapons of strife,
From stone and from wood,
From fire and from flood,
From the serpent's tooth,
And the beasts of blood:
From Sickness I charm thee,
And Time shall not harm thee;
But Earth which is mine,
Its fruits shall deny thee;
And Water shall hear me,
And know thee and fly thee;
And the Winds shall not touch thee
When they pass by thee,
And the Dews shall not wet thee,
When they fall nigh thee:
And thou shalt seek Death
To release thee, in vain;
Thou shalt live in thy pain
While Kehama shall reign,
With a fire in thy heart,

And a fire in thy brain;
And Sleep shall obey me,
And visit thee never,
And the Curse shall be on thee
For ever and ever.
Robert Southey, The Curse of Kehama

you are the dumbest thing
on the earth the slimiest
most rotten thing in the universe
you motherfuckin germ
you konk-haired blood suckin punks
you serpents of pestilence you
samboes you green witches gnawing the heads of infants
you rodents you whores you sodomites you fat
slimy cockroaches crawling to your holes
with bits of malcolm's flesh
i hope you are smothered
in the fall of a huge yellow moon.
Welton Smith on black people who failed to support Malcolm X, The Nigga
Section

Sadaam, oh Sadaam
Thou flesh-knotter you
Claim not to be Muslim
For you are truly a Jew
Your deeds have proved ugly
Your face is darkest black
And we will set fire

To your bottom and your back.
Poem on Sadaam Hussein, broadcast on Saudi television during the Gulf War

Son of a Scots manse though you were
I've take the rare scunner against you,
You who thieve the golden hours of bairns,
You who bitch up the world's peoples
With crystal images, pitch-black lies,
You who have ended civilized conversation
And dished out licenses to print banknotes,
May your soul shrink to the size of a midge
And never rest in a couthie kirkyard
But dart across a million wee screens
And be harassed by TV jingles for ever and ever,
For thine's the kingdom of the televisor,
You goddam bloody genius, John Logie Baird!
Robert Greacen, curse

May you wander over the face of the earth forever, never sleep
twice in the same bed, never drink water twice from the same
well, and never cross the same river twice in a year.
Gypsy curse

May you be cursed with chronic anxiety about the weather.
John Burroughs

Fuck you.
*Ed Koch, in response to a reporter's allegations of war criminality. And
countless others.*

I hope you will pray too that the Lord will smite him hip and thigh, bone and marrow, heart and lungs and all there is to him; that he shall destroy him quickly and utterly.

Bob Jones III, a Christian fundamentalist, on Alexander Haig, after the latter refused Ian Paisley a visa to visit the USA

The Rev Ian Paisley has died. The authorities have asked that we should all observe a minute's shouting.

David Baddiel

I fart in your general direction.

John Cleese, Monty Python and the Holy Grail

Now I can finally say what a diplomat normally cannot to those he comes into contact with: I hope you encounter every curse imaginable!

Koji Haneda, First Secretary, Embassy of Japan (London), wishing the editor of this book success in his collection of insults

Extra Bile: Brexit, Corbyn, Trump and Macron

EU Referendum

Unchallenged master of the self-inflicted wound.
Nicholas Soames on Boris Johnson

He's the life and soul of the party but he's not the man you want driving you home at the end of the evening.
Amber Rudd on Boris Johnson

He's 100 per cent political herpes. Back in six months whatever you do. Or three days, like last time.
Camilla Long on Nigel Farage's claim that he might quit politics if Britain leaves the EU. Long is referring to Farage's previous resignation as UKIP leader, which had lasted only days.

It's more than a U-turn. It's the U-turn of a man who has got himself trapped in a revolving door.
Martin Kettle on Michael Gove's referendum campaign

I think people in this country have had enough of experts.

Michael Gove

What they're offering instead of EU membership is a divorce where you can still have sex with your ex. They reckon they can get out of the marriage, keep the house, not pay alimony, take the kids out of school, stop the in-laws going to the doctor, get strict with the visiting rights, but, you know, still get a shag at the weekend and, obviously, see other people on the side.

AA Gill

A man who descends to the big occasion.

Michael Deacon on Jeremy Corbyn

All through this campaign we were told Britain is the greatest country on Earth. Can we all now just agree that we're a clueless shitheap? I mean, come on. A respectable nation would not have ended up like this. We are clowns. A crap cover version of a Victorian superpower.

Michael Deacon on Brexit

Britannia waives the rules.

Sinn Fein MEP on Brexit

If you need help identifying your current personal brand, it's weapons-grade treachery.

Marina Hyde on Michael Gove's leadership launch

We need to renegotiate a new relationship with the EU, based on free trade and friendly cooperation.

#Gove2016

Responses to this tweet called Gove:

One confused bag of mince. @Mr_Dave_Haslam
Boil-in-the-bag rent-a-clown. @PULPKetchup
Incompetent ventriloquist-dummy-faced spunktrumpet.
@MJ_Boh_
Reprehensible spam faced tool bag! @InvaderXan
Back stabbing cockwomble. @Brummiecris
Haunted pork mannequin. @AlexWattsEsq

I hate this referendum, for turning a question of unfathomable complexity into *Lord of the Flies*.

Hugh Laurie

The 2017 UK Election

A woman who always keeps her promises has called an election she promised not to, in order to obtain a mandate she says she already has, for a policy she said was a bad idea.

David Robjant, *letter to the* Guardian

If 38 per cent of voters genuinely go for pro-IRA anti-nuclear pro-mass-nationalisation Corbyn, UK voters are no longer mature enough for democracy.

Andrew Lilico, *before Jeremy Corbyn secured 40 per cent of the vote*

A mutton-headed old mugwump.
Boris Johnson on Corbyn

Boris, the dog was put down, when its master decided it
wasn't needed any more.
Theresa May to Boris Johnson, after he had compared himself to Michael
Heseltine's mother's dog

In an election, they would tear Corbyn's Labour party to
pieces. Will there be 150, 125, 100 Labour MPs by the end of
the flaying? My advice is to think of a number then halve it ...
Nick Cohen on 19 March

I was wrong.
Nick Cohen on 11 June

It's going to start earlier than I thought. Brace yourself for the,
'Jeremy Corbyn could surprise people' articles. He can't. He
won't.
Dan Hodges on 20 April

Dear Corbynites. There are lots of people out there who will
happily say 'I was wrong about Jeremy'. I'm not one of them.
Sorry.
Dan Hodges on Jeremy Corbyn

We were steaming under blue skies and then we created our
own iceberg and steered our campaign towards it.
Nigel Evans MP

We all f***ing hate her. But there is nothing we can do. She has totally f***ed us.
Senior Tory MP to Robert Peston

Had this weird dream Theresa May humiliated herself in snap election and clung to power with homophobe fundamentalist terrorist sympathisers.
Owen Jones on Twitter

Go away and learn some emotional intelligence.
Reputed comments from Theresa May to George Osborne when she sacked him

A dead woman walking.
George Osborne on Theresa May during election night

Queen of Denial.
Front page of the Evening Standard the day after the election, edited by George Osborne

Imagine any of the great Labour figures in history talking like this. I can't.
Marina Hyde quoting Clive Lewis MP's tweet about the Grenfell Tower blaze, 'Burn neoliberalism, not people'

The 2016 American Election and the Trump Administration

Nasty woman.
Donald Trump on Hillary Clinton

As you know, I have a running war with the media. They are among the most dishonest human beings on Earth.

Donald Trump to the CIA, in front of the memorial wall for agents who died in the field

Just arrived in Scotland. Place is going wild over the vote. They took their country back, just like we will take America back.

Donald Trump tweeting on 24 June 2016

All 32 regions of Scotland voted to remain in the EU. Get your facts right you rug-wearing thunder nugget.

@Peemo83, in response

Scotland hates both Brexit and you, you mangled apricot hellbeast.

@queenbernstein, in response

You tiny-fingered, Cheeto-faced, ferret-wearing shitgibbon.

@MetalOllie, in response

I'm not Steve Bannon, I'm not trying to suck my own cock. I'm not trying to build my own brand off the fucking strength of the president.

Anthony Scaramucci, the short-lived White House Director of Communications, to the New Yorker, on Steve Bannon

Reince is a fucking paranoid schizophrenic, a paranoiac.

Anthony Scaramucci to the New Yorker, on his boss, Reince Priebus

I bought avocadoes the day Scaramucci started and they're still ripe.

@HollynHeron, responding to Scaramucci's sacking, ten days after being appointed

Whenever you see the words 'sources say' in the fake news media, and they don't mention names, it is very possible that those sources don't exist but are made up by fake news writers. #FakeNews is the enemy!

Donald Trump on Twitter, 28 May 2017. In 2012, Trump claimed an 'extremely credible source' had told him Barack Obama's birth certificate was a 'fraud'.

Don Jr. has been accused of colluding with Russians. To defend himself he released the emails proving it.

Comedian Chelsea Handler on Twitter

Is President Obama going to finally mention the words radical Islamic terrorism? If he doesn't he should immediately resign in disgrace!

Donald Trump in June 2016

We condemn in the strongest possible terms this egregious display of hatred, bigotry and violence on many sides. On many sides.

Donald Trump's first statement after the Charlottesville attack, in which a car was driven into a group of people protesting a white supremacist and neo-Nazi march.

It is not too much to ask to have a president who explicitly condemns Nazis.

Senator Brian Schatz responding to Trump

Trump's face when he denounces White Nationalism and the KKK is the same face I made when my parents made me eat brussels sprouts.

@osullivanauthor after Donald Trump released a second statement, two days later, explicitly condemning far right groups

Made additional remarks on Charlottesville and realise once again that the #Fake News Media will never be satisfied … truly bad people!

Donald Trump on Twitter

The president never loses sight of the real victim in this tragedy: himself.

David Frum, quoting the above tweet

The 2016 French Election

To govern a country it is my conviction that one must be irreproachable. I support the principle that the President and ministers must lead by example.

Francois Fillon, tweeting in 2016

There is social injustice between those who work hard for little and those who don't work and receive public money.

Francois Fillon, tweeting in 2012

Many of my political allies, and the four million people who voted for me call this a 'political assassination'.

Francois Fillon after receiving a summons from judicial magistrates over accusations that he employed his wife as an assistant, a position for which she allegedly did no work and received hundreds of thousands of euros in payment.

They don't speak in the name of the people – they speak in the name of their bitterness, they speak for themselves, from father to daughter and daughter to niece.

Macron on Marine Le Pen and her father, Jean, and niece, Marion, both far-right politicians, at a campaign rally

He is a hysterical, radical 'Europeanist'. He is for total open borders. He says there is no such thing as French culture. There is not one domain that he shows one ounce of patriotism.

Marine Le Pen on Emmanuel Macron

The high priestess of fear.

Emmanuel Macron to Marine Le Pen during their head-to-head debate

Smirking banker.

Marine Le Pen to Emmanuel Macron during their head-to-head debate

Parasite.

Emmanuel Macron to Marine Le Pen during their head-to-head debate

Acknowledgements

Nothing in this book is new. To my helpers, Alex Dudok de Wit and George Morris, has fallen the task of gathering the mountain from which I have assembled this personal molehill of an anthology. They have worked hard for many months, and I am grateful. I have relied not only on their industry, but their judgement. Cecily Gayford, at Profile Books, has been a wise and helpful editor.

My thanks to those hundreds of friends and long-shot acquaintances whom we contacted for suggestions, many of which have found their way into the book; to my peerless agent Ed Victor; a special word of thanks to Andrew Franklin, my proactive and creative editor for the first, Penguin, edition of this book, and now my publisher. Thanks also to Dr Richard Parkinson at the British Museum and to the editors of dozens of dictionaries, anthologies and works of reference in this field, on whose research we have drawn. These are too numerous to list in full, but the following have been particularly useful:

An Anthology of Invective and Abuse, ed. Hugh Kingsmill (London, 1930); *A Dictionary of Contemporary Quotations*, ed. Jonathan Green (London, 1982); *A Dictionary of International Slurs*, ed. A. A. Roback (Wisconsin, 1979); *A Dictionary of Sexist Quotations*, ed. Selma James (Hemel Hempstead, 1984); *The Garden of Priapus: Sexuality and Aggression in Roman Humour* by Amy Richlin (London, 1983); *The Guinness Dictionary of Poisonous Quotes*, ed. Colin Jarman

(London, 1991); *Lexicon of Musical Invective* by Nicholas Slonimsky (Washington, DC, 1965); *Maledicta: The International Journal of Verbal Aggression*, ed. Rheinhold Aman (1977–86); *Picking on Men* by Judy Allen (London, 1985); *Shakespeare's Insults*, ed. Wayne Hill and Cynthia J. Ottchen (Cambridge, 1992); *Far Too Noisy, My Dear Mozart*, ed. Jennifer Higgie (Michael O'Mara Books, 1997).

Acknowledgement is also due to HarperCollins Publishers Limited and Germaine Greer for *The Female Eunuch*; to William Heinemann Limited for *Cakes and Ale* by W. Somerset Maugham; to Guy Lee for *The Poems of Catullus* (OUP, 1990) by permission of Oxford University Press; to The Society of Authors on behalf of the Bernard Shaw Estate; to John Murray (Publishers) Limited for *Slough* by John Betjeman; to Laurence Pollinger Limited and the Estate of Frieda Lawrence Ravagli for *How Beastly the Bourgeois Is* by D. H. Lawrence; to David Higham Associates and Osbert Sitwell for *A Certain Statesman*; and to Faber and Faber Limited for the following extracts: Philip Larkin's 'This be the Verse' from *High Windows*; and John Osborne's *Look Back in Anger*, and to Matthew d'Ancona, former editor of *The Spectator*, for permission to quote from the magazine's attack on Liverpool. For almost twenty years, *The Week*, has offered readers a discerning pick of pithy verbal insolence, and I have plundered this resource shamelessly.

The illustrations on pages 390 and 90 are reprinted courtesy of the British Museum Department of Egyptian Antiquities and the British Library respectively.

Every effort has been made to trace copyright holders. The author and publishers apologise for any errors or omissions, and would be grateful to be notified of any corrections that should appear in any reprint.

Finally I must acknowledge the intelligent energy of my assistant editor, Robbie Smith, in bringing this new edition to completion.

Matthew Parris, August 2016

Index